FROM PREFERENTIAL STATUS TO PARTNERSHIP

This book is dedicated to:
My parents
Samia, Amany, Raouf, Moujib, Ikram and Hasna.

From Preferential Status to Partnership
The Euro-Maghreb relationship

AHMED AGHROUT
University of Salford

LONDON AND NEW YORK

First published 2000 by Ashgate Publishing

Reissued 2018 by Routledge
2 Park Square, Milton Park, Abingdon, Oxon OX14 4RN
711 Third Avenue, New York, NY 10017, USA

Routledge is an imprint of the Taylor & Francis Group, an informa business

Copyright © Ahmed Aghrout 2000

All rights reserved. No part of this book may be reprinted or reproduced or utilised in any form or by any electronic, mechanical, or other means, now known or hereafter invented, including photocopying and recording, or in any information storage or retrieval system, without permission in writing from the publishers.

Notice:
Product or corporate names may be trademarks or registered trademarks, and are used only for identification and explanation without intent to infringe.

Publisher's Note
The publisher has gone to great lengths to ensure the quality of this reprint but points out that some imperfections in the original copies may be apparent.

Disclaimer
The publisher has made every effort to trace copyright holders and welcomes correspondence from those they have been unable to contact.

A Library of Congress record exists under LC control number: 00108817

ISBN 13: 978-1-138-73004-5 (hbk)
ISBN 13: 978-1-138-73001-4 (pbk)
ISBN 13: 978-1-315-18954-3 (ebk)

Contents

List of tables	*vi*
List of charts	*viii*
Acknowledgements	*ix*
List of abbreviations	*x*
Introduction	1
Part One: The Euro-Maghreb Relationship and its Environment	**9**
1 Nature, Characteristics and Determinants	11
Part Two: From Commercial to Enlarged Cooperation	**41**
2 A Partial and Limited Association: The Trade Arrangements	43
3 Broad-based Cooperation under the 'Global' Mediterranean Policy	67
Part Three: Maghreb Malaise since the 1980s and Europe's Response	**101**
4 Factors of Instability in the Maghreb	103
5 A Partnership Pact from Europe	126
6 Conclusion	155
Appendix One	163
Appendix Two	186
Bibliography	187
Index	201

List of tables

1.1	Share of intra-Maghreb trade in total trade	21
1.2	Recorded intra-Maghreb trade in 1996 and 1997	22
1.3	Extra-EU export and import share by selected partners	34
1.4	Principal Maghreb trade partners in the EC	37
2.1	Morocco's trade with the EC, 1963-1964	46
2.2	Tunisia's trade with the EC, 1963-1964	47
2.3	Value of EC imports from the Maghreb countries and share of total extra-EC imports, 1969-1975	61
3.1	Value of EC imports from the Maghreb countries and share of total extra-EC imports, 1976-1996	80
3.2	Structure of Maghreb countries exports to the EC, 1976 and 1995	82
3.3	Financial appropriations under the four protocols, 1976-1996	86
3.4	Financial implementation of the four protocols at the end of 1995	88
3.5	Net official development assistance to the Maghreb countries	90
3.6	Maghreb migrants in the EC, 1995	92
4.1	Demographic profile of the Maghreb countries	105
4.2	The growth of the labour force in the Maghreb countries	108
4.3	External debt indicators in the Maghreb countries	111
5.1	Share of trade taxes in the Maghreb countries' revenue, selected years (1990, 1993 and 1996)	141

| 5.2 | Cost of the overall adjustment measures | 144 |
| 5.3 | Cost of industrial restructuring by sector | 145 |

List of charts

2.1	Maghreb countries' trade balance with the EC, 1969-1975	62
3.1	Maghreb countries' trade balance with the EC, 1976-1996	78
3.2	Share of clothing products in the Maghreb countries' exports of manufactures to the EC in 1995	84
3.3	Annual remittances of migrants from the Maghreb countries, 1970, 1980 and 1995	93
5.1	Flows of net foreign direct investment to the Maghreb countries, 1990-1998	148

Acknowledgements

I have been given much assistance from many people during the production of this book. It would be impossible to name them all in a brief preface. However, I wish to acknowledge my deepest debt of gratitude to Professor Martin Alexander whose advice, encouragement and stimulating remarks have sustained my efforts throughout the preparation of this study.

I would also like to record my gratitude to Professor John Keiger for his time and efforts in reading and providing comments on the manuscript despite his busy schedule.

The professional support and encouragement from Professors Avril Horner and Geoff Harris at the European Studies Research Institute, the University of Salford, are also greatly appreciated.

I must extend my gratitude to Nacereddine Haddaoui and all staff at the Department of Economics, the University of Sétif, for their understanding and valuable cooperation.

I would also like to take this opportunity to thank Jocelyn Evans, Andrew Geddes and Paul Maddrell for their review of parts of the study.

A great debt is owed to the librarians at the University of Salford Library, particularly Helen Mills and John Percy for their valuable assistance in helping to obtain material for this research.

On a special note, I wish to express my sincere thanks to my family, most notably Rachid, Hassiba, Mouatez and Chouaieb for being a source of constant support and encouragement. My thanks also go to my friends, Djamel Ferradj, Hakim Meliani, Redha Bougherira, Fadhl al-Rashid, Chafik Allaoui, Nabil Bensabai and Hassan Lounis for their unwavering moral support.

My thanks are also due to Kath Capper, Elaine Smith, Lesley Harris, Wendy Dodgson and Louise Pickles for their help and understanding during the preparation and completion of this work. Finally, full responsibility for the content of the book rests with me.

List of abbreviations

ACP	African, Caribbean and Pacific countries
CAP	Common Agricultural Policy
CCP	Common Commercial Policy
CEEC	Central and Eastern European Countries
CET	Common External Tariff
CPCM	Comité Permanent Consultatif du Maghreb (Maghreb Permanent Consultative Committee)
EAGGF	European Agricultural Guidance and Guarantee Fund
EC	European Community
ECA	European Court of Auditors
Ecu	European Currency Unit
EDF	European Development Fund
EIB	European Investment Bank
EU	European Union
FLN	Front de Libération Nationale (National Liberation Front)
GATT	General Agreement on Tariffs and Trade
GDP	Gross Domestic Product
GSP	Generalised System of Preferences
IMF	International Monetary Fund
MFA	Multi-Fibre Arrangements
NATO	North Atlantic Treaty Organisation
OECD	Organisation for Economic Cooperation and Development
RCD	Rassemblement Constitutionnel Démocratique (Constitutional Democratic Rally)
SEM	Single European Market
UMA	Union du Maghreb Arabe (Arab Maghreb Union)
UN	United Nations
UNCTAD	United Nations Conference on Trade and Development
UNECA	United Nations Economic Commission for Africa
WTO	World Trade Organization

Introduction

The establishment of the European Economic Community was concomitant with a commitment in which the founding Member States emphasised their readiness to preserve and eventually develop the 'special' relationships that had previously existed between them and their former colonies. It was in this context that the Maghreb countries (Algeria, Morocco and Tunisia), which by virtue of the close relations they had developed with France during the colonial period, were first among the countries on Europe's southern borders to seek to establish with the then new entity links that would preserve their existing status and ensure their access to the European market on favourable terms. Originally that was the starting point for the inception of the Euro-Maghreb relationship. This relationship was to develop afterwards on the basis of the principle of association stipulated under the provisions of Article 228 of the Rome Treaty.

Within the Mediterranean policy of the Community, this relationship has undergone various stages in its evolution. These can be seen as a reflection of the different approaches attempted by the European Community/European Union (EC/EU hereafter) towards the Maghreb region. The first stage was associated with the trade arrangements which the Community concluded with Morocco and Tunisia in 1969. They were limited in both scope and time as they were solely commercial by nature and operational only for a five-year period. Though preferential in kind, they were subject to the granting of reverse preferences from the beneficiaries in favour of Community exports. In short, one way of characterising this initial approach is that it was no more than a partial EC response to what the Maghreb countries aspired to receive.

The second stage coincided with the overall policy for the Mediterranean which the Community had launched by the beginning of the 1970s. The belief in Brussels was that by embarking on a more comprehensive approach, the Community would provide a more favourable treatment to the problems and needs of its southern neighbours, including the Maghreb. In fact, the most salient feature of this approach was the enlarged scope of its development cooperation. In addition to trade questions, financial and social (migrant workers) issues were also included. Initially, for the Maghreb countries this represented an improvement in their relationship with Europe on two accounts. First, its content, which was previously confined to purely commercial aspects, became more broadly based in its coverage of areas and non-reciprocal in terms of trade relations. Second, the temporary nature of the relationship was to be substituted, at least at that time, by a long-term perspective via the conclusion, in 1976, of another generation of agreements to last for an unlimited duration.

A third and final stage relates to the partnership initiative that the Community began implementing in 1996 and under which Morocco and Tunisia signed new association agreements in 1995. Within EC circles the need for this initiative, while dictated by what was viewed as a mixed record for the overall Mediterranean policy so far, was made imperative by the implications stemming from the increasing vulnerability of the economic and political conditions of several neighbouring countries. This was particularly apparent and urgent in the case of those of the Maghreb. The thrust of this latest attempt, as it appears from its content, is that it goes beyond the traditional pattern of combining trade and aid, by involving other issues such as political dialogue and social and cultural cooperation which have become a standard part of the initiative. Despite its wide-ranging scope and its ambitious nature, however, its central pillar is and will remain the gradual establishment of a free trade area between the Community and individual Maghreb countries, along with the financial support from the EC and other sources to facilitate its materialisation. This phase may seem to illustrate a shift from a relatively favoured position towards a relationship based, albeit progressively, on *quid pro quo* principles with trade remaining at the centre of the whole process.

Through these various phases in the evolution of the Euro-Maghreb relationship, the Community has maintained its intention to build steadily improving links that would have a positive impact upon the economies of the Maghreb countries. This philosophy is, of course, part of its wider strategy in fostering relations with other parts of the developing world, evidenced in initiatives such as the successive Lomé Conventions with the African, Caribbean and Pacific countries (ACP). With respect to the Maghreb countries, the Community's policy has, for the most part, consisted of granting trade preferences, financial aid, and to a lesser extent a commitment to improve the social and professional conditions of migrant workers employed in the EU. These have been the principal policy instruments used to achieve the aims set out in the arrangements concluded between the EC and the Maghreb countries.

The recurring feature constantly emphasised in these arrangements is that they have been intended to make a contribution to the economic development process of the beneficiaries through close economic cooperation. Trade is the most distinctive area in which they have been assumed to assist the efforts of the Maghreb countries in their quest for development. The fact that it is the key dimension of the relationship is more likely to be associated with the assumption that trade serves as a vehicle for potential economic growth. Therefore, the granting of preferential treatment to the exports of the Maghreb countries into the EC market would be expected to be beneficial to the recipient countries in a number of ways.

The value or importance of this preferential trading status lies first in the provision of a stimulating environment which would lead to an increase in the exports of the countries concerned to the European market. This would help promote economic development in the beneficiary countries through an increase in their export earnings. It would also provide the spur to diversify the composition of their exports, especially in certain products in which they estimate that they have a comparative advantage. This aspect may have been of certain relevance to Tunisia and Morocco which have given a positive encouragement to the export sector. Finally, this preferential system, by offering security of access to a larger market, particularly for manufactured products, would be expected to exert an attractive effect on the foreign direct investment which was and is much needed in countries like those of the Maghreb at an early stage of their development.

In addition to the provision of trade concessions as the most important facet of the relationship, the Community committed itself to the task of taking part in the development process in the Maghreb countries by means of financial assistance. The financial aid programme consisted of a mixture of commercial loans, loans on easy terms and grants. Such aid had to be used wholly or partly to finance capital projects in the areas of production and infrastructure, as well as technical cooperation and training schemes. The logic behind this additional dimension in the form of direct aid implied and still implies that the development needs of the Maghreb countries cannot be met by the preferential trade regime *per se* on its own. To enable these countries to take advantage of the opportunities offered by this regime, more financial resources would be required to improve and diversify their production potential and thus their capacity for supplying existing and new products.

Another area of no less significance in the relationship is that of migrant labour. Both the EC and the Maghreb countries committed themselves to a non-discriminatory policy to each other's workers in terms of working conditions, remuneration, and social security benefits. However, it is the Maghreb side which was expected to benefit the more, not least because of its important community working and living in Europe. Although not explicitly stated, the treatment to be given to the Maghreb migrant workers would have positive implications for the economies of the labour-exporting countries. Not only would workers received into EU countries relieve them to a certain extent of pressure on their labour markets but, more importantly, it would provide the Maghreb countries with a significant source of revenue in the form of remittances from their migrant workers.

Overall, these have been the principal areas in which the EC has sought to strengthen its links with the Maghreb countries and, at the same time, provide them with opportunities deemed to be essential factors in assisting their economic development. Therefore, for the Maghreb countries the incentives for the maintenance of the relationship with Europe and, of course, its improvement would seem quite obvious.

However, the development of the relationship and the subsequent changes brought to it, at least during previous phases, seem not to have produced an outcome as good as anticipated. A Commission statement echoed this by pointing out that: 'The record of almost twenty-five years of cooperation between the Maghreb and the Community is disappointing when compared with the hopes cherished by the two sides.'[1] An assessment of this kind, while generally accepted by both parties to the relationship, does not, of course, reflect identical grievances and/or perceptions on either side.

For obvious reasons, which have to do with the importance of the relationship for them and their status in it, the Maghreb countries have been the more concerned about its outcome. Despite the several approaches successively attempted by the EC, the Maghreb countries consider that, overall, its policy has not fulfilled their expectations. The rhetorical shift in policy content, they argue, has been one thing and the reality has been another. Whatever the good intentions underlying the relationship, it is believed that its development has suffered the consequences of Community practices or policy actions. In this regard, their dissatisfaction has been mainly concerned with the gradual whittling away of the advantages originally granted; the protectionist trend of the trade policy, not least because of the Common Agricultural Policy (CAP) mechanisms and restrictions on imports of certain industrial products regarded as sensitive; the inadequacy of financial aid; and finally the situation of migrant workers which has hardly seen any significant improvement since the conclusion of the original agreements.

On the European side, the disappointment in question does not equate with a failure of its policy towards the Maghreb region. Rather it illustrates occasional weaknesses due to internal and changing external circumstances which the EC claims to have taken into account, via appropriate measures, in order to mitigate their effects on the normal course of the relationship. Notwithstanding certain shortcomings, the EC points to essential achievements particularly in terms of market access to imports from the Maghreb countries. Without this opening-up, the Community contends that there would not have been any development, however slight, in the manufacturing sector (clothing, leather, electronics and chemicals) with its corollary impact on employment and income in both Morocco and Tunisia.[2] Access for their agricultural exports is also perceived to have substantially improved over the last two decades (1970s and 1980s).[3] On the financial side, the Community assistance, which has quantitatively increased over the years, is believed to have had in certain instances a beneficial impact on the recipient countries.[4] By and large, the EC maintains that the current economic and social situation of these countries would have been less favourable if they had not engaged in a cooperation policy with the Community since the 1960s and, in a more reinforced manner, since the mid-1970s.[5]

Given this background of arguments from both sides about the performance of their relationship, this study seeks to investigate the validity of these claims by examining the apparent effect of the provisions, as appropriate, of the various arrangements, including the most recently concluded ones in 1995 -- in admittedly only a tentative way with respect to the latter.

Aims and Motives

This study takes stock of the Euro-Maghreb relationship now that it has been in effect for more than three decades. Its main purpose is to find out the extent to which the EC policy has, in its successive phases, lived up to its intended objectives.

In assessing the impact of this policy on the Maghreb countries, the study focuses upon the structural arrangements of the different agreements and their performance in those spheres for which they have been assumed to be supportive to the process of development within the countries concerned. Nevertheless, since this study is concerned with a succession of phases in the lifetime of the relationship, the first two stages, corresponding to trade and then cooperation arrangements, will be dealt with in a fairly detailed way. This is because they reflect previous policy initiatives/attempts in the relationship and, empirically, they are supported by quantities and a quality of data which will normally allow the drawing of a final judgement. As for the third stage, where the recently concluded agreements are at an initial phase of implementation and thus have not yet had time to produce results, an attempt will be made to look into their immediate effect and forecast their likely future prospects.

The adoption in this study of a relatively long-term perspective makes it possible to gain insight into how the relationship has developed. This may be justified by the fact that in the relationship between both sides, certain periods need to be distinguished which show an increase in the activities or instruments in the EC policy towards the Maghreb region. Moreover, the effects of this relationship on the countries concerned can only be adequately appreciated by ranging over the long-run.

Having said that, it is worth noting some of the reasons that motivated the undertaking of this study. These may be grouped under two main heads.

First, the Euro-Maghreb relationship has been and continues to be a matter of primary concern particularly for the Maghreb countries for which it remains a determining framework for cooperation for development. Although the same cannot be said about the EC, the latter's partnership initiative, endorsed at the Barcelona Conference in November 1995, may also suggest on its part a renewed interest in the relationship. This is an ongoing process that is still the subject of a continual and somewhat divergent official debate from both sides. This study, by contributing to this debate, looks into the evolution of that relationship in order to draw some lessons from its past, present and eventually future patterns. The conclusions arrived at may be taken into consideration by either those policy-makers from both parties -- who are at the moment entering what is called a new phase in their relationship -- and interested researchers within the academic community.

In the second place, the Euro-Maghreb relationship has so far received scant attention, when not downright understudied, when compared, for example, to other EC regional links such as Lomé or even the recent experience towards central and eastern European countries (CEEC). In general, besides a few sparse research materials, a great deal of the studies published to date have concentrated on selected aspects covering certain periods of EC relations in a rather wider geographical scope, that is, in regard to the Mediterranean basin as a whole. These, while having the merit of giving a broader perspective on EC cooperation policy, have in certain instances tended to deal with the whole area as a single unit for their analysis. The result is that they do not give an adequate account of the implications of EC policy, with its range of instruments over time, on any individual country or group of countries which, by and large, differ from the others in several respects. Thus this study attempts to fill this gap by seeking to examine specifically the Euro-Maghreb relationship in a more comprehensive way from its inception until the present time.

The methodological thrust of this work is analytical, descriptive and to a certain extent policy prescriptive at a later stage.

Structure of the Book

The study is an examination the Euro-Maghreb relationship which, after being preceded by an attempt at identifying the nature, characteristics and some of the determinants of this relationship, follows a chronological sequence moving according to the successive phases in the EC policy towards the region. Its main structure is arranged in an introduction and three parts including the final conclusion.

The first part, consisting of one chapter, sets the general background. Thus this opening chapter surveys some of the major theoretical debate on the concepts of 'dependence' and 'interdependence' and attempts to define the nature of, and characteristic features associated with, the Euro-Maghreb relationship. This is followed by an examination of a number of factors, both in the Maghreb and Europe, deemed of particular importance as a background in understanding the environment in which this relationship has evolved.

Following this preliminary overview, the second part of this book takes stock of, and evaluates the comparative successes/failings of the previous phases of the EC policy *vis-à-vis* the Maghreb countries. Chapter two addresses the initial or first phase corresponding to the 1960s arrangements whose content was entirely confined to trade matters. Chapter three investigates the subsequent 'global' approach of the 1970s in its broadly-based coverage of issues, encompassing trade, financial assistance, and labour.

Finally, the third part deals with the EU's partnership initiative articulated in the 1990s which, in essence, is a European response to the implications of the increasing instability of the Maghreb region. Accordingly, chapter four examines the sources of that potential instability. Chapter five attempts an appraisal of the recently concluded schemes in terms of their immediate effects and future prospects, focusing in particular on their central component, the establishment of a free trade area. Chapter six, as a conclusion, summarises the findings of the study and makes some recommendations as for the future development of the Euro-Maghreb relationship and possible areas for further academic research.

Notes

1   Commission of the European Communities, *The Future of Relations between the Community and the Maghreb*, SEC(92) 401 final, Brussels, 30 April 1992, p. 14.
2   *Ibid.*, p. 13.
3   Commission of the European Communities, *Strengthening the Mediterranean policy of the*

European Union: Establishing a Euro-Mediterranean Partnership, COM(94) 427 final, Brussels, 19 October 1994, published in *Bulletin of the European Union*, supplement no. 2, 1995, p. 22.
4 Commission of the European Communities, *The Future of Relations...*, *op.cit.*, p. 14.
5 *Ibid.*

PART ONE
THE EURO-MAGHREB RELATIONSHIP AND ITS ENVIRONMENT

1 Nature, Characteristics and Determinants

Introduction

Prior to the examination of the successive phases in the Euro-Maghreb relationship, an attempt is made here to convey a definition of the nature of this relationship along with a number of characteristic features associated with it. It is also the case that this chapter provides a background about the environment in which this relationship has been evolving. Despite not being an exhaustive review, it does, however, address some of the actual and possible developments or issues that, on both sides, have affected and might affect the course of its development. These include not only an examination of the state of regional integration among Maghreb countries and their external position towards Europe but also, on the Community side, those aspects relating to trade policy, the Single Market, treatment reserved to central and eastern Europe, and somewhat different perception of interests amongst Member States.

This chapter is divided into two main sections. The first one focuses on the integrative process in the Maghreb along with the coordination of relations with the EC. The second one considers the impact of Community policies in external trade, completion of the internal market, association of CEEC, and the divergent interest of Member States towards the Maghreb region.

Defining the Relationship

In the field of North-South relations, and more particularly Euro-South regional economic arrangements, the numerous studies undertaken have given analytical consideration to the concepts of dependence (or more commonly dependency) and interdependence.[1] Therefore, it would seem appropriate at this point to shed some light on these two key concepts prior to the attempt to define the Euro-Maghreb relationship.

Concepts of Dependence and Interdependence

The academic literature on interdependence and dependence is vast and in many instances controversial (Baldwin, 1980, pp. 471-506). In his study on the international political economy, Timothy Shaw notes that both concepts have come 'to characterise and symbolise rather different world views and visions'. He argues that whereas the former tends to be proposed 'as both approach and ideology' by various individuals and institutions in the developed countries, the latter is seen by many developing countries as 'their major problem and constraint, resulting in underdevelopment rather than development' (Shaw, quoted in Asante, 1986, p. 187).

James Caporaso, like Shaw, distinguishes the two concepts as follows:

> The dependence orientation seeks to probe and explore the symmetries and asymmetries among nation-states. This approach most often proceeds from a liberal paradigm (...)The dependency orientation, on the other hand, seeks to explore the process of integration into the international capitalist system and to assess the development implications of this peripheral capitalism (1978, p. 2).

During the 1970s the concept of dependence, either mutual or otherwise, had stimulated an interesting theoretical debate among social scientists. For instance, Robert O. Keohane and Joseph S. Nye regard it as helpful in explaining the distribution of power in world politics (1977, pp. 3-19), while Sanjaya Lall rejects it on the ground that it is an 'unhelpful' and 'misleading' analytical category (1975, p. 808). Other scholars such as Richard Rosecrance and Arthur Stein complain about the lack of conceptual clarity (1977, pp. 425-426), and some even deny that there exists any generally accepted definition of the term (Alker et al., 1974, vol. 1, p. 2). As these concepts appear to be contested ones in contemporary social thought, there will be no attempt here at theoretical exactitude, nor will there be an attempt to discuss in detail the various contending stances. Rather, the aim is limited to a summary of some of the attempts at defining them.

Two basic meanings can be distinguished with respect to the concept of dependence. For Lall dependence would, in conventional economic usage, mean a state of being determined, or significantly affected by external forces. A country may, for instance, be described as being dependent on foreign trade or foreign technology, and in such a context, he argues that:

> There is no hint of anything undesirable, nor there is any implications of a process of causation. Dependence is defined with reference to some particular

objective economic fact and says nothing in a descriptive or causal sense about the condition of the economy as whole (1975, p. 800).

In another respect, this concept has been associated with the post-colonial economic situation of developing countries. In this context, dependence is meant to describe certain characteristics of the economy as a whole and is intended to trace certain processes which are causally linked to its underdevelopment and which are expected to affect adversely its development in the future (Lall, 1980, p. 800). As such a distinction should, therefore, be made between dependence as alluding to 'external reliance on other actors' and dependency as referring to 'the process of incorporation of less developed countries into the global capitalist system and the structural distortions resulting therefrom' (Caporaso, 1978, pp. 18-20). In this latter usage, the concept is commonly associated with the writings of some scholars from, and working on, Latin America in particular. One of the most frequently quoted definitions of dependence is that of Theotonio Dos Santos:

> By dependence we mean a situation in which the economy of certain countries is conditioned by the development and expansion of another economy to which the former is subjected. The relation of interdependence between two or more economies, and between these and world trade, assumes the form of dependence when some countries (the dominant ones) can expand and can be self-sustaining, while other countries (the dependent ones) can do this only as a reflection of that expansion, which can have either a positive or a negative effect on their immediate development (1970, p. 231).

The concept of interdependence, on the other hand, carries various connotations or meanings thus making the task difficult to single out a commonly accepted definition (Baldwin, 1980, pp. 471-506). This being so, some attempts at defining this concept warrant some attention. According to Graham Evans and Jeffrey Newham: 'Interdependence in world politics implies that actors are interrelated or connected such that something that happens to at least one actor, on at least one occasion, in at least one place, will affect the actors' (1990, p. 182). Such a definition more or less joins that of Rosecrance and Stein for whom, in the most general sense, this concept consists of 'a relationship of interests such that if one nation's position changes, other states will be affected by that change', or in an economic sense 'interdependencies are present when there is an increased national 'sensitivity' to external economic developments' (1977, p. 2).

A fundamental question that can be raised in this regard is whether all actors (states or others) in such a relationship are equally affected. And this question will determine whether interdependence is symmetrical or not. A pure symmetry in an interdependent situation is a very rare case, if not an ideal type. Most cases display asymmetries rather than symmetries, but with varying degrees. For instance, if one actor is less affected by some change in a relationship, whereas the other partner is crucially affected, then the interdependence is asymmetrical. In other words, interdependence, in this case, suggests that the dependence of one side is much greater than that of the other side. This means, as aptly observed by R. Harris Wagner that: 'One party needs the benefits derived from a relationship more than the other' (1988, p. 461). In relation to power, an asymmetrical interdependent relationship is seen by Keohane and Nye as follows: 'A less dependent actor in a relationship often has significant political resources, because changes in the relationship (which the actor may be able to initiate or threaten) will be less costly to that actor than to its partners' (1977, p. 11).

Nature and Features of the Euro-Maghreb Relationship

After this succinct background on both concepts of dependence and interdependence, a major point that remains to be tackled here is the identification of the nature and distinguishing characteristics of the relationship between the EC and the Maghreb countries.

The characteristic feature in this relationship is that it involves two economically unequal parties. On the one hand is a highly developed and integrated European economy progressing towards self-sufficiency in many respects. On the other, there is the Maghreb economy at an early phase of its development. This situation may convey the image of a centre-periphery/metropole-satellite relationship or dominance-dependence pattern as described by dependency theorists. Approaching it from a dependency perspective would suggest first and foremost the exposition of some of the major tenets of this perspective and their relevance to the specific case of the Euro-Maghreb relationship. In this context and generally speaking, a dependent relationship assumes, among other things, domination and exploitation of the peripheral economy via capital investment from the centre; penetration of the dependent country by multinational corporations based in the centre and alliances of convenience; and common interest existing between the centres of international capitalism and the clientele class that wields power in the dependent economy (Gilpin, 1987, pp. 281-290). Instead of contributing to the economic development of peripheral countries, altogether these characteristics are seen as perpetuating the dependence of these countries on the capitalist system which maintains them in an underdeveloped position.

If one looks at these features, the dependence may seem to be more applicable in accounting for the Latin American experience. Even in this case, however, the concept of dependence, as used in the analysis of underdevelopment was not accepted. Lall argues that the characteristics to which underdevelopment in dependent countries is generally attributed are not exclusive to these economies, but are also found in those economies categorised as non-dependent countries. He found that the dominance of foreign capital -- one of the most important aspects of dependency -- was more important in the latter than in the former countries (1975, p. 800).

In the context of this study, these characteristics cannot adequately account for the Euro-Maghreb relationship. With varying degrees, the economic development of the Maghreb countries has not been primarily dependent upon foreign investment.[2] Morocco and Tunisia (the latter since 1969), which more or less opted for liberal economic policies, resorted to a great extent to local investment either in its public or private form. The penetration of multinational corporations has remained limited and the scope of their potential operation will have to be seen in the light of the ongoing economic reforms under way in this region. Such reforms are given much emphasis by the present partnership agreements with Europe.

Another aspect that can be charged against the dependency perspective relates to its pessimism regarding the export-oriented policies pursued by the developing countries. Recent experience shows that their share of manufactures in total exports is increasing and both Morocco and Tunisia can relatively be categorised as 'new emerging exporting countries' (David, 1987, p. 142).

Finally, this study, while mainly concerned with the successive phases in the Euro-Maghreb relationship, will suggest, at a later stage, some policy measures destined to its improvement which, overall, makes inappropriate the use of dependency perspective, especially when it comes to the breaking away from the world market economy and the option for self-reliant development policy.

For the reasons outlined above, the Euro-Maghreb relationship could rather be defined as one of high asymmetrical interdependence. And because the concept of interdependence has also been a subject of a large and controversial debate among social scientists, the task ahead would be to formulate or produce a clear statement of its meaning in this respect. 'If one is to theorise about interdependence or attempt to measure it' argues David A. Baldwin, 'the first step is a clear conceptualisation of the nature of interdependence' (1980, p. 472). Here interdependence is used to mean that both parties would incur costs if the relationship were broken. It does not, however, suggest that each party would bear equal costs, that is, it does not imply that each actor is equally dependent upon the other (Habeeb, 1988, p. 19). Asymmetrical interdependence, exemplified by the Euro-Maghreb relationship, means that the latter needs the benefits derived from such a relationship more than the former and, therefore, would bear far greater costs if the relationship came to an end. In other words, this typical characterisation suggests that the dependence of one side (the Maghreb) is clearly much greater than that of the other side (EU) (Aghrout and Geddes, 1996, p. 228). Viewed from an economic angle, the reality of this asymmetrical pattern of relationship was candidly expressed by Eberhardt Rhein, a former European Commission official, for whom the relationship: 'continues to be one of "giant" to "dwarf". Europe can therefore, economically speaking, largely ignore what goes on in the Maghreb but not the other way round' (1989, p. 3).

The dimension of this asymmetry are glaring when one considers some key economic indicators. The available data show that the gross domestic product (GDP) of the EU reached 8,330 billion dollars 1998,[3] compared to about 106.1 billion dollars in the Maghreb,[4] thus representing nearly 1.3 per cent of that of the EU during the same year. One other noteworthy trend to stress is that the Maghreb countries only account for around 2.3 per cent and 2.4 per cent of the extra-EU imports and exports respectively.[5] By contrast, the EU is their major trading partner with which an average of 65-67 percent of their total trade is conducted.[6]

In sum, over its evolution, this asymmetrical interdependence between two unequal actors has displayed a number of features. First, the policies of the EC and economic development in Europe have exerted and continue to exert a greater determining impact on the Maghreb countries' economic development. While this fact denotes the vulnerable position of the Maghreb countries in this relationship, it does not suggest that there is no sensitivity on the EC side. Energy supplies and migration are areas of clear European interest, and may be felt particularly strongly by southern EU Member States (see Chapter Five). Furthermore there is a growing awareness on part of the EU of the implications of economic and political instability, the implications of which, in terms of security and potential migratory pressure, seem potentially very large.

Second, production structures of Maghreb economies are to a certain consideration oriented towards Europe and not vice versa, thus making the process of their development policies fragile and insecure. Finally, as a result of these two inter-related facets, the EC as a less dependent actor enjoys a greater capacity to determine the outcome of interaction than do the Maghreb countries.[7]

In terms of power, there is an unbalanced relationship to the detriment of the latter which -- because of the few alternatives available to them -- have limited margin for manoeuvre.

Maghreb: Regional Unity and Coordination of Relations with Europe

Attempts at Regional Integration

One of the most significant features of Maghreb countries is their historical, cultural and geographical unity. All these aspects may be considered as factors impelling any process of integration. While this propitious environment may have served as an initial stage or 'trigger' to a number of collective integrative efforts, it has, however, been overridden by constraints of a political, economic, and institutional nature.

The move towards integration among the Maghreb countries goes back to the early 1960s. Its beginning coincided with the euphoria of independence and the widely accepted notion of regional integration as a potentially effective medium for helping bring about rapid economic development. In this respect, two main phases can be singled out: 1964-1975 and the late 1980s onwards.

The first multilateral attempt was fostered by numerous contributing factors including the continuing belief in the necessary unity of the Maghreb. This was particularly underlined on economic grounds as emphasised in the conclusions of an official meeting of the Maghreb foreign ministers in Rabat in February 1963.[8] The declared goals included, among other things, harmonising policy towards other groupings and coordinating development plans and trade policy. The next force that helped to bolster this process was the relative settlement of tension and border disputes that emerged following independence, and which degenerated into an armed conflict between Algeria and Morocco. A final factor was the contribution of the United Nations Economic Commission for Africa (UNECA) which, in a report tabled after a visit to the region, drew the attention of these countries to the possibilities of industrial development, especially projects that could benefit more than one country, and made suggestions for coordinated policy among the countries concerned.[9] All these forces prompted the first conference of economic ministers of Algeria, Libya, Morocco, and Tunisia in Tunis in 1964 that launched a regional institution, the *Comité Permanent Consultatif du Maghreb* (CPCM), to coordinate and harmonise economic policies (Slim, 1980, p. 325).

Agreements signed afterwards provided for the coordination and harmonisation of development plans, including those for industries and services as well as intra-regional trade and relations with the EC (Aghrout, 1990, pp. 139-162). A Maghreb Centre for Industrial Studies was set up during 1968 in Tripoli, with financial and technical assistance from the United Nations Development Programme, to promote joint projects. However, cooperation broke down because each country's industrial policy ignored those of its neighbours, resulting in the proliferation of rival industries and sectoral over-capacity. For instance, by 1968 the competing steel industries had achieved a production capacity of almost one million tonnes, compared with a regional consumption of slightly more than a half that figure (560,000 tonnes) (Mokaddem, 1987, p. 445). Similarly, each of the Maghreb countries developed its own fertiliser plants, despite the UNECA suggestion of only one, and again production capacity exceeded the demands of the regional market.[10] Meanwhile in the area of trade, *'le principe de l'approvisionnement prioritaire dans les pays du Maghreb'* was not implemented, not least because most of their commerce was conducted with third countries.

A renewed interest in regional integration in the late 1980s culminated in the establishment of the *Union du Maghreb Arabe* (UMA) in February 1989, between Algeria, Libya, Mauritania, Morocco, and Tunisia. This time a number of factors made the creation of this regional economic grouping a matter of survival. Among these factors were the heightening of the internal economic crisis in oil-producing countries such as Algeria and Libya since 1986, the global trend towards the formation of regional trade blocs, the southern enlargement of the EC to include Greece, Spain and Portugal, and the imminent completion of the European internal market (Aghrout, 1992, p. 579).

Among the central objectives of the UMA Treaty was the strengthening of links between member countries in order to ensure stability and enhance policy coordination, as well as gradually to introduce free movement of goods, services, and factors of production.[11] It also highlighted the broad economic strategy to be pursued, namely the development of industry, agriculture, and commerce by means of specific joint ventures and general programmes of cooperation.[12] An institutional machinery for taking and administering decisions was put in place consisting of the council of heads of state, the council of foreign ministers, the follow-up committee, the consultative assembly, and the various specialised commissions (food security, economic and financial affairs, basic infrastructure, and human resources).

After the signing of the Treaty a number of economic decisions were taken. At the second meeting of the heads of state in Algiers in July 1990, a common development strategy was formulated. It was adopted during the third meeting in Libya in March 1991 as a basic document entitled '*Les grandes lignes d'une stratégie maghrébine de développement*'. These guidelines outlined four steps of economic integration with fixed deadlines for establishing a free trade area by the end of 1992, a customs union by the end of 1995, a common market by the end of 2000, and at a later stage with no specified date, an economic and monetary union.

Up to April 1994, the UMA member countries had signed around thirty-six multilateral agreements, concerning diverse economic, social, environmental and cultural areas.[13] Only five of them have been ratified. These relate to trade in industrial products; trade in agricultural products; regional investment guarantees; avoidance of double taxation; and phytosanitary standards. The first two agreements which aimed to establish a free trade area through removal of tariff and non-tariff barriers, have partially been implemented (agricultural products only) as of January 2000. At the same date, the remaining three agreements have not yet come into operation. Therefore, any tangible success that the UMA can point to, more than eleven years since its inception, is rather modest, if not disappointing. Despite its scope for multilateral integration, it has proved to be neither a substitute for, nor a complement to, those relations which largely continue to be confined to the bilateral or sometimes trilateral level.

All in all, no single factor is in itself sufficient to account for the poor performance of past and present experience. Instead it is the result of the accumulation and interaction of several political, economic, and institutional considerations, all of a handicapping nature. The most crucial one has been the lack of unwavering political commitment. Economic issues of 'high politics' remain dependent on the fluctuating political will and enthusiasm of the partner countries (Ravenhill, 1979, p. 228). In the Maghreb, the manifestation of this will has always been both ephemeral and occasional. To varying degrees, the effects of divergent ideologies among the governing political regimes, frequent inter-state conflicts, and struggles for regional leadership have raised obstacles to the necessary building of consensus politics. The incidence of these may have been compounded in recent years by the still unresolved Western Sahara issue, the internal difficulties in Algeria, and the fallout of United Nations (UN) sanctions on Libya, with which the UMA partners have no other alternative than to comply. In retaliation, Libya seems to have defected from the organisation, especially when it announced on 30 January 1995 that it would not take over the UMA chairmanship from Algeria.[14] Libya's position, however, comes as an additional constraint since the future of the grouping was put in doubt during the foreign ministers' council meeting on 11 January 1993, at which the Algerian representative attributed the serious problems facing the UMA to: 'The Western

Sahara, which needs to be settled before the construction of the Maghreb Union, and the differences in economic orientation in the member countries at present.'[15]

The different economic policies embarked upon by the Maghreb countries since the 1960s have also created major obstacles to regional integration. Though it had been agreed at that time that Maghreb unity was the theoretical solution to many of the most difficult problems besetting North African states in the field of economic development (Rivlin, 1966, p. 286), the newly-independent nations in practice pursued more individualistic and distinctive patterns of development.

Algeria opted for a non-liberal path based on a central planning development model. Morocco's economic development assumed rather more of a capitalist nature where private, and public (state participation) investments coexisted. As for Tunisia, it followed a middle-of-the-road plan, which changed course in 1969 from an initial phase of collectivisation to a more pronounced liberal system. These divergent paths proved difficult to reconcile at regional level. Indeed, they surfaced at the Rabat meeting in 1970, when the approach favouring a global integration -- instead of a sectoral integration -- was subordinated to the right of each government to exercise its own fundamental choices in the political and economic field alike. Moroccan and Tunisian attachment to western capitalism did not find favour with the Algerian conception, any more than did the former's preference for a European-Mediterranean Maghreb (Aghrout and Sutton, 1990, pp. 118-119).

Although all the Maghreb nations have since the 1980s embarked on economic reforms aimed at either increasing the role of market forces and the private sector or reorientating economic management towards a market system, there are still few significant signs of converging policies at the regional level.

Their trade relations can serve as a case for argument about the effect of economic policies. As illustrated by table 1.1, trade among the Maghreb countries has been characterised by its small size and volatile nature. The figures suggest a decline in their regional trade between 1970 and 1985. Whereas in 1970, the process of integration seemed imminent, intra-regional trade accounted for less than 2 percent of total trade at that time. This decline mirrors the then prevailing political climate characterising inter-state relations, especially the Algerian-Moroccan conflict over the divisive issue of Western Sahara and its corollary, the emergence of regional alliances and axes. From 1985 onwards, one can discern a reversed trend where a small but steady improvement in intra-Maghreb trade is registered. It coincides, among other things, with the relative rapprochement between the Maghreb countries and may even be associated with

Table 1.1 Share of intra-Maghreb trade in total trade

	Total trade (million dollars)		Intra-Maghreb (%)	
	Imports	Exports	Imports	Exports
1964	1,695	1,996	4.4	1.6
1970	2,805	4,047	2.3	1.6
1975	13,827	13,418	0.8	1.0
1980	26,007	40,011	0.4	0.2
1985	22,148	27,911	1.4	1.1
1990	28,808	33,368	3.2	2.8
1993	28,858	27,340	3.3	3.5
1996	32,043	35,353	3.8	3.1
1997	29,719	36,702	2.8	2.1

Source: Calculations based on data derived from the International Monetary Fund (IMF), *Direction of Trade Statistics Yearbook* (Washington, DC: IMF, 1972, 1982,1992,1993,1994,1997 and 1998).

the trading position of both Morocco and Tunisia. As can be seen from table 1.2, Morocco and Tunisia are, proportionally to their total exports, the biggest exporting countries to the Maghreb, accounting for nearly all the imports of Algeria and Libya from the region in 1996.

On the institutional side, a noteworthy factor is the weakness of the

Table 1.2 Recorded intra-Maghreb trade in 1996 and 1997 (million dollars)

	Total exports		Algeria		Libya		Mauritania		Morocco		Tunisia		Maghreb (%)	
	1996	1997	1996	1997	1996	1997	1996	1997	1996	1997	1996	1997	1996	1997
Algeria	12,555	13,923	–	–	8	ntr	19	22	106	103	116	92	2.0	1.6
Libya	10,033	9,816	5	5	–	–	1	1	51	140	213	228	2.7	3.8
Mauritania	573	540	ntr	ntr	ntr	ntr	–	–	ntr	ntr	2	2	0.3	0.3
Morocco	6,973	7,060	56	40	134	ntr	8	10	–	–	53	25	3.6	1.1
Tunisia	5,519	5,363	96	68	196	ntr	1	1	38	38	–	–	6.0	2.0

Source: Calculations based on data derived from the IMF, *Direction of Trade Statistics Yearbook* (Washington, DC: IMF, 1997 and 1998).
(ntr): no trade recorded.

various regional structures that are considered of an overriding importance in any integrative process. This fact has been common to both experiences (the CPCM and the UMA) the region has known so far. The lack of unwavering commitment to the regional construct, mentioned above, has had the effect of reducing the role and effectiveness which those established institutions were normally supposed to assume in this context. It is noticeable that their tasks have been mainly confined to producing feasibility studies and making proposals for policy coordination which, in most case, have not been implemented. A plausible explanation for this lies in the deliberate intention of the member countries not to surrender decision-making powers to a regional body and hence to subordinate the whole regional construct to the will of the governments, previously the conference of economic ministers and currently the council of heads of state. In the UMA Treaty, the council of heads of state is the only body empowered to take decisions. Consequently, as far as the present scheme is concerned, this means that this council is the motor that drives or stalls the regional project (Mortimer, 1993, p. 18).

The centralisation of decision-making power in the hands of an intergovernmental institution is, to a significant extent, responsible for the slow, if not the limited progress thus far achieved. This is always likely to be the case when for more than a decade (1964-1975), the economic ministers met only seven times to discuss and attempt to decide on important regional matters. Similar observations are equally valid for the council of heads of state which has met only six times since the UMA's foundation, with intervals sometimes reaching sixteen months as was the case between the two last summit meetings (November 1992-April 1994). More disappointing is the fact that more than six years have elapsed since the last summit meeting and still there is no indication of a date for the next one. In addition, though now abandoned, the need for unanimity proved to be a stumbling block when key decisions were vetoed by one or more member countries. One example was, for instance, the need for unanimity which faced the sixth conference of Maghreb economic ministers in Rabat in 1970, which failed to endorse a global integrative approach because of a single veto from Algeria (Aghrout and Sutton, 1990, p. 135). The end result is an array of institutions whose functioning and performance are not only hampered by their denial of any decision-making power but also by the volatile political will of the partner countries.

Coordination of External Positions

It was argued that, in principle, the degree of coordination of external relations is a measure of the unity of a regional grouping *vis-à-vis* the outside world (Dusan, 1974, p. 136). Despite being made more than two and a half decades ago, this observation from a United Nations Conference on Trade and Development (UNCTAD) expert on regional economic integration among developing countries, may still be applicable to the Maghreb countries' case. Indeed, these countries have, on several occasions, pointed to the importance of their relations with the EC and pledged to work towards coordinating them. In so doing, this would enable them to obtain more favourable conditions in the European market than would have been available to them acting independently.

As a starting point, such a commitment to act in concert was made at the Tunis conference of 1964 where the Maghreb economic ministers stressed the urgency of hammering out a coordinated external trade policy. In this respect, the ministerial conference 'taking account of the importance of economic relations between the different Member States of the European Community, has recognised the necessity of defining new relations with the EEC' and decided 'to widen contacts with a view to coordinating the respective positions *vis-à-vis* the EEC, and entrusted the Permanent Committee [CPCM] to study the various aspects of this coordination'.[16]

An institution created under the auspices of the CPCM, the Maghreb Commission for Trade Relations, was assigned the task of preparing a study on the coordination of member countries' export policies. The objectives sought were as follows:

- Coordinating the export of similar agricultural products;
- Creation of specialised agencies for each export;
- Possible creation of a central agency to coordinate and monitor the activities of the specialised agencies;
- Taking into consideration existing trade links of each member country as well as each member's economic conditions.[17]

Though these commitments could be seen at the time as an explicit recognition of the seriousness of the matter, they were accompanied by no significant achievement in practice. The only concrete accomplishment was the establishment of a marketing and export agency, *Comptoir Maghrébin de l'Alfa*, which was concerned with the exports of esparto-grass. It investigated markets, centralised orders, fixed each member country's quota, and established floor prices (Aghrout and Sutton, 1990, p. 117). From 1967, the shrinking international markets limited this agency's role and led to its dissolution in 1975.[18]

Apart from this exceptional case which had little impact on their relations with the EC, there were no other joint arrangements of the kind and for which they might be credited. Neither was there a harmonised attitude when the Maghreb countries negotiated the agreements with their European partners. While in principle a common policy had been accepted in this regard and despite the Community's desire to favour joint negotiations towards a single free trade area encompassing the whole region, the Maghreb countries never coordinated their positions for even one round of EC negotiations (Zartman, 1971, p. 119). Thus each country went its own way, negotiating on an individual basis for a separate association. This led to trade agreements in 1969 for Morocco and Tunisia. Again and including Algeria this time, they individually negotiated the 1976 cooperation agreements.

In this regard, a number of reasons can be adduced to account for the absence of a coordinated external policy and thus the undertaking of separate negotiations. One reason had to do with their different status *vis-à-vis* the EC. Whereas comparatively Algeria inherited a more advantageous position, Morocco and Tunisia did not. The latter were particularly worried about their trade relations with the Community following France's commitment to the CAP. This difference in respective positions and preoccupations had an adverse effect on the necessary coordination of their negotiating status as a group. Such an argument is validated by a late 1966 internal report from one member country which stated that:

> The need to conclude an agreement rapidly with the European Market has led to undertaking separate contacts because the search for a complete Maghreb agreement prior to these contacts has appeared susceptible to pushing [back] new economic and commercial relations with the Common Market to an infinite date (cited in Zartman, 1971, p. 157).

A further reason of no less importance to pinpoint in this context was the reluctance of the Maghreb countries to engage in the harmonising of their development plans based on different political and economic orientations. Having opted for different economic strategies, they have consequently manifested non-convergent interests in their links, both to the outside world generally, and in relations with Europe in particular.

The formation of the UMA, though it was not exclusively dictated by the necessity to bring about an improvement to existing Euro-Maghreb relations, did, indeed, constitute a renewed interest in improving links with Europe. Thus a large part of the rationale behind the launching of this regional arrangement was to allow the founding members to bargain collectively with the EC.

Indicative of this concern is the proposals made by some member countries in two official documents.[19] The first document initiated by Morocco in August 1989 and entitled *'Les relations de l'UMA et de la CEE: bases et axes'* identified two inter-related factors which would underlie the conduct of these relations. On the one hand, it emphasised the appropriateness of the UMA as a viable vehicle through which Maghreb countries could articulate their external relations and thereby increase their bargaining leverage. On the other hand, the realisation of this was made conditional on the definition and adoption by member countries of a common strategy for the UMA in its external relations, mainly those with the EC.

The second document on *'Les mécanismes de concertation entre l'UMA et la CEE'* was put forward by Tunisia in March 1990. Relative to the Moroccan proposal, it can be viewed as a further step in the process of devising a commonly coordinated and unified position for the UMA member countries. Essentially concerned with procedural matters, the Tunisian document implicitly deplored the fact that while contacts between the Community and other regional organisations in South-East Asia, Central America, and the Gulf (Gulf Cooperation Council) continue to be conducted at the level of foreign affairs ministers on both sides, this has not been the case with respect to Maghreb countries. Hence the Tunisian proposal insisted on the necessity for similar procedures or contacts between the UMA members and those of the EC which would be organised on a regular basis.

These proposals were initially realised when two meetings were held in Brussels on 13 November 1990 and 4 November 1991, and brought together the UMA foreign ministers and those of the EC. During the second meeting, political dialogue and economic cooperation were identified as key issues in their future contacts. These were further elaborated in a Commission communication in April 1992 to the Council and the European Parliament entitled *'The Future of Relations between the Community and the Maghreb'*.[20]

This communication, which outlined the Community's new type of 'partnership' with the Maghreb countries, did not, however, envisage a 'global' deal that would involve both organisations. Indeed, the European side, though not ruling out the eventuality of such a deal in the long-term, made it explicitly clear that for the time being only 'the three individual states [Algeria, Morocco and Tunisia] will remain the Community's main negotiating partners in the Maghreb' thereby excluding in the process the two remaining members of the UMA, Libya and Mauritania. Even for those countries targeted, the new Community approach 'will be implemented through agreements concluded with each of the three states separately' that would form part of the group of Mediterranean non-member countries and this group, rather than the UMA, would be the main building block for relations between the two flanks under the new Euro-Mediterranean policy.

By emphasising separate arrangements to be negotiated on a country-by-country basis, the Community rendered the already fragile consensus amidst the Maghreb countries, in their initial intention to coordinate respective positions and even reach a global deal, more difficult to achieve. While that was the position firmly defended by the Community, Maghreb countries were unable, or perhaps more accurately, unwilling to express their disagreement. It is clear that it is the European side which carries more weight in determining the outcome, but it should also be borne in mind that the Maghreb countries manifested no strong commitment to their collective endeavour.

In fact, over recent years, Maghreb countries tended towards negotiating the new Euro-Mediterranean agreements on a bilateral basis. By way of illustration, Morocco showed less enthusiasm about developing a relationship with the EC as part of a regional grouping. For many years, Morocco had strived for special attention from its European partners. Its official application for Community membership in July 1987 can be seen as an early signal in this direction. As the alternative of membership was ruled out -- being solely open to European countries -- Morocco had instead sought a status similar to that provided for in the association of CEEC. An aspiration of the kind is reflected in a statement made by Abdelatif Filali, former Prime Minister and head of the Moroccan diplomatic service, who argued that: 'Morocco was within its right to demand a different status from the other countries of North Africa [because] of all the Maghreb countries, Morocco is closest to Europe by virtue of its economy and internal politics.'[21] This assertion is a clear indication of the fact that Morocco's priorities tilted away from those of the Maghreb as a group. Thus it is not surprising that it was the first country which not only welcomed with great interest the EU offer for a free trade zone but also pioneered the negotiations towards the implementation of such a scheme.

Until recently, Tunisia seemed probably the only country in the region to have attached more importance to the UMA as a potential partner with Europe. In an address to the European Parliament in Strasbourg on 22 June 1993, President Zine el-Abidine Ben Ali of Tunisia was quoted as saying:

> I would call on the European Community and its Member States to convene a conference on development in the countries of the Arab Maghreb, with the purpose of concluding a contract for progress and solidarity that could set in motion mechanisms for cooperation based on a political, economic, social and cultural partnership between the two communities.[22]

For Tunisia, Europe is seen both as a challenge and an example that could inspire the building of a Maghreb community and even stimulate its anchoring into the dynamic European space. It is this perception which might have motivated Tunisia's call to the EC regarding the Maghreb countries' debt to Europe in 1990. It suggested the conversion of this debt, or part of it, into financial means to support regional environmental and productive programmes. It also called for the development of new instruments of financial cooperation such as the establishment of a 'Euro-Maghreb Development Bank'. Besides this, Tunisia went even further by proposing a *'Commissariat Maghrébin Commun'* to represent the interests of UMA member countries in the EC.

However, these appeals were, in fact, met with neither any exceptional attention from Europe nor a resolute commitment from the other Maghreb countries. Feeling somewhat disappointed as a result, Tunisia had no other alternative than to fall back on bilateral relations and negotiate individually with Brussels at a moment when Morocco was already doing so and Algeria was almost fully absorbed by its domestic problems.

Once again, it appears that in failing to take adequate account of regional interests shared in common *vis-à-vis* Europe, the Maghreb countries have demonstrated the ephemeral or circumstantial nature of their collective endeavour. So long as the logic of national interest and, to a certain extent, political problems continue to be a stumbling block, any move to embrace a common front towards the EC can be considered merely as a weighty addition to the long-standing rhetoric. This is because the reality seems to reflect a situation where the UMA is still far from being a reality, and its members, in particular, fear that multilateral cooperation may call into question bilateral cooperation to which they are tremendously attached.

Actual and Potential Impact of the EC Policies

Aspects of External Trade Policy

Because of its economic size, the EC occupies a major place in the international trading system. In 1997, it accounted, in value terms, for 37.8 per cent of the world's exports and 35.1 per cent of the world's imports, compared to 12.4 per cent and 16.0 per cent for the United States and 7.6 per cent and 6.0 per cent for Japan.[23] Being by far the biggest trading bloc reflects, to a certain extent, the Community's world-wide trade links.

The most developed instrument available to the Community in dealing with third countries in this respect is the Common Commercial Policy (CCP), which is regarded as a natural extension of both the Customs Union and the Common External Tariff (CET) (Church and Phinnemore, 1994, p. 183). It mainly covers trade in goods and services while trade in agricultural and steel and coal products are governed by the CAP and the European Coal and Steel Community respectively.

In the course of its development, the EC has become an important partner in numerous bilateral and multilateral trade agreements. Very briefly, among these arrangements one can cite the following:

- The European Economic Area whose aim is the setting up of a free trade area between the EU and the EFTA (European Free Trade Association) countries, excluding Switzerland, with the extension of most aspects of the Single Market to the latter. Moreover, a number of them such as Austria, Finland, and Sweden have already become full members since January 1995.
- The Europe agreements (also known as association agreements) with CEEC designed to establish on a step-by-step basis a free trade zone, with the EU removing its trade barriers faster. The ultimate objective is that some of these countries are most likely to be included in the next wave of of enlargement.
- The Mediterranean agreements, which under their trade heading, provide for free access to industrial products into the EU, subject to certain exceptions in the textile and clothing sector, and restricted access for agricultural products covered by the CAP. A new generation of agreements, launched under the partnership initiative, is expected to replace those concluded in the 1970s.
- The Lomé Convention grants, on a non-reciprocal basis or one-way preferences, free entry to all manufactured goods and certain agricultural products outside the framework of the CAP. This convention is to be replaced by a new ACP-EU partnership agreement in June 2000 which, in its trade component, provides for non-reciprocal preferential treatment over a preparatory period of eight years.
- The Generalised System of Preferences (GSP) which applies to other developing countries in Asia and Latin America. Under this scheme, a broad range of manufactures may enter the EC duty-free, subject to quota or a safeguard provision, as well as a preferential treatment for a limited range of agricultural products. The preferences granted are temporary and non-binding.

- The most favoured nation status or non-preferential treatment according to General Agreement on Tariffs and Trade (GATT)/World Trade Organization (WTO) rules is reserved to non-European developed countries, including the United States, Japan, Canada, Australia, and New Zealand.

Although all these preferential and non-preferential trade links may be indicative of the dynamic and important external dimension of its trade relations, the EC trade pattern, however, shows an increased regional concentration. In 1998, intra-EU trade in total trade was 62.9 per cent for exports and 62.4 per cent for imports, therefore indicating that the links among Member States' economies have become stronger since the establishment of the EC.[24] Such relatively strong internal trade expansion, according to a previous GATT study, was, indeed, a hallmark of the 1980s.[25] For instance, available estimates of import penetration indicate that the share of third country imports in apparent consumption declined from 18 to nearly 15 per cent in the case of agricultural products while it remained in the vicinity of 11 per cent in the case of manufactures between 1982-1983 and 1986-1987 (apparent consumption is defined as EC gross domestic production plus imports minus exports of merchandise). Over the same period, in contrast, the share of intra-EC imports in apparent consumption increased from 11 to 13 per cent for agricultural products and 17 to 19 per cent for manufactures.

This trend of relative decline in penetrating the European market can be linked with the Community's search for more intensified exploitation of potential gains from trade primarily through measures to achieve greater integration in intra-trade (McAleese, 1993, p. 35). In pursuit of this objective, the Community presided over a number of protective measures. While through successive rounds of negotiations within the GATT/WTO, tariff barriers have been reduced to fairly low levels reaching on average about 5 per cent, the resort to non-tariff mechanisms has, instead, proliferated (Hine, 1985, pp. 259-264). This kind of 'new protectionism' can be identified with, among other things, quotas, subsidies, voluntary export restraints, and countervailing and anti-dumping measures. According to the World Bank, for instance, between 1966 and 1986, the share of imports affected by all non-tariff measures grew by more than 20 per cent for the United States, almost 40 per cent for Japan, and 160 per cent for the EC.[26]

The growing tide of non-tariff trade measures has been perceptible in sensitive sectors particularly agriculture and textiles and clothing. These are sectors where developing countries, including the Maghreb countries, are assumed to have a strong comparative advantage resulting from lower costs. It is also agreed that trade in textiles and clothing is the single most important source of developing countries' foreign exchange earnings from manufactures as well as an important source of employment (Faini et al, 1995, p. 113).

In the agricultural sector, Article 39 of the Rome Treaty outlined the main aims of the CAP (to increase agricultural productivity; to improve farm incomes; to stabilise markets; and to ensure regular supplies to consumers at reasonable prices). By emphasising Community preference, the CAP has served as a stimulus to increasing reliance on domestic production thus reducing the scope for imports from outside suppliers. This preference is achieved mainly through two instruments: import levies and export subsidies. Subsequent enlargement to the South has exacerbated the situation of Maghreb agricultural exports especially Morocco, as the new members, with their similar pattern of Mediterranean produce, have made the EC self-sufficient in many areas of Maghreb production such as olive oil, tomatoes, fruits and vegetables, and wine.

As for textiles and clothing, they were governed until 1995 by bilateral agreements which the EC and other industrialised countries had negotiated with developing countries through the framework of Multi-Fibre Arrangements (MFA). These agreements imposed quantitative restrictions on low-cost competitive products originating from developing countries. Around 70 per cent of total EC imports were subject to quotas (Tsoukalis, 1993, p. 292). Although the Maghreb countries' exports were not subject to MFA treatment, certain of them were, nevertheless, monitored under self-restraint arrangements. This, in a way, acted as a disincentive to both local and foreign investment and even resulted in a crisis of confidence in the EC by its Maghreb trade partners.

The 1992 Programme

The rationale behind the Single European Market (SEM) is the removal of physical, technical, and fiscal barriers, allowing people, goods, services, and capital to move freely across the Community's territory. According to its proponents, this process, by generating growth effects on the European economy, would have a positive impact on outsiders as well. That is why the EC has, on several occasions, given assurances that Europe 1992 would not be an inward-looking 'Fortress Europe' but rather a 'World Partner'.

The concern of developing countries, as a group, over the implications arising out of the completion of the internal market can be discerned in the reactions of UNCTAD and the South Commission.[27] In their reports, while stressing certain positive prospects, they expressed uncertainties about what they regarded as a 'distinct tendency towards the formation of large trading groups of developed countries', in particular the EC of 1992, and the 'drift towards greater protectionism' which, by and large, may lead to a less open trade policy with potential adverse effects impinging upon developing countries.

Along the same lines, numerous studies attempted to estimate the likely implications on these countries.[28] In his study, Christopher Stevens identifies two types of effects that are likely to have an impact upon particular groups of countries. First, there are direct effects consisting of trade creation attributable to faster economic growth in the EC and trade diversion attributable to increased competitiveness, and hence lower costs of production in the Community. While trade creation would result in increased imports of primary products and some manufactures from developing countries, trade diversion would tend to prompt increased competition of domestic supplies relative to these imports. Second, indirect effects are the outcome of political decisions taken to influence the impact of the direct effects. In this respect, some Member States benefiting from existing trade barriers can be expected to lobby for increased protectionism even at the expense of third countries (Stevens, 1990, pp. 220-221).

The various studies of the SEM's impact on particular groups of countries do not convey an encouraging picture, at least in the short and medium term. The Maghreb countries will probably be affected by a certain amount of trade diversion, investment diversion, and restricted migration (Stevens, 1990, p. 225; Bourrinet, 1993, p. 32). In the area of trade, the erection of a series of non-tariff barriers linked to the new European-wide industrial standards -- 5,000 of them are being introduced -- will have a major impact on Maghreb industrial exports as further important investment costs will be required to meet these standards (Joffé, 1994, p. 262; Khader, 1992, pp. 131-139). On the investment side, there are poorer prospects as better and more attractive opportunities are offered either inside the EC or in other regions such as CEEC and Asian new industrialising countries.

Overall, since the Community's motive for the 1992 programme has to do with internal needs associated with its own development, its economic impact on the rest of the world is a factor that will be determined primarily by the way in which Community dynamics unfold (Izam, 1993, p. 151). Such dynamics will also be, to a certain extent, determined by the degree of commitment to the GATT/WTO deal concluded at Marrakech in 1994.

Expansion towards CEEC

The late 1980s marked an important stage in the evolution of CEEC. It coincided with the collapse of the Soviet Union's sphere of influence and the undertaking of drastic political and economic reforms. To this radical change, the EC responded by taking measures to bring these countries 'back to Europe'. In a first phase, the Community's support took three main forms: aid to the countries most affected by the economic crises; improved access to the EC market of these countries' exports; and the development of an institutional framework to deal with political and economic relations between both sides (Grilli, 1993, pp. 308-316). This was topped by the establishment of a multilateral financial institution, the European Bank for Reconstruction and Development, to encourage and provide financial means to help smooth the transition to market economies in the CEEC and thus to anchor them to Western Europe.

A second phase, as a step further, corresponds to the conclusion of the association agreements or 'Europe Agreements' which, in addition to aspects of commercial and economic cooperation, include a political dialogue dimension and a cultural component. They provide for the gradual establishment of free trade areas over a period of ten years. The ultimate objective, as made clear by the final declaration of the EC heads of state and government following their meeting in Copenhagen in June 1993, is the accession of the CEEC to the Community.

It is this rapidity of response unparalleled in EC history towards these countries that heightened the worries of the Maghreb countries. The distinctive treatment accorded to them was interpreted in the Maghreb as an expression of a declining interest in the North African region by the EC. This took place at a time where much was at stake in the Euro-Maghreb relationship with its possible impacts affecting, or perhaps more accurately, displacing Maghreb interests.

There are good reasons lending credibility to the appearance of such concerns. First in order to reply to the urgent economic needs of the CEEC, The Community not only mobilised its own resources and those of Member States, but also got other countries and international financial institutions involved in this process. For instance, between 1992-1994, the Union aid granted to these countries under PHARE and TACIS programmes amounted to 2,997 million European Currency Unit (Ecu) and 1,350.4 million Ecu respectively.[29] Generally, the amount committed especially by the EC, and the remarkable speed of decision-making on the matter, led a former Spanish Foreign Affairs Minister, M. Ordonez, to observe that: 'The EU's assistance to Hungary and Poland alone was more than the total given to Maghreb states in previous years.'[30]

In addition to the important financial support, the increasing improved market access granted to these countries has been showing signs of adverse consequences for the exports of the Mediterranean. Indeed, given the strong

Table 1.3 Extra-EU export and import share by selected partners

Partners	Exports			Imports		
	1990	1995	1998	1990	1995	1998
CEEC	6.2	10.2	13.5	5.4	8.7	10.1
Mediterranean	12.4	11.3	11.9	10.1	8.3	8.0
ACP	4.5	3.1	3.1	4.8	3.6	3.0

Source: Eurostat, *External and Intra-European Union Trade: Statistical Yearbook 1958-1998* (Luxembourg: Office for Official Publications of the European Communities, 1999), pp. 15-16.

association between trading patterns of the Mediterranean basin, including the Maghreb, and the CEEC with the EC, the risk of 'displacement' has become apparent (see table 1.3). Trade between the EC and the CEEC saw an unprecedented expansion during 1989-1992 where Community exports and imports grew by 56 per cent and 87 per cent in value terms respectively. This fact means that Community imports from this region grew more than six times faster than imports from the Mediterranean basin that experienced a decline in Community demand for its products.[31]

Divergent Interests of Member States

Within the Mediterranean basin, it is rather difficult to assert convincingly that the Maghreb countries are seen as particularly significant by all the EU Member States. This is, to a considerable degree, reflective of different perceptions of interest that Member States have in this particular region.

For quite a long time, though less commonly nowadays, the Maghreb has been regarded as a 'French preserve' not only because of historical considerations but also because of the close nature of economic, social, and cultural ties which France has maintained with its former colonies since their independence.[32] By virtue of these vested interests, France championed the cause of association of former colonies to the then European Economic Community. Despite being not actively supported at the time by all founding members, especially Germany and the Netherlands which saw it as a narrowly-motivated French national interest, France, by making its participation in the nascent Community conditional on association, finally succeeded in getting its partners involved. This meant extending to them its exclusive markets in those former colonies or remaining colonies, and at the same time making them share the economic burden the latter represented for the French treasury (Grilli, 1993, p. 8).

Subsequent enlargements of the EC, particularly southwards to include Mediterranean countries like Greece, Portugal and Spain, made the Maghreb region a focal point of increasing importance. Indeed, besides the obvious motive of protection against competition because of a marked similarity in the pattern of production with that of the Maghreb, these Member States have been recently expressing great concern about economic dislocation and political instability noticeable in the Maghreb societies (see Chapter Four). Owing to geographical contiguity in large part, they consider themselves likely to be the most to feel the knock-on-effect stemming from such situation. This risk also seems to be shared in the EC, at least in the official rhetoric. A Commission document, while highlighting a situation of political instability, high demography, important population movements, and high unemployment rates in the Mediterranean, viewed these problems in the case of the Maghreb as those of the whole Community.[33]

Probably it is this state of growing sensitivity to these problems and in an attempt to mitigate their effect that the EC southern states (France, Italy, Portugal, and Spain) initiated the so-called 'Five plus Five' approach in 1990. It brought together these four EC Member States, those of the UMA, and later Malta. It set the stage for dialogue and a number of outstanding issues of common interest were identified. Various working groups were set up to deal with policy areas such as regional financial institutions and easing of debt, food self-sufficiency and protection against the encroaching desert, migration, and cultural safeguards.[34] On the whole, increased cooperation on a wide-ranging agenda of issues was seen as the effective way to remedy the Maghreb's socio-economic and political problems and thus to bolster stability and security in the region.

However, this initiative proved to be a short-lived experience. Its process was halted following alleged Libyan involvement in the Lockerbie air disaster of December 1988 and the deteriorating political situation in Algeria. More importantly, apart from its instigators, it did not stimulate any enthusiasm on the part of other Community Member States.

This first initiative demonstrated that in reality there exists differences of attitude among Member States towards the problems of the Maghreb region. At the root of this split is the disagreement over the appropriate policy to be adopted in this context. Indeed, whereas southern Member States prefer aid to trade concessions, their northern partners take an opposite view. In the whole process, the interest in the region continues to be predominantly subordinated to well-defined national, rather than to supranational (EU), considerations.

As they face no competition, those favouring trade such as Germany and the UK feel that they would be less affected by the Community opening its market via further preferential concessions to agricultural produce of a Mediterranean type. Moreover, being in the main net contributors to the Community budget, they seem unwilling to bear the burden of increased financial flows as this may mostly benefit those Member States with an already established influence and great involvement in this part of the Mediterranean. It is a concern that is clearly valid in terms of trade links.

In fact, as table 1.4 shows, a significant proportion of Maghreb trade is mainly conducted with those southern Member States (France, Italy, and Spain) plus Germany. However, when it comes to the latter's direction of trade towards the Maghreb, this concentration is relatively more pronounced in southern Member States than in Germany. In 1997, while the share of the Maghreb in their total exports was 2.3 and 1.8 per cent in each of both France and Spain respectively and 1.2 per cent in the case of Italy, it was only 0.4 per cent in that of Germany.[35]

This being so, it is also precisely those southern Member States which face direct competition from Mediterranean agricultural produce and textiles/clothing. According to them, granting more trade preferences will have little impact as previous experience has shown and what it is needed is the injection of more EC cash.

Such divergent attitudes are, to a certain extent, reminiscent of the existing gap between national and Union development cooperation policy which the Maastricht Treaty -- by providing a legal basis in Part three Title XVII -- and more recently a Commission communication attempt to narrow, with an ultimate aim to achieve a greater collective effectiveness in this regard.[36]

Table 1.4 Principal Maghreb trade partners in the EC*

	Exports					Imports				
	1987	1990	1993	1996	1997	1987	1990	1993	1996	1997
World total (million dollars)	13,686	19,021	18,868	24,744	26,316	14,123	22,757	22,985	26,270	26,828
EC (million dollars) of which (%)	9,428	12,879	13,358	16,918	17,713	8,434	13,522	14,945	17,660	17,553
France	33.9	32.4	30.7	31.5	31.7	39.2	39.8	41.4	40.9	40.0
Italy	19.4	25.5	20.0	23.8	23.8	16.1	18.6	17.7	17.1	16.8
Germany	10.1	7.7	18.2	13.9	11.2	16.5	16.4	12.8	12.4	11.6
Spain	6.6	8.9	9.0	10.8	12.6	9.8	10.0	12.4	11.3	11.2

Source: Calculations based on data derived from the IMF, *Direction of Trade Statistics Yearbook* (Washington, DC: IMF, 1994, 1997, and 1998).
(*): Maghreb comprises Algeria, Morocco and Tunisia.

Conclusion

By considering the nature of, and a range of policy issues in, the Euro-Maghreb relationship, this chapter has attempted to define this relationship and provide a balanced analysis of the underlying environment of its development. It is the case of a relationship involving two economically unequal parties and featuring high asymmetrical interdependent pattern both in terms of interaction and outcome. As for the environment, it can be characterised, on the one hand, by the fragile status of the Maghreb countries which remains noticeable not only in their repeated efforts to build a sound and lasting economic community but also in their external attitude, particularly towards Europe. The failure to make the regional integration process move ahead has undoubtedly rendered the constitution of a united front, when dealing with the EC, difficult to achieve.

On the other hand, this has been compounded by other developments at the EC level. The protectionist trend in its trade policy in certain economic sectors may further develop as a result of the completion of the internal market, especially those non-tariff barriers concerned with, among other things, the new pan-European industrial standards. Moreover, the rapid and distinctive treatment reserved to the CEEC was parallelled by rather protracted haggling among Member States over the policy to be adopted towards the Maghreb region.

In sum, the development of the EC-Maghreb relationship is to be understood against a background of a weak and divided Maghreb facing a more integrated Community whose policies have a more determinant effect on that relationship than do the actions of the fragmented Maghreb countries.

Notes

1   The literature on Lomé Conventions involving the EC and the African, Caribbean and Pacific states is an illustrating case in this respect. For examples of this literature, see R.H. Green, 'The Lomé Convention: Updated Dependence or Departure towards Collective Self-Reliance?', *African Review*, vol. 6, no. 1, 1976, pp. 43-55; Isebill Gruhn, 'The Lomé Convention: Inching towards Interdependence', *International Organization*, vol. 30, 1976, pp. 241-262; I.W. Zartman, 'Europe and Africa: Decolonisation or Dependency?', *Foreign Affairs*, vol. 54, 1976, pp. 325-343; S.K.B. Asante, 'The Lomé Convention: Towards Perpetuation of Dependence or Promotion of Interdependence?', *Third World Quarterly*, vol. 3, no. 4, Oct 1981, pp. 658-672; Guy Martin, *The Political Economy of African-European Relations from Yaoundé I to Lomé II, 1963-1980: A Case Study in Neo-Colonialism and Dependency*, PhD dissertation, Indiana University (USA), 1982; Ravenhill, Collective Clientelism - The Lomé Conventions and North-South Relations (New York: Columbia University Press, 1985), p. 17.

2   In Morocco, foreign capital investment represented 2.4 per cent in 1973, 3.7 per cent in 1980 and 3 per cent in 1986 of the total investment. As for Tunisia, while accounting for 10 per cent in the 1970s, it slightly decreased to 9 per cent in 1986; quoted from Larbi Talha, 'Relations Europe - Maghreb: La Question des Investissements Directs', *Revue Tiers Monde*, vol. 34, no. 136, October-December 1993, pp. 928-931.
3   Author's calculations based on data from Euromonitor, *European Marketing Data and Statistics 2000* (London: Euromonitor Plc, 2000), p. 131.
4   Author's calculations based on data from Euromonitor. *The World Economic Factbook 1999-2000* (London: Euromonitor Plc, 1999), pp. 48, 298 and 420.
5   Author's calculations based on data from Eurostat, *External and Intra-European Union Trade: Statistical Yearbook 1958-1998* (Luxembourg: Office for Official Publications of the European Communities, 1999), pp. 46 and 50.
6   Author's calculations based on data from IMF, *Direction of Trade Statistics Yearbook* (Washington, DC: IMF, 1998).
7   Some of these features are drawn on W.M. Habeeb's work , 'The Maghribi States and the European Community', in W. I. Zartman and W. M. Habeeb (eds), *Polity and Society in Contemporary North Africa* (Boulder, Colorado: Westview Press, 1993), p. 204.
8   *Annuaire de L'Afrique du Nord*, vol. 2, 1963, p. 965.
9   See UNECA, *Industrial Coordination Mission to Algeria, Libya, Morocco, and Tunisia*, UN Document E/CN 14/248, February 1964, p. 1.
10 *Economic Bulletin for Africa* (UNECA), vol. 7, nos. 1-2, 1968, p. 65.
11 See Article 2 of the AMU Treaty.
12 See Article 3 of the AMU Treaty.
13 For a list of accords and conventions, see F. Oualalou, *Après Barcelona - Le Maghreb est nécessaire* (Casablanca: Editions Toubkal, 1996), pp. 320-323.
14 *Keesing's Record of World Events*, vol. 41, no. 10, 1995, p. 40385.
15 *Africa Research Bulletin* (Political, Social, and Cultural Series), vol. 30, no. 1, 1993, p. 10843.
16 See Protocol of Tunis, 1 October 1964.
17 See Protocol of Tripoli, 26 May 1965.
18 See Final Declaration of the 7th Conference of the Maghreb Economic Ministers, Algiers, 23 May 1975.
19 These two basic documents can be found in M. Alaoui, *La Coopération entre l'Union Européenne et les Pays du Maghreb* (Paris: Editions Nathan, 1994), pp. 201-204.
20 Commission of the European Communities, *The Future of Relations between the Community and the Maghreb*, SEC(92) 401 final, Brussels, 30 April 1992.
21 Cited in *Middle East International*, 5 March 1993, p. 9.
22 Speech published in *Etudes Internationales* (Tunis), vol. 48, 1993, p. 151.
23 Author's calculations based on data from the IMF, *Direction of Trade Statistics Yearbook* (Washington, DC: IMF, 1998).
24 In 1960 the figures were 46 per cent for imports and 49.4 for exports; see Eurostat, *External and Intra-European Union Trade: Statistical Yearbook 1958-1998* (Luxembourg: Office for Official Publications of the European Communities, 1999), pp. 21-22.
25 This study is part of the GATT's Trade Policy Review Mechanism which became a permanent feature of the WTO after its establishment in January 1995. See GATT, *Trade Policy Review: The European Community*, vol. 1 (Geneva: GATT, 1991), p. 21.
26 Figures derived from the World Bank, *World Development Report* (New York: World Bank, 1991), p. 105.

27 For more details on this issue, see UNCTAD, *Trade and Development Report* (New York: UN, 1990 and 1991), pp. 79-87 and 60-65; and South Commission, *The Challenge to the South* (Oxford: Oxford University Press, 1990), p. 242.
28 See for instance, Vincent Cable, '1992 and its Implications for Developing Countries', in Horst Siebert (ed.), *The Completion of the Internal Market* (Tubingen: Mohr, 1990), pp. 205-275; special issue of *Journal of Common Market Studies*, vol. 29, no. 2, 1990; special issue of *Journal of Development Planning*, vol. 21-22, 1991; Michael Davenport and Sheila Page, *Europe: 1992 and the Developing World* (London: Overseas Development Institute, 1991); and Dermot McAleese et al. (eds), *Africa and the Community after 1992* (Washington, DC: World Bank, 1993).
29 *Official Journal of the European Communities*, no. C 88, 10 April 1995, p. 30.
30 *Le Monde*, 3 February 1990.
31 *European Economy*, no. 6, 1994, pp. 95-99.
32 A more detailed account on these links is provided by Riffi El-Meloukhi, *La Politique Française de Coopération avec les Etats du Maghreb 1955-1987* (Casablanca: Editions Toubkal, 1989).
33 See Commission of the European Communities, *From the Single Act to Maastricht:The Means to match our Ambitions*, COM(92) 2000 final, Brussels, 11 February 1992, p. 17.
34 *El-Moudjahid*, 23 September 1991.
35 Author's calculations based on data from the IMF, *Direction of Trade Statistics Yearbook* (Washington, DC: IMF, 1998).
36 Commission of the European Communities, *Complementarity between the Community's development cooperation policy and the policies of Member States*, COM(95) 160 final, Brussels, 3 May 1995.

PART TWO
FROM COMMERCIAL TO ENLARGED COOPERATION

2 A Partial and Limited Association: The Trade Arrangements

Introduction

The starting point for the institutionalisation of Euro-Maghreb relations occurred in the late 1960s. It gave concrete meaning and form to the willingness expressed by Member States to reach association accords with the Maghreb countries at the time the European Economic Community was formed. Indeed, the conclusion in 1969 of the trade agreements marked the beginning of the first phase of the EC development cooperation policy towards these countries. Through these arrangements the Community intention was to foster closer links with the Maghreb region and thus to assist the countries concerned in their socio-economic development. However, instead of a comprehensive package, the EC approach was only and exclusively confined to trade. The instrument employed consisted of granting trade concessions which were expected to strengthen the trading position of the Maghreb countries in the European market as a result of the preferential treatment. Other issues viewed of significance by these countries to their economic development, such as financial assistance and labour relations, were ignored.

Thus this chapter will be concerned with the examination of this first generation of agreements between the EC and the Maghreb countries. First, a background traces both the situation of Morocco and Tunisia on one side and, on the other, the specific case of Algeria, in their relationship with France and the Community. Next, the long and protracted negotiations leading to the conclusion of these agreements are reviewed. Finally, this chapter provides an analysis and evaluation of their content and scope.

State of Relations prior to Association

When the European Economic Community was founded, some Member States were still administering important colonial territories. In this respect, the Fourth Part of the Rome Treaty had been exclusively devoted to the particular links between these states and their colonies by providing for their association. As for those states already independent at the signing of the Treaty and having retained a special relationship with their former coloniser, as was the case for Morocco and Tunisia, they could benefit from two dispositions contained in the annexes to this Treaty. These consisted of the Protocol 1/7 and the Declaration of Intent.

The Protocol was concerned with:

> Certain goods originating in and from certain countries and enjoying special treatment when imported into a member state [thus] the application of the Treaty establishing the European Economic Community shall not require any alteration in the customs treatment applicable, at the time of the entry into force of this Treaty, to imports into France of goods originating in and coming from Morocco and Tunisia.[1]

Once these goods are imported on a preferential basis into a member state, they shall not be considered to be in free circulation when re-exported to another member.[2]

In the Declaration of Intent, the founding Member States:

> Taking into consideration the economic, financial and monetary agreements and conventions between France and the independent countries of the Franc Area, [and] anxious to maintain and intensify the traditional trade flows between the Member States of the European Economic Community and these independent countries and to contribute to the economic and social development of the latter, declare their readiness, as soon as this Treaty enters into force, to propose to these countries the opening of negotiations with a view to concluding conventions for economic association with the Community.[3]

It was under this Protocol that France managed to preserve its previous preferences especially those related to goods originating from Morocco and Tunisia. This was despite the provisions of the customs union which bound the six Member States to adopt the CET towards third countries. In fact, these preferences were regarded as a reflection of France's intention to keep its former North African countries closely linked to its economy through cooperation arrangements.[4] As for Algeria, it was still under French rule and that being so, its case witnessed a different pattern from that of neighbouring countries. Considered as a French territory at the time, Algeria saw various provisions of the Rome Treaty extended to its status. However, this status was to change after independence.

Morocco and Tunisia

The Protocol enabled certain Member States to preserve their preferences towards their former colonies. This arrangement was not a sort of convention linking these countries to the Community but simply a legal recognition of existing specific relationships between these Member States and their independent ex-colonies. In this respect, the Member States concerned were sovereign in granting as well as ending their preferential treatment. Because of this fragile position and the almost complete economic dependence on France, the Maghreb countries sought to set up contractual relations with the Community. For its part, France largely resorted to this Protocol to retain the already existing specific relationship with its former North African colonies.

With Morocco, France had no trade agreement. The regime governing their commercial exchanges was subject to periodic revision. In general, Morocco's exports were granted duty-free access to the French market on the basis of fixed quotas. In 1957 these amounted to 90 per cent of all exports. Parallel to these preferences, Morocco maintained its tariff system concerning French exports and only privileged access in terms of quotas was granted. The reason, at the time, rested on the fact that Morocco was bound by the Act of Algeçiras of 1906 which provided for equal treatment in the country's commercial relations.[5] Despite this situation, France remained the principal trading partner of Morocco. As can be noted from table 2.1, about 60 per cent of its external trade was conducted with the EC, of which more than two-fifths were with France during 1963-1964.

Relations between France and Tunisia were different from those with Morocco since they were based on a bilateral agreement. Before the end of the protectorate on 3 June 1955, an accord was concluded establishing a customs union between both sides. This remained effective until 5 September 1959 where another accord was signed, thus ending the previous arrangement. The fundamental principle of this accord was free movement of goods on both sides with possible exceptions in favour of Tunisia. As a consequence, 75 per cent of Tunisian exports benefited from duty-free access into the French market. In return, two-thirds of French exports were allowed in on the basis of a minimum tariff.

Table 2.1   Morocco's trade with the EC, 1963-1964

	Exports (%)		Imports (%)	
	1963	1964	1963	1964
World	100	100	100	100
European Community *of which*	55	61	61	54
France	41	42	45	41
West Germany	7	9	6	6

Source: G. Vallay, 'La Communauté Economique Européenne et les Pays du Maghreb', *Revue de l'Occident Musulman et de la Méditerranée*, no. 2, 1966, p. 205.

On 12 May 1964, the Tunisian government decided to nationalise the foreign-owned lands. France reacted not only by ending its financial flows towards Tunisia but equally by renouncing the Franco-Tunisian trade accord of 5 September 1959. Since then, Tunisia had been treated as a third country in its relationship to France. The immediate effect on Tunisia was an increasing disequilibrium in its trade balance resulting mainly from the cut-off of French financial aid. However, the political tensions that surfaced between the two countries did not severely affect the size of their trade exchanges. As indicated in table 2.2, more than 50 per cent of Tunisian exports went to the French market and 44 per cent of Tunisian imports came from France in 1964.

As time went by, the Maghreb countries realised that preferential treatment would be deteriorating as a result of the establishment of the CAP and the provisional nature of the Protocol. Within the CAP, for example, France renounced the benefit Morocco and Tunisia enjoyed from previous concessions and decided to apply a third country levy to their exports of cereals. In this context, faced by a strategic commercial choice between maintaining its particular relationship on the one hand and the advantages stemming from a common organisation of agricultural markets on the other, France opted for the

Table 2.2 Tunisia's trade with the EC, 1963-1964

	Exports (%)		Imports (%)	
	1963	1964	1963	1964
World	100	100	100	100
European Community *of which*	69.9	65.2	65.5	64,9
France	49.9	51.3	48.2	44.1
Italy	17.5	10.2	9.8	5.0
West Germany	--	--	4.5	5.6

Source: G. Vallay, 'La Communauté Economique Européenne et les Pays du Maghreb', *Revue de l'Occident Musulman et de la Méditerranée*, no. 2, 1966, p. 207.

second formula (Vallay, 1966, p. 210). Thus the preservation of preferences had been ultimately dependent on the economic interests of France. As far as the Protocol was concerned, its primary purpose was to maintain those preferences on a provisional basis, that is not exceeding the transitional period, while the countries concerned negotiated the conclusion of association agreements with the Community as a whole. In such conditions, the Maghreb countries had no other alternative than that of trying to secure their relations with the EC on a contractual basis. But because of political considerations, they were reluctant to engage in any talks with the Community until the end of the liberation struggle in Algeria.

The Situation of Algeria

In 1957, Algeria was under French occupation as part of metropolitan France. Therefore, its relationship to the EC had not caused any sort of major concern in comparison to other already independent countries that maintained closer ties with their former coloniser. France, moreover, had not shown the slightest intention to grant the country its independence. As a special exception to the Rome Treaty, the legal basis of its status was provided for in Article 227, Paragraph 2, which was concerned with French overseas territories including Algeria.

The provisions of this Article that were to be applied to Algeria, were the free movement of goods (Articles 9 to 37); agriculture (Articles 38 to 47 except for Article 40, Paragraph 4); the liberalisation of services (Articles 59 to 66); the rules on competition (Articles 85 to 90); the protective measures (Articles 108, 109 and 226); and the institutions (Articles 137 to 198). Consequently, customs duties were lowered towards Algeria and quantitative restrictions were abolished as was the case for the rest of the Community members. Rules of competition and rules on capital mobility were also applied following a decision taken by the Council on 11 May 1960 in accordance with Articles 67 to 73 and 106 of the Rome Treaty. In addition, Algeria benefited from the European Development Fund (EDF) conforming with Article 6 of the convention relative to the association of the overseas territories to the Community (Dupouy, 1979, p. 9).

On the eve of independence in July 1962, the integration of Algeria into the Common Market was not fully accomplished. In many respects, it was excluded from certain provisions embodied in the Treaty of Rome. By way of illustration, Algeria was excluded from the European Agricultural Guidance and Guarantee Fund (EAGGF) whose aim is to finance a price support system and the development of the structure of European agriculture.[6] Except in France, the situation of Algerian migrants was a subject of restrictions especially in terms of free movement and right of establishment.[7] It was equally excluded from those provisions regarding the Community's economic and social policies.[8]

When Algeria achieved independence in 1962, its relationship to the Community became a matter of great concern. Article 227 that had been applied so far could not be maintained in force. Under such circumstances, Article 238 concerned with association agreements with a third country might be applied to Algeria. According to the principle of state succession (Reuter, 1965, p. 125), an attempt was made to provide Algeria with grounds to choose between two legal options because the newly-established state had acquired competence in the administration of the Algerian territory upon obtaining independence. According to M. Flory these two options were:

- The non-recognition of the Article 227 provisions. This could be interpreted

as an end to the conventional obligations in force;
- The recognition of these conventional obligations and thus the maintenance of the inherited status (1966, p. 11).

The second option was legally impossible because Article 237 of the Rome Treaty states that only European countries are eligible for membership within the Community. Some believed that it might be possible for Algeria to be represented at the EC institutions by the organs of the French Republic. This, however unlikely, was to be accepted by the then-revolutionary Algeria (Muzikar, 1967, p. 56). Nevertheless, and because of economic considerations in particular, the Algerian government, in a letter of 24 December 1962 addressed to the Council expressed its wishes for the preservation on a temporary basis of Article 227 until a further and definitive settlement of the future relations between both parties.[9] In replying to this request, the Community declared its willingness to ensure the provisional continuation of this status and particularly its financial pledges.[10]

From independence onwards, relations between France and Algeria were supposed to develop on the basis of the Evian Accords signed on 19 March 1962. Article 6 of the Declaration of Principles of these Accords, concerned with economic and financial cooperation, emphasised the specific nature of their future links. In reality, however, France unilaterally decided on 19 September 1962 to maintain previous preferential arrangements regarding its trade regime with Algeria. Hence exports from Algeria into the French market were granted duty-free entry except goods such as wine, certain fruits and vegetables and cereals which were respectively subject to gradual increasing quantitative restrictions or customs duties. Wine exports, for instance, were to be decreased in terms of quotas from 8,760,000 hectolitres in 1963-1964 to 7,000,000 hectolitres in 1967-1968 (Vallay, 1966, p. 217). As for French exports, between 30 to 40 per cent of them were exempt from customs duties. To the remaining proportion of exports was applied a preferential treatment corresponding to 50 per cent of the minimum tariff.

With respect to other members of the EC, Algeria's customs regime evolved differently. During the two successive intra-community tariff cuts on 1 July 1963 and 1 January 1965, Member States were unanimous in consenting that such cuts be extended to it. From 1966, nevertheless, a growing disagreement surfaced among the Community partners over the continuation of this distinctive treatment. Consequently, the Council decided to exclude Algeria from further intra-community cuts and various members granted it an intermediate customs position between intra-community and CET levels

(Zartman, 1968, p. 2). Since then, its *de facto* status had been slowly eroding.

Whereas France maintained its preferential treatment of Algeria, the other Member States decided to apply their particular regimes taking into account strictly national considerations. As a result, the years 1967-1968 witnessed a period during which Member States employed or resorted to different preferential systems in a way that would suit their own interests. Italy adopted the less favourable position because Italian farmers feared direct competition from Mediterranean products. Thus it decided to treat Algeria as a third party. West Germany, like the Benelux countries, applied the intra-community customs of 1 January 1965. As for those products subject to common market organisation, however, they were allowed in on a third-country basis. The new members that joined the Community in 1973 -- United Kingdom, Denmark and Ireland -- treated all products originating from Algeria in a similar way.

Aware of its precarious and provisional relationship with the EC, Algeria expressed its desire to engage in negotiations with the aim of concluding a more solid and comprehensive overall agreement. By 28 February 1964, preliminaries opened in Brussels. On the Algerian side, emphasis was placed upon the need to expand outlets for agricultural products, free movement with improved social conditions and training for Algerian workers in the Community and financial cooperation. The European Commission proposed only an association in accordance with Article 238 of the Rome Treaty which provides for a customs union or a free trade area. The proposal for an association was not accepted by Algeria because of its political connotation that was thought or believed likely to compromise its independence (d'Yvoire, 1965, p. 44). After further rounds of talks that lasted until 18 December 1964, the Commission handed to the Council on 24 February 1965 a final report and after that the Algerian case remained open until 1968 (Muzikar, 1967, p. 56).

This lack of progress in hammering out a bilateral arrangement between both sides could be explained by a number of reasons. On the Algerian side, the option for an international policy of non-alignment made Algeria less enthusiastic to take a decision regarding the EC which it viewed either totally or partially as a bloc whose policies were incompatible with its own (Mameri, 1968, p. 434). Another reason put forward is that Algeria was better accommodated with the provisions of Article 227, Paragraph 2, at least for some time, and therefore any new accord would not, at the best, be more advantageous than its existing situation. On the European side, and essentially for political considerations, some Member States were reluctant to conclude a final agreement despite their growing disapprobation of Algeria's *de facto* status. Several Member States resented and even disagreed with Algeria's position in international politics, which, at the time, they regarded as radical as that of a number of other Third World regimes. In 1967, Algeria broke diplomatic relations with West Germany because of the latter's support of Israel during the six-day war in June 1967.[11]

Because no tangible progress seemed to be achieved, the Community established, on a provisional and unilateral basis, a regime whereby wines originating from Algeria would benefit from a substantial reduction of the CET, though still not as much as had been desired. Agricultural products were subject to a 50 per cent reduction of this tariff and industrial products a 70 per cent reduction. This was interpreted as largely an extension of the *status quo*, a partial *de facto* membership based on the Franco-Algerian 'special relationship' (Sutton, 1972, p. 199).

By 1972, the Community decided to resume negotiations with Algeria. This coincided with the shift in EC policy towards its Mediterranean neighbours (Siotis, 1974, p. 76). The main principles relating to a more comprehensive approach, known as the 'global' Mediterranean policy, were laid down. Besides trade relations, this approach embodied issues of technical and financial cooperation as well as social provisions for migrant labour. And it is within the framework of such an approach that an agreement was concluded for the first time between Algeria and the Community in 1976, enabling the former to institutionalise its relationship with the EC on a contractual basis.

The Negotiation Process

Both Morocco and Tunisia could have started negotiations with the EC as early as 1958. It was six years after the signing of the Rome Treaty, however, when they first expressed their wish to enter into negotiations. A number of constraining factors can be adduced to explain the causes behind this dearth of initiatives on both sides.[12]

Because Algeria was still at war with France, it was rather difficult for neighbouring countries, which were providing political and material support to the Algerian *Front de Libération Nationale* (FLN), to start any kind of official talks with the Community. Moreover, they were reluctant to enter into a formula of association that might, in their opinion, compromise their newly-recovered sovereignty. At the time, the EC appeared to a great number of Third World countries as a grouping of colonial powers attempting through economic arrangements to establish some sort of neo-colonialism.[13]

As the EC was preoccupied with its internal integration, Morocco and

Tunisia equally feared that the time was not appropriate for them to obtain better concessions from the Community. But with the passage of time, they realised that their trade relations were more and more threatened, particularly when the Community adopted, within its CAP, the five regulations in relation to products such as cereals, pork, poultry and eggs, fruit and vegetables, and wine on 4 April 1962.[14] For the first three products, the regulations in question introduced levies with respect to their imports from non-member countries. This was seen as an additional pressure on the economic situation because a number of Moroccan and Tunisian agricultural exports such as cereals and eggs were hit by these measures.[15] For instance, while the EC market represented 88 per cent of Moroccan exports of cereals in 1957, this proportion decreased to only 2.7 per cent in 1964.[16] The association of Greece and Turkey and the conclusion of the Yaoundé Convention during 1961-1963 provided another motivating force for them to re-assess the importance of working out a deal with the Community.

With respect to the EC, the Declaration of Intent stipulated that it was incumbent upon the Community to propose the envisaged association. To the disappointment of Morocco and Tunisia, the Community did not undertake any initiative in this context. A plausible explanation was the success of France in convincing the other Member States to conclude association arrangements with the African countries (Yaoundé Convention). This was viewed by the other Member States as an important concession to France. Later in fact, the functioning of the association revealed that the assistance given to the eighteen African states signatories of this convention essentially favoured French sales in Africa.[17] The other EC Member States therefore merely perceived an association with Morocco and Tunisia as a further concession to France. Furthermore, France in its turn at that time showed no hurry to proceed as it already enjoyed a privileged relationship with these countries.

The association of the Maghreb countries, moreover, would have required the Community to devise and implement a Mediterranean policy which would have proven difficult to achieve at that moment. In the case of the Maghreb region, one of the reasons, as explained by H. Andresen from the European Commission, was that: 'Several Community Member States considered their relations with the Maghreb to be a burden rather than a benefit' (1977, p. 16).

By 1963, the Maghreb countries engaged in exploratory discussions with the Community. On 8 October and 14 December 1963, Tunisia and Morocco respectively requested the opening of exploratory talks.[18] In expressing the desire to conclude a comprehensive agreement, during these preliminary negotiations that took place between January and June 1964 in particular, they stressed the following issues:

- Establishment of an adjusted free trade area taking into account the difference in the economic development between them and the Community;
- Application of a scheme as similar as possible to that in force among the Community members on their farm products;
- Initiation of financial (via EDF) and technical cooperation;
- Provision of better conditions for their nationals employed in the Member States in terms of remuneration, social security, vocational training and so forth.[19]

After these preliminaries, it took the Community a year, that is until mid-June 1965, to resume negotiations on a partial mandate with Morocco and Tunisia. This mandate was extremely limited in scope as it was only concerned with trade relations leaving out financial and labour issues. Even in the sphere of trade, products of importance to the Maghreb countries, especially in the agricultural sector, were partially addressed. As a result, no clear offer was made as regards the export of their two major products, citrus fruit and olive oil, for which there were no import regulations yet. In the absence of these and because of the potential impact of the products in question on Community own production, it proved difficult for Member States to agree on a common position. For instance, the Italian government, in a memorandum issued on 4 May 1964, expressed its opposition to the granting of any concessions particularly in the agricultural sector to the Maghreb countries without prior protection for its own production.[20]

In this context of disappointment and dissatisfaction coupled with increasing economic difficulties, the late President Habib Bourguiba of Tunisia was reported to have said that: 'It is in the interest of Italy, as well as France, to obtain a more favourable situation in Tunisia, to show a little comprehension.'[21] This situation was further underlined on the Moroccan side which stated that: 'We have a hard time understanding why the countries of the Maghreb must pay the costs of the internal differences of the EEC.'[22]

After an interruption of more than two years, a new mandate was issued by the Council at its meeting of 24 October 1967. This was possible because a number of issues were settled which in turn enabled the negotiations to move ahead. First, to the opposition to any arrangement with the Maghreb countries, especially in the area of agricultural products, Italy finally accepted a compromise over the issue of citrus fruit products.[23] Second, were two major events in respect of the CAP. The financing of the agricultural policy was brought to a conclusion by the important agreement of 11 May 1966 and the adoption of certain regulations concerned with the establishment of a single market for olive oil especially in terms of imports and exports in July 1966.[24] Under this second mandate the Community made the following proposals:

- An intra-community system for industrial products -- with reservations on origins and safeguard clauses -- and oil products up to 100.000 tons for each country;
- A reduction of 80 per cent of the CET was proposed for citrus fruit provided that a minimum price was respected by the Maghreb countries' exports into the Community (Morocco was the most concerned). The EC was insistent upon this minimum price to be observed in order to prevent dumping;
- No quota restrictions and a reduction of 5 dollars per 100 kilogrammes in third country levy for olive oil provided that the country concerned (Tunisia) would accept a minimum price.

However, products such as wines, tomatoes, tinned fruit, vegetables and cork -- representing about 40 per cent of Moroccan and Tunisian trade -- were excluded in this mandate.[25]

In spite of the insistence of Morocco and Tunisia upon a comprehensive deal, issues regarded of importance to the development of their economies were not taken into account. Indeed, neither the situation of migrant workers in the EC, nor financial and technical cooperation were considered. The community justified this partial approach by the fact that a global agreement would require much more time and involve the parties concerned in difficult negotiations because of the so-called sensitive products (wine, tomatoes, and so forth) and because of the pressure put upon it by other potential Mediterranean countries offering similar products and requiring preferential treatment as well such as Yugoslavia, Israel and Spain (Zartman, 1971, p. 137). Combined with this was also the fact that the EC was still in the process of shaping its CAP.

Both Morocco and Tunisia reacted vehemently to the exclusion of the afore-mentioned issues. But considering the difficulty of reaching an overall deal and the position of the Community as dominant actor both in terms of interaction and outcome, the Maghreb countries resignedly opted for the speedy conclusion of partial arrangements. On the European side, this was also acknowledged by Gaston Thorn, the President of the Commission, who stated that:

> Insofar as we have seen difficulties that would satisfy both sides, we thought that the essential, after such very long negotiations, was to give concrete

expression to the political will by concluding an association even if it is a limited one.[26]

This culminated in the signing by the EC of trade agreements on 28 March and 31 March 1969 with Tunisia and Morocco respectively.

Analysis of the Agreements

Characteristics of the Association

It was stipulated in the preamble that these agreements were concluded according to 'the desire that a first application should be given to the Declaration of Intent annexed to the Rome Treaty'.[27] They were also based on Article 238 of this Treaty which provides for the 'creation of an association characterised by reciprocal duties and obligations in common, and particular procedures'.[28]

Association, indeed, can be considered as an intermediate status between full membership in the Community and third country status. For some countries such as Greece and Turkey, the ultimate objective of their association status, as a preparatory stage at the time, was to lead to eventual accession. With the Maghreb countries, it was rather intended to establish a free trade area.

Three main features underlay the nature of the Maghreb countries' association to the EC. First, it was partial since it was only confined to commercial matters thus leaving out other issues such as, for instance, economic aid and labour. Comparatively, the type of association that the Community developed within the framework of the Yaoundé Convention was more comprehensive as it covered besides trade, financial aid from the EDF set up for this specific purpose, as well as the provision for free circulation of labour between the EC Member States and their associates.

Second and even in terms of trade, it was limited to a certain number of products. Products that were not provided for in the agreements could continue to benefit from French preferences in accordance with the Protocol 1/7 annexed to the Rome Treaty which, in this regard, remained in force. The preferences given to the Maghreb countries' exports entering the European market were subordinated to the granting of reciprocal treatment for the Community's exports to these countries.

This principle of trade reciprocity was maintained despite being called into question by the UNCTAD in its resolution 21 relative to the application of the GSP in New Delhi in 1968. This resolution requested the developed countries to grant a one-way preferential access to the developing countries' exports which meant that the latter were not expected to reciprocate in the same way. Moreover, one can discern a certain contradiction between the trade provisions of the association agreements and GATT regulations since customs duties were maintained on a substantial part of Maghreb exports to the EC. In contrast, Article XXIV of the GATT which defines the free trade area, stipulates that customs duties must be removed for the essential part of trade exchanges.

A final feature relates to the transitional nature of these association agreements. As set out in Article 14, these were concluded for a period of five years but negotiations could be started by the end of the third year with a view to reaching an eventual accord on a wider basis. Through this commitment, the Community seemed to be taking into account the initial demands of Morocco and Tunisia for a global and permanent arrangement involving trade relations, financial and technical assistance and migrant labour. As they were at the time, however, these association arrangements would have had a rather modest impact on the development prospects of the Maghreb countries because their limited duration could not induce a propitious long-term climate either for local or foreign investment.

Trade Provisions

Within the framework of these agreements, the intention of the Community was to make a contribution to the economic development of both Morocco and Tunisia by two means: on the one side favouring their industrialisation, viewed as an essential factor for economic take-off in the developing countries, and on the other side, improving their export earnings as a necessary factor to meet their investment needs required by the development process.[29]

Overall, the agreements covered respectively 60 per cent and 70 per cent of Moroccan and Tunisian industrial and agricultural exports. The industrial products were granted free access, both in terms of customs duties and quantitative restrictions, to the European market. Two categories of products, nevertheless, were excluded. These were products which came under the European Coal and Steel Community Treaty and cork products. With respect to refined petroleum products, they were limited to a quota of 100,000 tons per year for each country.

The Community reserved the right to re-establish customs duties when importing them was to cause serious difficulties on the market of one or more Member States and, without having to provide detailed justification, when these imports were to exceed 100,000 tons from either of the two countries.[30] In certain circumstances as stipulated in Article 8 of the agreements, the Community could take preventive measures or resort to the safeguard clause if any Maghreb industrial exports were to cause sectoral disturbances within its market. The Community also retained the right to modify the arrangements provided for in the industrial sector especially when decisions were to be taken in the context of a CCP or when a common energy policy was to be established.[31] In sum, the bulk of industrial exports of the Maghreb countries to the Community consisted of raw materials. Manufactured products accounted for only a small proportion ranging between 7 to 8 per cent of total exports originating from these countries.

It was essentially in the agricultural sector, which accounted for 60 per cent and 45 per cent of total exports of Morocco and Tunisia respectively, that the Community was expected to contribute to the preservation and even the amelioration of these countries' export earnings. In the event, this was not the case since a significant part of their exports were in competition with similar products of the Community members like Italy and to a certain extent France. Thus the arrangements made in terms of the conditions of market access for the agricultural produce were not only designed to maintain the protection and the preferences enjoyed by Community producers but also to keep a certain balance between competing Mediterranean producers.[32]

Crude olive oil, representing 20.6 per cent in the total exports of Tunisia in 1969, enjoyed an economic advantage in the form of a reduction of 5 units of account (ua) per 100 kg on the levy applicable to third countries. This advantage could be automatically abolished if the Maghreb exporters did not abide by a minimum price. Over and above this economic advantage there was a commercial advantage in the form of a standard abatement of 0.5 ua per 100 kg. Refined olive oil, while subject to the variable component of the levy, was exempt from its fixed part.[33] However, these reductions meant almost no preference *vis-à-vis* other exports from Spain which enjoyed a reduction of 4 ua per 100 kg and Turkey 4.5 ua per 100 kg. The granting of these preferences seemed to be a 'blanket' approach and had not taken into account the difference in the level of economic development among the Mediterranean countries.

As for citrus fruits (oranges, tangerines, clementines and lemons), accounting for 27.6 per cent of Moroccan exports to the Community in 1969, an 80 per cent reduction of the CET was granted. This could be automatically ended if the prices of these products on the Community's internal market were below the reference price, and therefore the application of the third country clause. This preference brought nothing new because citrus fruits used to enjoy free access into the French market which, indeed, was their principal destination in Europe. Furthermore, a 40 per cent tariff preference was granted to Spain, Israel and

Turkey for their exports of citrus fruits.[34] Despite the fact that Morocco had a larger preference than them, they were considered to be in a better position, particularly Spain for its geographical proximity and Israel for its high productivity. Some tinned food and vegetables benefited from preferences ranging from nil duty to 50 per cent of CET. Concessions for fish products, representing an important sector for Morocco and to a lesser extent Tunisia, came within the scope of provisional national arrangements and, being so, could be changed at any time as long as the common policy was not yet operating for these products. In general, tariff preferences were subject to tariff quotas or quantitative restrictions.[35]

As a *quid pro quo*, the Maghreb countries were required to offer a certain preferential treatment to products originating from the EC. In the tariff sector, Morocco was asked to grant concessions that represented 10 per cent of the total volume of imports from the Community.[36] In terms of quotas, the concessions made accounted for 88 per cent of the total volume of imports from the EC. However, Morocco reserved the right to resort to a safeguard clause through for instance the introduction of quantitative restrictions on products which might have an adverse affect on its infant industries. By doing so, Morocco undertook to grant the Community similar concessions on other products in order to preserve the equilibrium of the agreement.[37]

In the tariff sector, Tunisia conceded to the EC a reduction on a certain number of products corresponding to 70 per cent of the preference which France enjoyed at the time on these products. Such a preferential treatment represented 40 per cent of Tunisia's total volume of imports from the Community.[38] Like Morocco, Tunisia was also required to grant quota concessions covering 73 per cent of the total volume of imports from the EC. In a similar vein, any modification to the concessions granted by Tunisia should not put into question the equilibrium on which the agreement was based.

Implications

The association arrangements, as a policy instrument, were designed to assume a prominent character of development policy towards the associates. Their stated objective was therefore to make a contribution to the economic development of Morocco and Tunisia. It was in the industrial sector in particular that the potential impact was considered beneficial to the Maghreb economies. The basic argument put forward was that the opening up of a larger market, stemming from the prospect associated with preferential access, would inevitably lead these countries to concentrate their efforts on the launching and development of export-oriented industries as they enjoyed local favourable conditions in terms of relative access to raw materials and availability of a low-wage labour force. An argument of the sort was also emphasised when the Community concluded the cooperation agreements in 1976. However, the aim of promoting the industrial development of the associates was questionable because of a number of interrelated considerations.

First, at that time in the late 1960s, the Maghreb countries were not only lacking a viable industrial basis but the handful of manufactured products supposed to be exported could not reach a level of competitiveness that would normally enable them to benefit from this greater openness.[39] And the least that can be said is that the granting of zero-tariffs was not to lead to a market increase of their exports in the short or even medium term because of their economic structure. It seems, therefore, that the assertion that these countries would enjoy overall unrestricted access for their manufactured goods was of purely academic interest to them. Even by the end of the lifetime of the trade agreements, that is the mid-1970s, the proportion of these goods in total exports destined to the EC had remained nearly unchanged since 1969, amounting to 8.7 per cent and 9.2 per cent for Morocco and Tunisia respectively. Furthermore, in the case of Morocco, the concessions granted in this sector were rather of marginal significance as they merely represented 7-8 per cent preference *vis-à-vis* third countries.[40] The reduction of the CET following the Kennedy Round, resulted, from 1972, in the reduction of this average marginal preference to 5-6 per cent. The preferential treatment granted was also to be affected by the Community's policy of extending trade concessions to other developing countries through its GSP which came into effect in 1971.

Second, the development of trade under the association seemed not to have had the expected effect. The initial objective was that an improved access to the Community market particularly for primary products, of which agricultural products made up a significant proportion of Morocco's exports and to a lesser extent those of Tunisia, would enable them to generate some of the financial needs to develop, among other things, their industrialisation in particular. Because of this acute reliance on foreign trade, the Maghreb countries were not yet able to obtain capital goods locally and investment therefore depended on imported equipment whose financing in turn depended on proceeds from exports (Robana, 1973, p. 75). This is typical of many other developing countries which were concerned about the possibility of expanding their exports as a means of financing their economic development in general. The contribution of these exports was already anticipated in the 1968-1972 Moroccan development plan for which the association:

> Will have the great advantage of normalising Morocco's relations with the EEC. The great uncertainty hanging over the future of our exports will be to a large extent eliminated. Moreover, the opportunities which will be offered to Moroccan products in a market of European size, with a greater consumer base, should stimulate industrial investment in our country.[41]

Once the agreements were concluded, it was more specifically the contribution from agricultural exports which was singled out in a statement made by the late King Hassan of Morocco, who said that:

> It is on the basis of a modern and competitive agricultural sector (...) that Morocco will, with much more chance of success, embark on an accelerated phase of industrialisation in which the EEC Member States will actively participate within the framework and perspectives offered by the present accord.[42]

Although certain Moroccan farm produce (tomatoes, potatoes and other vegetables and fruits) were not included in the trade arrangement -- which in 1968 amounted to 18 per cent of total exports in value terms to the Community market -- indicators from trade statistics pointed to an effective expansion of total trade between the two regions. Nevertheless, whereas from 1969 to 1975 the value of Community imports from both Morocco and Tunisia increased by an annual average rate of 18.6 per cent, its exports to these countries achieved a much higher average growth rate, that is 24.7 per cent.[43] The market share provides no strong evidence to demonstrate the beneficial effects that these countries' preferential trade relationship with the EC had on their exports. As illustrated by table 2.3, their share of the Community market was in the range of 0.9 per cent in 1969 and 1975 alike, indicating no improvement at all. If account is taken of their export performance in the pre-association period, one can notice something of a deteriorating trend. Indeed, in the last two years before association, that is 1967 and 1968, both countries' share of the European market was 1.1 per cent and 1.0 per cent. From this it can be argued that the export-promoting effect of preferences had not been a strategic factor in promoting the growth of their exports to the European market. In other words, it seems as if these preferences, by attempting to consolidate and even improve an earlier trading position *vis-à-vis* France, have had the opposite effect of what was expected when such a position was extended to cover the whole Community.

That poor performance in the EC market was marked by a continuing trade deficit, especially in the case of Tunisia (see chart 2.1). This contrasted with the period prior to association where, from 1958 to 1968, Tunisia enjoyed

Table 2.3 Value of EC imports from the Maghreb countries and share of total extra-EC imports, 1969-1975

	1969		1970		1971		1972		1973		1974		1975	
	Eua mn	%	Eua mn	%	Eua mn	%	Eua mn	%	Eua mn	%	Eua mn	%	Eua mn	%
Morocco	377	0.7	408	0.7	379	0.6	435	0.6	582	0.7	912	0.7	808	0.6
Tunisia	103	0.2	121	0.2	134	0.2	193	0.3	192	0.2	423	0.3	357	0.3
Total	480	0.9	529	0.9	513	0.8	628	0.9	774	0.9	1,335	1.0	1,165	0.9

Source: Calculations based on data derived from Eurostat, *Monthly External Trade Bulletin/Special issue 1958-1976* (Luxembourg: Office for Official Publications of the European Communities, 1977), pp. 12-14.

62 *From Preferential Status to Partnership*

Chart 2.1 Maghreb countries' trade balance with the EC, 1969-1975

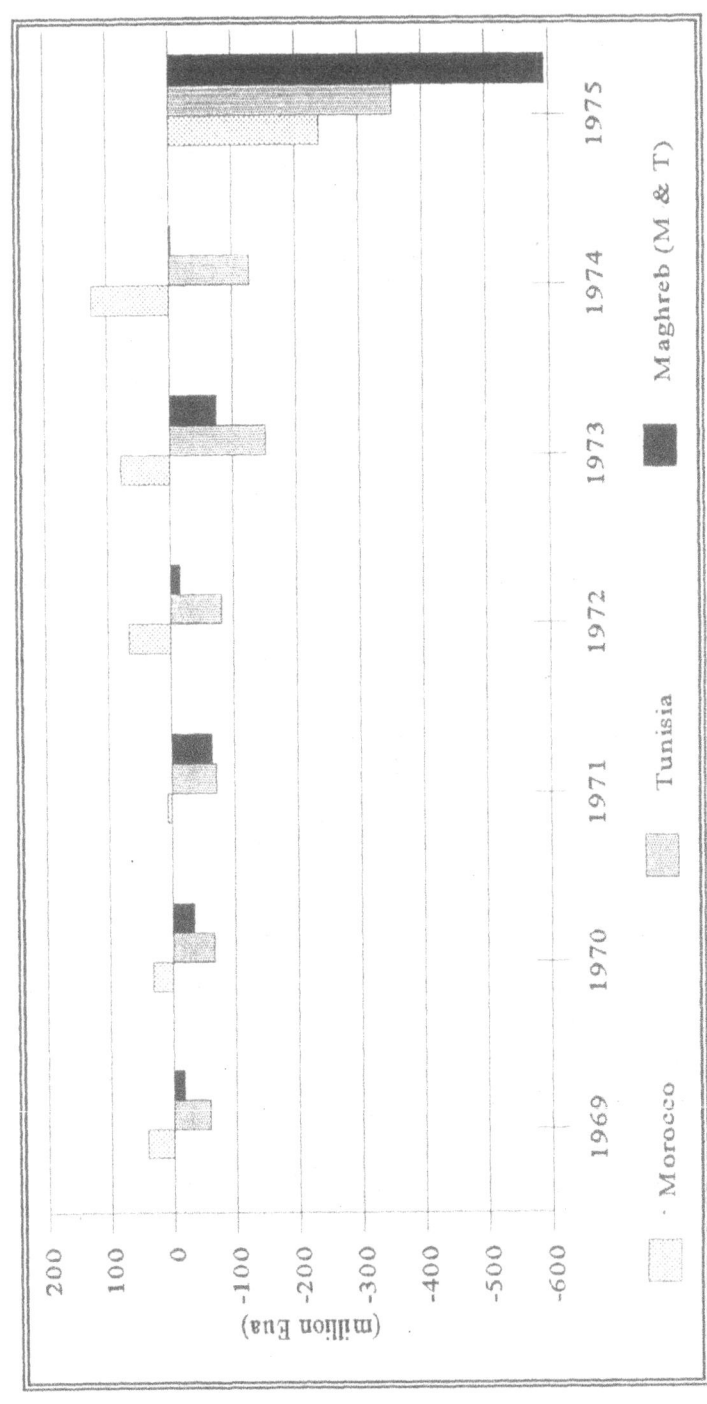

Source: Calculations based on data derived from Eurostat, *Monthly External Trade Bulletin/ Special issue 1958-1976* (Luxembourg: Office for Official Publications of the European Communities, 1977), pp. 12-14.

a surplus in its trade relations with the Community.⁴⁴ A situation of the sort was to represent a limiting factor to the industrialisation prospects. It meant obstacles to maintaining a steady flow of investment for long-term economic development and thus increasing capital was necessary if this trade deficit was not to be a major constraint in this respect.

Third, unlike the association schemes concluded with Greece, Turkey and the Yaoundé countries, the association of Morocco and Tunisia had not envisaged any financial assistance from the Community. For instance, Greece and Turkey received 125 million dollars and 175 million dollars during the first five years of their associated status.⁴⁵ As for the Maghreb countries such aid, if provided, might have served as an additional support to, among other things, infrastructure projects designed to facilitate and encourage the flow of investments.

On the absence of this one wonders whether the association, solely confined to trade matters, was in itself sufficient to provide a viable environment for capital inflow. In fact, it is doubtful that the precarious nature of the preferences conceded, partly because of their limited duration, had acted as a strong stimulus to the attraction of potential investors. Neither had the incentives and guarantees offered by the Maghreb countries to foreign investors during that first phase of association with the EC. The fact that yearly average net foreign direct investment in each of the countries had not exceeded 19 million dollars between 1970-1975 might have to a certain extent been associated with the modest prospects the association was expected to offer.⁴⁶ This limited interest shown in the region by European private investment in particular was understandable. Coinciding with a period of construction associated with high economic growth across Europe, the latter would, obviously, had been a much more attractive place for European capital than the Maghreb region.

Conclusion

In the foregoing examination of the first phase of Community policy towards Morocco and Tunisia, one can argue that its trade agreements fell short of meeting the aspirations held by the associates. Whereas these countries sought, through an arduous and lengthy process of negotiations, to accomplish a global arrangement that would in their view provide a viable framework to help them tackle their economic difficulties, the Community's response was a distinctly partial approach. Surprising was the fact that such an approach was far behind what was already admitted -- and in certain cases even put into practice -- in EC circles as necessary instruments to assist the development needs of developing countries. The Yaoundé convention, with its enlarged instruments, was a prime example.

Being exclusively confined to trade relations, the development contribution presumed to lie within this approach was from the start questionable. In fact the benefits derived by the Maghreb countries, when measured in terms of stimulus to their economic development, were decidedly insignificant. This had to do with the unbalanced content of the Community approach, which by favouring a liberal policy on industrial products, was to place its exports at an advantageous position while providing only limited concessions in the agricultural sector. And it was in this area that the Maghreb countries had a bigger potential for exports and a comparative advantage as well. The restricted access meant not only a constraint on the growth of their exports but also, as a corollary, a limited prospect for their industrialisation which, in the absence of any aid programme from the EC, was to hinge to a certain degree on the income generated by these exports.

It was in an acknowledgement of the limits that characterised this first phase of relations that the EC decided to reconsider this initial attempt with a view to establishing a comprehensive approach, involving additional instruments, towards its Mediterranean neighbours including the Maghreb countries. From 1972, therefore, the Community launched its 'global' cooperation policy as a framework for the conclusion of a new generation of agreements, coinciding this time with the second phase in its relations towards the region.

Notes

1   *Treaties establishing the European Communities* (Luxembourg: Office for Official Publications of the European Communities, 1987), p. 531.
2   *Ibid.*
3   *Ibid.*, p. 603.
4   See in this context 'Le Protocol Annexe à la Déclaration Franco-Marocaine relative à l'Etablissement de l'Indépendance dans l'Interdépendance' of 2 March 1956; 'La Convention Financière et Economique Franco-Tunisienne' of 3 June 1955 and 'La Déclaration Franco-Algérienne sur la Coopération Economique et Financière des Accords d'Evian' of 18 March 1962. For a detailed account on these accords, see Riffi El-Meloukhi, *La Politique Française de Coopération avec les Etats du Maghreb 1955-1987* (Casablanca: Editions Toubkal, 1989).
5   The Act of Algeçiras was signed by the following countries: Austria-Hungary, Belgium, France, Great Britain, Italy, Morocco, the Netherlands, Portugal, Russia, Spain, Sweden and the United States of America.
6   Article 40, Paragraph 4 of the Rome Treaty. The EAGGF was established by the Council

Regulation no. 25, 4 April 1962, *Journal Officiel des Communautés Européennes*, vol. 5, 1962, pp. 991-993.
7   Articles 48 to 58 of the Rome Treaty.
8   Articles 103 to 116 for economic policy and 117 to 127 for social policy.
9   *Maghreb-Etudes et Documents*, no. 49, January-February 1972, p. 31.
10 *Sixth General Report on the Activities of the Community*, June 1963, p. 201.
11 *Annuaire de l'Afrique du Nord*, vol. 8, 1969, p. 185.
12 *Revue du Marché Commun*, March-April 1971, p. 4.
13 *Maghreb-Etudes et Documents*, no. 26, March-April 1968, p. 46.
14 *Fifth General Report on the Activities of the Community*, June 1962, pp. 150-154.
15 *Revue du Marché Commun, op.cit.*, p. 6.
16 *Ibid.*
17 *Maghreb-Etudes et Documents, op.cit.*
18 *Seventh General Report on the Activities of the Community*, June 1964, pp. 286-287.
19 *Eighth General Report on the Activities of the Community*, June 1965, pp. 300-301.
20 Memorandum on 'Les Principes directeurs d'une politique globale de la Communauté en ce qui concerne les relations avec les pays tiers'; quoted by J. d'Yvoires, 'Le Maghreb et la Communauté Economique Européenne', *Etudes Maghrébines* (Fondation Nationale des Sciences Politiques), no. 4, April 1965, pp. 63-70.
21 *La Presse* (Tunis), 26 January 1967.
22 Cited in M. Pellerin, 'La Communauté Economique Européenne et les Etats du Maghreb', *Le Mois en Afrique*, September 1966, p. 65.
23 *Annuaire de l'Afrique du Nord, op.cit.*, p. 181.
24 *Tenth General Report on the Activities of the Community*, June 1967, pp. 203-211.
25 *Jeune Afrique*, no. 360, 3 December 1967.
26 *Revue du Marché Commun, op.cit.*, p. 94.
27 *Journal Officiel des Communautés Européennes*, vol.12, no. L 197 and L 198, 8 August 1969.
28 *Ibid.*
29 *Revue du Marché Commun*, July-August 1969, p. 362.
30 *Bulletin of the European Communities*, no. 4, 1969, p. 26.
31 See Annex 1 on the implementation of Article 2 (1) of the association agreements, *Journal Officiel des Communautés Européennes, op.cit.*, p. 10.
32 *Bulletin of the European Communities, op.cit.*, p. 27.
33 *Journal Officiel des Communautés Européennes, op.cit.*, p. 11.
34 *Bulletin of the European Communities, op.cit.*, p. 28.
35 *Journal Officiel des Communautés Européennes, op.cit.*, p. 13.
36 See Annex 3, List 1 and 2 of the Agreement establishing an Association between the European Economic Community and the Kingdom of Morocco.
37 In accordance with Article 7 of the Association Agreement.
38 See List 1 of the Agreement establishing an Association between the European Economic Community and the Tunisian Republic.
39 *Annuaire de l'Afrique du Nord, op.cit.*, p.190.
40 *Revue du Marché Commun*, March-April 1971, p. 115.
41 Cited in F. Oualalou, *L'Assistance Etrangère Face au Développement Economique du Maroc* (Casablanca: Editions Maghrébines, 1969), p. 212.
42 Quoted in *Revue du Marché Commun, op.cit.*, p. D.

43 The figures on trade in this paragraph are the author's calculations based on data from Eurostat, *Monthly External Trade Bulletin/ special issue 1958-1976*, 1977, pp. 12-14.
44 *Ibid.*
45 *Fourth General Report on the Activities of the Community*, May 1961, p. 214, and *Seventh General Report on the Activities of the Community*, June 1964, p. 263.
46 World Bank, *World Tables 1992* (Washington, DC: World Bank, 1992), pp. 426 and 610.

3 Broad-based Cooperation under the 'Global' Mediterranean Policy

Introduction

The second phase in Euro-Maghreb relations started when the EC introduced what was then called the 'global' Mediterranean policy. Reflecting a broader approach, its coverage of areas was, in addition to trade, extended to include financial aid and social provisions in respect of migrant workers from the Maghreb. This approach came as a result of the dissatisfaction with the previous attempt both in its scope, judged to be too narrow, and length of time, judged to be too short. The belief in Brussels was that enlarging the scope of the relationship, by combining different means of action for an indefinite period of time, would not only more effectively take into consideration and satisfy the aspirations of the Maghreb countries, but also make the Community intervention more substantive and forward-looking.

After briefly tracing the formulation of this approach, the chapter investigates in the following sections its different components -- that is, trade, financial assistance and migrant labour. This is primarily done by exploring the objectives pursued in each of these areas and assessing their record on the ground.

The Community's 'Global' Mediterranean Policy

During the 1960s there was no tangible success in working out a global approach as the Community's attention was much more directed to its internal construction. Thus, given the lack of an agreed overall conception of its own, the Community simply reacted to the requests of its neighbours by concluding a set of association agreements, preferential trade agreements and non-preferential trade agreements (Shlaim and Yannopoulous, 1976, p. 2). The result was regarded as a mosaic of arrangements that gave the impression of a jigsaw puzzle which had never properly been put together. This complex state of relations led Community decision-makers to take a determined step in the direction of establishing a global policy (Siotis, 1974, p. 77).

From the 1970s onwards, a shift in the Community policy towards the Mediterranean countries became discernible. A first step in this direction came from the European Parliament in its debate on 9 February 1971. The debate centred on M. Rossi's report on the commercial policy of the Community in the Mediterranean basin.[1] This report, while deploring the policy pursued hitherto, stressed the need to lay the foundations of a Mediterranean global approach that would combine trade, development aid and increased consultation on issues of common interest. During this debate, Ralf Dahrendorf, then the Community's Commissioner for external trade relations, expounded in his statement to the Parliament a set of principles that should guide the Community in devising a credible policy in the Mediterranean area. Underlying Dahrendorf's vision was a wish to see the extension of existing purely commercial relations to other fields in such a way as to contribute to the economic development of the region. His argument was:

> The commercial policy instruments available to us under our existing agreements with the Mediterranean countries can make only a very slight contribution towards achieving the goal we have set ourselves, i.e., our contribution to the creation of the long-term conditions [required] for the economic development and stability of the countries bordering on the Mediterranean.[2]

Parallel to these developments and despite earlier disagreements, the attitude of the individual Member States seemed to have evolved towards a common acceptance of a comprehensive formula for the whole Community with respect to Mediterranean countries. France and to a certain extent Italy played a major role as the main proponents of such an undertaking. France's support was dictated by its economic and political weight in North Africa and by its desire to develop better relations with the rest of the Arab world. The Community's expansion towards this region would in the words of the late French President Georges Pompidou: 'improve Europe's equilibrium by making Mediterranean and Latin influences more apparent' (quoted in Pickles, 1973, p. 326).

The growing interest in designing a common Mediterranean approach was also given impetus by the need to adapt the already existing trade arrangements concluded by the six original members in the 1960s to the changed situation created by the admission of new members in 1972. Furthermore, the planned negotiations were to be undertaken with the objective of concluding a second generation of agreements that would take into consideration the claims of the Mediterranean countries for wider and improved arrangements.

During the Council of Ministers' meeting on 6 June 1972, Maurice Schumann, the French Foreign Minister, made a broad proposal for the establishment of a free trade zone embracing all Mediterranean countries.[3] On the basis of his proposal, the European Commission, in September of the same year, drew up an outline plan aiming at setting up trade and cooperation agreements between the Community and all the Mediterranean countries within the framework of an overall and uniform scheme. The principles embodied in such a plan received the blessing of the Council of Ministers on 9 October 1972 as well as the support of the Paris summit meeting. The final communiqué of this summit stated that:

> The Community attaches essential importance to the policy of association as confirmed in the Treaty of Accession and to the fulfilment of its commitments to the countries of the Mediterranean basin with which agreements have been or will be concluded, agreements which should be the subject of an overall and balanced approach.[4]

Subsequently, the Community activated the process of finalising its overall approach which was endorsed afterwards by the Council of Ministers in its meeting on 6 November 1972. The negotiations with the Maghreb countries which started in June 1973 were -- after arduous bargaining mainly over trade concessions in the agricultural sector -- completed in January 1976. The agreements were signed in April 1976.

These arrangements represented for Morocco and Tunisia a substantial improvement over those established by the association agreements of 1969. For Algeria, this arrangement was of particular significance since for the first time it enabled the Community to end the previous *de facto* status and place its relations with that country on a contractual basis.[5]

Trade

The explicit objective of the agreements was the promotion of trade between the Community and the Maghreb countries in three ways: ensuring a better balance in their trade; increasing the rate of growth of Maghreb countries' trade or exports; and improving the conditions of access for their products to the Community market.[6] On this basis, provisions were made whereby the exports from the Maghreb countries would benefit from preferential treatment.

Trade Regime

Under the terms of the agreements, the trade regime applicable to the Maghreb countries' exports consisted of combined free and preferential access to the Community market. Accordingly, exports of raw materials and industrial products were allowed to enter the Community duty-free and without any quantitative restrictions. There were three exceptions to this principle which involved temporary restrictions on cork and petroleum products along with motor vehicles. They were, however, totally lifted at the end of 1979 for the first group of products and in 1985 for the second. As a proportion of total exports, the products concerned accounted at that time for 92 per cent of Algeria's exports to the Community, and in the case of Tunisia and Morocco 65 and 42 per cent respectively. The exports in question consisted mainly of raw materials (crude oil and phosphates) which were already admitted duty-free under the Community's CET.[7] In this sector, therefore, the value of the agreements was not immediate as substantial benefits were to hinge on the progressive industrialisation of the Maghreb countries.

As for agricultural products, they were the object of a system of preferential access. This consisted of tariff concessions ranging from 20 per cent to 100 per cent, which covered between 80 per cent and 90 per cent of the Maghreb countries' exports of agricultural products. Certainly these concessions represented an improvement on their 1969 agreements which covered about 50 per cent of their exports in this sector. For its part, the Community claimed that, despite its limitations, the whole system was explicitly intended to boost trade and, because it was to be a permanent feature and thus provide security, to contribute towards the industrialisation of the partner countries.[8]

As such these trade concessions may at first glance seem to have been of great benefit to the Maghreb countries as they provided them with a better security of access for their exports and therefore with a favourable trade position in the Community market. But this preferential regime can only be appreciated if considered within a context which takes account of certain policy changes or developments in the EC's external trade policy, as well as of limitations inherent in the agreements.

To start with, the EC was involved in a series of multilateral trade negotiations within the framework of the GATT. The successive rounds have resulted in a reduction of the Community's CET to an average level estimated at 4.3 per cent following the Tokyo Round (started in 1973 and completed in 1979) and it decreased further in the aftermath of the conclusion in December 1995 of the Uruguay Round in Marrakesh (Evans and Walsh, 1994, p. 72). Given the low level of the CET, the importance of the discriminatory tariff treatment granted to the Maghreb countries' exports of industrial products, that is duty-free, was of marginal value when compared with the EC's non-preferred trading partners.

The extension of the Community's preferential trade arrangements to other countries or groups of countries was a cause for disappointment for the Maghreb countries. Their argument was that the extension of trade concessions through the GSP and the conclusion of further preferential trade schemes had had the effect of undermining their 'special' status *vis-à-vis* the EC. In this regard, the Moroccan economist, Fathallah Oualalou, observed that:

> In the name of globalism, the Community has granted similar status to the agricultural exports originating from other Mediterranean nations, which would have affected countries such as those of the Maghreb that used to have a monopoly of tariff preferences long before independence (1989, p. 5).

There is no doubt that global trade liberalisation and the trend towards increasing the number of beneficiaries from trade concessions caused an erosion in the value of the preferences granted to the Maghreb countries. This was only one part of the story as the preferential regime in question was also affected by the Community's protectionism that was not only embodied in certain clauses of a restrictive nature but also manifest in some trade-related areas.

Among the restrictive measures on market access were the rules of origin and the safeguard clause. In principle, the rules of origin were intended notably to determine which of the products exported to the Community would be eligible to benefit from preferential access. Their main purpose was to prevent deflection of trade whereby a third country or countries might use this preferential arrangement to gain access to the Community market. Hence, as set out in the agreements, tariff concessions were to be granted only to products originating in the Maghreb countries.[9] In general, the EC approach was that a good must be 'wholly obtained' or 'substantially transformed' in a particular country for it to be regarded as originating there (Hine, 1985, pp. 84-85).

The determination of origin seemed less complicated in the case of products completely obtained in the Maghreb countries than it was with respect to goods produced with imported materials (industrial products in particular).[10] In this latter context, a main alternative way to confer the origin status was the value-added rule. This means in the case of processed or manufactured goods that 50-60 per cent of the final value should have originated in the Maghreb countries. However, evidence shows that such a percentage requirement was unrealistic as it was in practice difficult to achieve in countries such as those of the Maghreb which until now have had limited industrial bases.

In fact, on the basis of available data from the UN *Yearbook of Industrial Statistics*, and taking the whole manufacturing sector into consideration, none of the Maghreb countries -- excluding Algeria for which there were no data -- seemed to have achieved such a percentage level.[11] On average, between 1987 and 1991 Morocco only succeeded in adding as much as 27 per cent and the figure for Tunisia was about 29 per cent for the period 1977-1981. Over the same periods and with respect to certain products of export potential such as textiles and clothing, the average of value-added to these goods was respectively 30 per cent and 33 per cent for Morocco and 25 per cent and 41 per cent for Tunisia.

When these record levels are taken into consideration, it is unquestionable that the requirements under the rules of origin did represent a serious hurdle to the Maghreb countries in respect of export of manufactures. These rules thus also inhibited the prospects of their export-oriented industrialisation which the preferential access to the Community market was intended to encourage.

A concession was made whereby all the Maghreb countries and the Community could be treated as a single territory for origin purposes.[12] By allowing cumulation to meet the percentage requirement of domestic added-value, this certainly gave these countries an advantage over the Machrek countries for whom cumulation was only permitted bilaterally, that is between each of them and the Community. Although in part the intention behind this concession was to encourage regional industrial cooperation among the Maghreb countries, its practical effect was limited. As already mentioned (Chapter One), trade between the Maghreb countries has been very low and regional cooperation relatively weak, if not quite insignificant.

Given the incorporation of these restrictive rules of origin into the agreements, one may question their consistency with the basic provision of promoting trade, especially on the Maghreb side. In reality, the rules can be interpreted as a means designed to provide protection for European industries from potential external competition. Even the principle of cumulation was mainly intended to benefit European firms. As such it discouraged not only the acquisition by the Maghreb countries of inputs for their manufactures elsewhere but also would-be investors from third countries.

Another restriction on market access is to be found in the provision of a safeguard clause. A measure of this type is taken by the concerned party when 'serious disturbances arise in any sector of the economy or if difficulties arise which might bring about serious deterioration in the economy'.[13] Therefore, its use was to protect local producers of one party from severe market disturbances caused by unexpected trends in the exports of the other party. The provision made for prior joint consultation so as to take the appropriate measures with the least disturbing effect on the functioning of the agreements was weakened by the inclusion of a special derogation. This derogation opened the way for possible unilateral and immediate action under 'exceptional circumstances'.[14]

Although the safeguard measure was never used by the Community, its existence and the threat to resort to it might have affected the development of the Maghreb countries' export potential because of the uncertainties it created. As Miles Kahler put it: 'With a safeguard clause poised in the background, few European firms were likely to invest, risking later loss of their market' (1982, p. 202). In addition to having possibly generated a welfare loss for these countries in this context, the threat of its imposition was effectively used by the Community as a means of extracting concessions from them which could not be obtained under the provisions of the agreements. Here the typical case was that of requesting them to agree to voluntary restraint arrangements for their exports of textiles and clothing. The Community action was described by the former Algerian ambassador to the EC, Sid-Ahmed Ghozali, as:

> A way that does not give the appearance of running counter to the legal stipulations [of the agreements], a manner that consists in telling the other partner, here a door that must be closed (...) We leave it to you to do it yourselves (1986, p. 71).

Besides the restrictive effect of these provisions, there were other protectionist measures which also tended to limit the preferential treatment accorded to the Maghreb countries. They related principally to products covered by the CAP and certain processed or manufactured goods that came to be regarded as sensitive.

As already indicated, varying levels of tariff concessions were granted to the Maghreb countries' exports of agricultural produce.[15] However, this advantage was hedged with non-tariff restrictions specific to regulations deriving from the CAP's respective market organisations. The preferential tariff treatment was therefore subordinated to mechanisms such as calendars, tariff-quotas, reference prices and import levies. For instance, tariff cuts for a wide range of fresh fruit and vegetables mostly applied within the limits of a calendar covering off-season production periods in the Community -- usually some interval between November and May. Exports in periods other than these meant the reestablishment of the full rate of customs duties. Equally, this applied to certain products (fruit salad, tomato concentrate and so on) once their tariff-quotas were used up. The common market organisation for fruits and vegetables provided an additional means of protection as products falling under this category were subject to countervailing entry levies, when imported into the Community market at prices below the level fixed as the reference prices.

Arguably, the existence of such mechanisms and the way they operated together acted as a deterrent to the potential increase in the exports of the Community's immediate neighbouring partners. The emphasis on Community preference through high prices to European farmers to encourage greater domestic supply restricted the export opportunities available to these partners. Exports of the Maghreb countries did experience a decline over the years. Morocco was a case in point, not least because of the relative importance of farm produce in its exports to the EC. Morocco regularly expressed its displeasure at the level of reference prices and calendar constraints on its sale of tomatoes (Morocco's second major agricultural export after citrus fruit) which caused a loss of its market share in the Community to the benefit principally of Dutch greenhouse production (Cherkaoui, 1987, p. 61). The accumulation of increasing quantities of unsold oranges was also attributed to the restrictive effect of the reference prices as well as to the gradual erosion of the tariff concessions for citrus fruit, particularly in favour of Spain, even before the latter country's accession to the Community in 1986 (Duchêne and Holmes, 1984, p. 60).

The restricted market access and its consequences for the potential exports of the Maghreb countries was exacerbated by the Community's subsequent enlargement to the south to include Greece (1981) and later Portugal and Spain (1986). The Iberian extension of the EC was the major source of concern. Spain, with its productive potential, was to enable the Community to reach a very high degree of self-sufficiency in the Mediterranean type of products. Hence, in the area of farm produce the 'Europe of the Ten' had deficits of between 6 and 20 per cent for tomatoes, small fruit and vegetables, wine, and olive oil, and a 55 per cent deficit for citrus fruit (Aghrout and Sutton, 1990, p. 60). By comparison, the post-1986 Community has only a 10 per cent deficit for citrus fruit, and will be sufficient or in surplus for the rest.

All this meant that among the North African Mediterranean countries, especially Morocco and to a lesser extent Tunisia, with the widest range of similar agricultural exports, there was an expectation of being adversely affected by Spanish accession to the EC. It was not merely the loss of an EC market that these countries were concerned about, since their production was geared to it, but also the difficulties in finding alternative outlets that might result from the effects on third markets of subsidised Community exports (Taylor, 1980, p. 10; Duchêne and Holmes, 1984, p. 57). Obviously, the second concern had to do with anticipation of the Community becoming a potential exporter itself of

Mediterranean products which the CAP mechanisms were to boost.

In order to cushion the impact of the enlargement,[16] the EC concluded additional protocols of adaptation with the Maghreb countries with a view to maintaining these countries' traditional flow of agricultural exports.[17] Without going into the details of these arrangements,[18] certain remarks about their scope ought to be made. First, the continuance of traditional trade flows, determined in accordance with the average exports to the EC of the partners concerned over the period 1980-1984, was one that corresponded with lower export growth. Second, the cornerstone of the adaptation process consisted of gradually phasing out the remaining duties on the agricultural exports of the Maghreb countries, in parallel with similar measures for Portugal and Spain, over the transitional phase 1986-1995. The phasing out was to begin only once the rate of customs duties applied to the exports of the then new members fell below those applied to the Maghreb. In point of fact, this could not be equated with an additional trade concession as, in general, the Maghreb countries already had a more preferential tariff treatment than that enjoyed by both countries prior to their accession. Finally, there was no improvement in terms of non-tariff barriers since the Community maintained those existing mechanisms of protection such as calendars, tariff-quotas and so forth.

By and large, in addition to the CAP instruments, the enlargement was to place a further limitation on the potential growth of exports from the Maghreb countries. At the same time, it rendered the future prospects of the whole exporting sector of farm produce uncertain. The point was clearly made by Oualalou who stated that:

> For 1996, Spain and Portugal know that they will enjoy member state status with similar rights and obligations. The Maghreb countries, in contrast, have no assurance about the nature of links they will have with the Community. This impossibility of forecasting what will occur prevents them from preparing the future in order to manage it better and from initiating development programmes that enable them to take their place in the environment that surrounds them. This means that, during the coming ten years, they will once again continue to negotiate with Europe the shape of an uncertain future (1989, pp. 11-12).

A final area where the protectionism of the Community affected the trade regime established by the agreements was the one that related to processed or manufactured goods. The preferential treatment provided for in these agreements -- that is, secured market access -- was considered to be a determinant factor for the industrial development of the Maghreb countries, at least in terms of increased local processing of raw materials.

The processing of agricultural products destined mainly for export to the European market was one sector in which restrictive practices were experienced. The Community provided support, in the form of subsidies, to European processors of agricultural products such as olive oil, tomato concentrate and a number of fruits. This system of assistance was viewed by the Community as a way of providing some sort of 'compensation' for the preferential tariff treatment granted to external suppliers. These subsidies, along with the minimum producer prices fixed by the Community, resulted in the generation of surpluses (Duchêne and Holmes, 1984, p. 75). For the Maghreb countries, this had the effect of discouraging investment, particularly in certain areas of the food-processing industries. Again the experience of Morocco is instructive in this context. This country which was exporting around 7,500 tonnes of tomato concentrate during 1975-1976 became, a few years later, unable to compete successfully with the heavily-subsidised Community production, namely that of Italy (Cherkaoui, 1987, p. 61). This situation was largely responsible for the closure of many factories, among them a big plant set up by the Heinz Company in the late 1970s for exports to the UK.

Measures of limitation were also extended to other industrial products that involved labour-intensive manufacturing. The textiles and clothing sector was the most targeted by these measures. In the Maghreb countries, this type of industry, which was already established, received an initial boost from the prospects of a guaranteed market in Europe. A direct effect of this was that further development of these countries' production capacities, as in other Mediterranean countries, was often to be built up with European financial assistance and joint ventures and processing deals with Community companies (Taylor, 1980, p. 12; Hamill, 1989, pp. 1-9). Their comparative advantage -- cheap labour and better geographical location -- combined with the free access were expected to make the expansion of exports in this sector a promising route to industrialisation.

However, from the late 1970s onwards as the crisis hit the EC textiles and clothing manufacturing sector,[19] the Community, in order to protect its own industry, requested the Maghreb countries -- Algeria was not included because of the small volume of its exports -- and other Mediterranean partners to consent to measures of self-limitation of their exports. This meant renouncing 'voluntarily' an advantage offered by the cooperation agreements, otherwise they would have run the risk of unilateral action by the Community under the safeguard clause. Protesting against the introduction of these quantitative restrictions, the Tunisian Foreign Minister, Mohamed Fitouri, was reported to have said in 1978 that: 'They conformed neither to the spirit nor the letter of the agreements and have delivered a whiplash to our young industry which has just started growing.'[20]

While there is no available data regarding the effect that these self-limitation arrangements might have had on Morocco, it was believed that, as far as Tunisia was concerned, their immediate impact was the closure of seventeen textile and clothing mills and the loss of several thousand jobs.[21] Nevertheless, as the Community repeatedly claimed, such measures were not so restrictive as those applied, under the MFA, to the exports of other suppliers, mainly Asian countries. Indeed, though both Morocco and Tunisia managed to register a steady increase in their exports of the products concerned, they would be better off without them.

The Community measures were considered in the Maghreb to mark a breach of the EC's legal commitment to the principle of free access for manufactured products. Such restraints were interpreted by the Maghreb countries as a serious obstacle to their industrial development, especially in their export-oriented sector. Not only was this likely to discourage potential investors from committing capital to the affected sector, but also from withholding investment from other sectors for fear of further restrictive measures.

Overall, the trade regime, by virtue of its preferential nature, was geared to the improvement of the Maghreb countries' trading position in the European market. Nevertheless, its initial scope was weakened by the restrictions intrinsic to the agreements themselves as well as by the Community's changing circumstances that affected its external trade policy. This is the background against which the trade relations, under the 1976 agreements, evolved between the two parties.

Trends in Trade Performance

One ultimate aim of the preferential access granted to the Maghreb countries was to improve their trade performance. This was intended to serve as a Community contribution to their overall socio-economic development. Accordingly, the improvement in question was to be reflected in the achievement of a better trade balance; increasing these countries' share of the EC market; and giving a boost to the diversification in the composition of their exports away from the predominance of primary products.

First, one of the means deemed essential in the promotion of their trade relationship was to ensure a better balance in their trade exchanges. Despite such a claim, the development of the trade balance saw an overall deterioration to the detriment of the Maghreb countries (see chart 3.1). Over the period 1976-1996,

78 *From Preferential Status to Partnership*

Chart 3.1 Maghreb countries' trade balance with the EC, 1976-1996

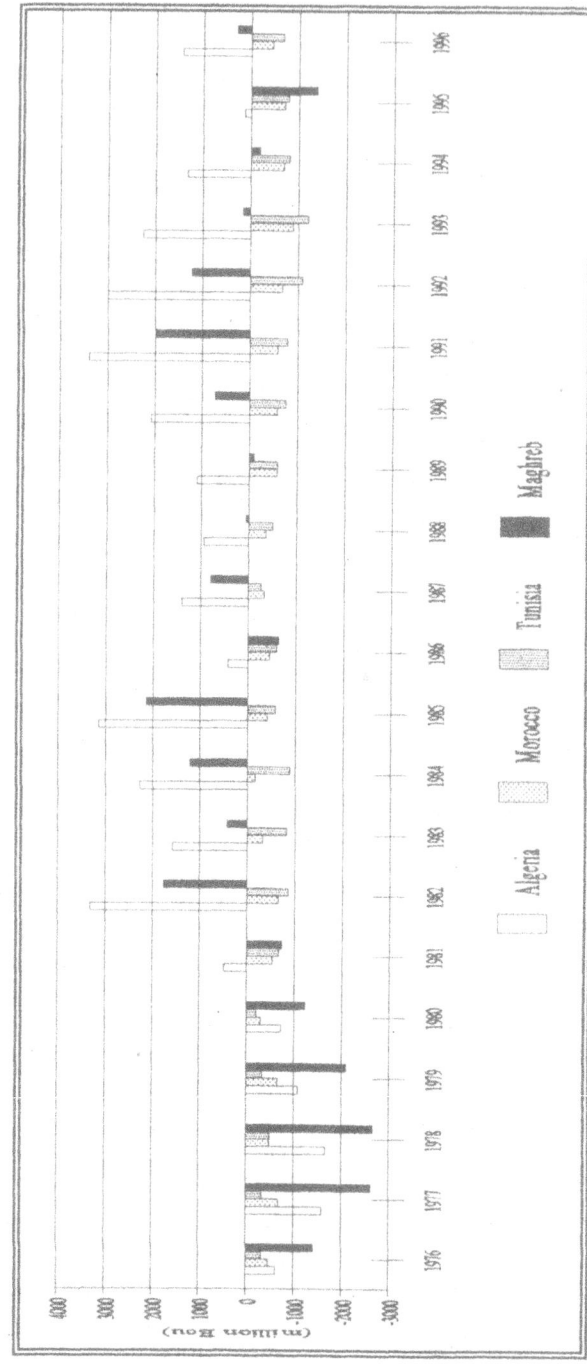

Source: Calculations based on data derived from Eurostat, *External Trade Statistical Yearbook* (Luxembourg: Office for Official Publications of the European Communities, 1986 and 1997).

that is, almost the lifetime of the 1976 agreements, the accumulated global trade deficit with the Community amounted to merely 2.3 billion Ecu.[22] However, a more detailed analysis reveals that the actual position varies among the countries concerned.

Algeria was the only country which reversed the trend, and its trade balance passed from a deficit to a surplus from 1981 onwards. This shift was due in particular to the soaring of oil prices until the mid-1980s and the subsequent massive cut in imports when these prices collapsed. By contrast, Morocco and Tunisia experienced a chronic trade deficit with the Community which, for both countries, was estimated at 24.9 billion Ecu in the period 1976-1996, representing an annual average of almost 1.2 billion Ecu.[23] Put in a comparative perspective, this tendency had not changed for Tunisia since the 1969 arrangements, while in the case of Morocco the situation seemed to have rather deteriorated mainly from the mid-1970s.

It can be argued that developing countries may increase their imports of capital goods for their economic development. Thus in the short run their trade deficit, reflecting a deliberate policy, cannot be seen as a serious problem to their economies. But, as indicated, for both Morocco and Tunisia such a deficit was a persistent feature in their trade with the Community for a long period of time (more than two decades). A possible explanation for the failure of the preferential access to produce a balanced trade relationship between the two sides can be found in the Maghreb countries' comparatively weak export performance in the European market.

Second, the preferential nature of the trading status accorded to these countries was expected to lead to an increase in their exports to the EC. From 1976 to 1996, the Community remained their largest single market. It took about 60 per cent of their exports and provided more than 64 per cent of their imports on an annual average.[24] Whilst this demonstrates the importance of the European market, it does not show whether there was a growth in these countries' exports to the Community.

In order to obtain some indication of the Maghreb countries' export performance, one can consider changes in the share of the European market. Table 3.1 shows that after the rise in exports experienced during the first decade, from 3.5 billion Ecu in 1976 to 15.3 billion Ecu in 1985, total exports went down to 13.3 billion Ecu in 1996. Despite this fact, the value of their exports as such improved substantially relative to 1976. More importantly, nonetheless, is their share of EC total imports from outside Member States which, apart from the increase registered by the mid-1980s, had subsequently dropped to reach a proportion quite similar to that of 1976.

Table 3.1 Value of EC imports from the Maghreb countries and share of total extra-EC imports, 1976-1996

	1976		1980		1985		1990		1996	
	Ecu bn	%	Ecu bn	%	Ecu bn	%	Ecu bn	%	Ecu bn	%
Algeria	2.1	1.3	4.6	1.6	11.6	2.9	7.3	1.7	5.5	0.9
Morocco	0.9	0.5	1.4	0.5	2.1	0.5	3.1	0.7	4.2	0.7
Tunisia	0.5	0.3	1.4	0.5	1.6	0.4	2.3	0.5	3.6	0.6
Maghreb	3.5	2.1	7.4	2.6	15.3	3.8	12.7	2.9	13.3	2.2

Source: Calculations based on data derived from Eurostat, *External Trade Statistical Yearbook* (Luxembourg: Office for Official Publications of the European Communities, 1986, 1994 and 1997).

One must also bear in mind the fact that the Maghreb countries' exports were heavily influenced by the importance of fuel products and their fluctuating prices. These accounted for 34 per cent of their total exports (in value terms) to the EC in 1995, compared to 65 per cent in 1985 and 53 per cent in 1976.[25] Excluding these products, the relative importance of their market share in the EC showed no sustained improvement over the years, and thus remained less significant.

This trend in the Maghreb countries' export performance was not very different from that of other Mediterranean countries. Although they were close to the top of the 'pyramid of preferences', their share of the European market had hardly changed at all between 1976 and 1995. The exports of the Mediterranean countries accounted for 8.4 per cent of total EC imports from outside the Member States in 1976 and 8.5 per cent in 1996.[26]

The less satisfactory export performance of the Maghreb countries was, nevertheless, apparent when compared to other developing countries which benefited from limited trade concessions in the Community market. For instance, the Asian countries, whose preferential access was available under the Community's GSP scheme, experienced a steady rise in their exports to the EC. This resulted in them becoming the first main trading partner of the Community among the developing countries. Within the Asian countries, the dynamic Asian economies and China saw their share of the European market increase respectively from 3.8 per cent and 0.5 per cent in 1976 to 10 per cent and 4.8 per cent in 1995.[27] In the period 1976-1995, their respective average annual growth rates of exports to the EC were 13 per cent and 18 per cent whereas for the Maghreb countries it was about 7 per cent.[28] A situation of the sort may be reminiscent of an old adage, quoted elsewhere, that some countries trade and others sign preferential trade agreements (Tsoukalis, 1997, p. 228).

Third, the preferential trade treatment was seen as an incentive that would favour the process of industrialisation in the Maghreb countries. Indeed, the provision for free access for industrial products was expected to boost, in the longer run, the endeavour of these countries to develop a manufacturing capacity, especially through an increasing degree of processing of traditional agricultural and mineral exports, and possibly by launching new export lines of manufactured goods.

Table 3.2 gives a view of the changes in the overall commodity composition of Maghreb countries' exports to the EC in 1976 and 1995. Algeria appears as the only country the structure of whose exports had hardly diversified at all. Energy products were, and remain, the major export commodities to the European market. Of course, the most plausible explanation for this lies in

Table 3.2 Structure of Maghreb countries exports to the EC, 1976 and 1995 (percentage value)

	Algeria		Morocco		Tunisia	
	1976	1995	1976	1995	1976	1995
Food, beverages and tobacco	2.1	0.4	36.9	20.4	9.1	3.5
Raw materials	1.9	0.6	41.6	7.5	27.6	8.9
Energy	94.6	95.0	0.4	0.9	23.1	7.0
Chemicals	0.2	1.1	2.1	9.2	12.8	6.1
Machines and transport equipment	0.1	1.6	0.3	11.2	1.8	10.2
Other manufactured goods	1.1	1.2	18.6	50.2	25.6	63.8

Source: Eurostat, *External Trade Monthly Statistics* (Luxembourg: Office for Official Publications of the European Communities, 1977 and 1996).

Algeria's development policy which, roughly until the end of 1980s, was based on a state-oriented strategy of import-substituting industrialisation. Only in recent years has a gradual shift away from this inward-looking policy towards a more export-oriented strategy been noticeable, with private capital being encouraged to play an increasing role in the economic sector.

With the exception of Algeria, evidence from table 3.2 suggests that both Morocco's and Tunisia's export structures changed since 1976. One apparent feature in their export profiles was the decline of primary products and the growth of manufactures.

As far as primary commodities were concerned, their declining share in the total value of exports during the period under review may be attributed to two factors. On the one hand, the CAP mechanisms and the southern enlargement of the EC had the effect of placing limits on the potential increase of exports of agricultural products from Morocco and Tunisia. On the other hand, the fluctuation in mineral export prices, and thus of mineral export revenue, had tended to affect the proportional value of their total exports, with phosphates being a major example of this.

Apparently, the share of manufactures in exports significantly expanded. At first glance, it seems that attempts were made to achieve some degree of diversification from traditional exports. Yet this pattern needs to be differentiated as it was mainly in the category of other manufactured goods, consisting of textiles-clothing and leather products, that the expansion was quite considerable, accounting in 1995 for more than 50 per cent in the value of Morocco's total exports and nearly 64 per cent of that of Tunisia. Clothing and clothing accessories made up the bulk of these products (a proportion of more than 80 per cent).[29]

While there was an alteration in the composition of Maghreb countries' exports to the Community, this does not mean a dramatic breakthrough in the process of diversification. Their exports of manufactures to the European market still gave evidence of a high concentration on a commodity level, that was essentially in the area of clothing products (see chart 3.2). In general, these are all products that require low technology and are based on labour-cost comparative advantage.

Financial Assistance

The inclusion of financial aid in the 1976 agreements constituted an innovative feature which the 1969 accords had not provided for. The objective, by adding

84 *From Preferential Status to Partnership*

Chart 3.2 Share of clothing products in the Maghreb countries' exports of manufactures to the EC in 1995 (percentage value)

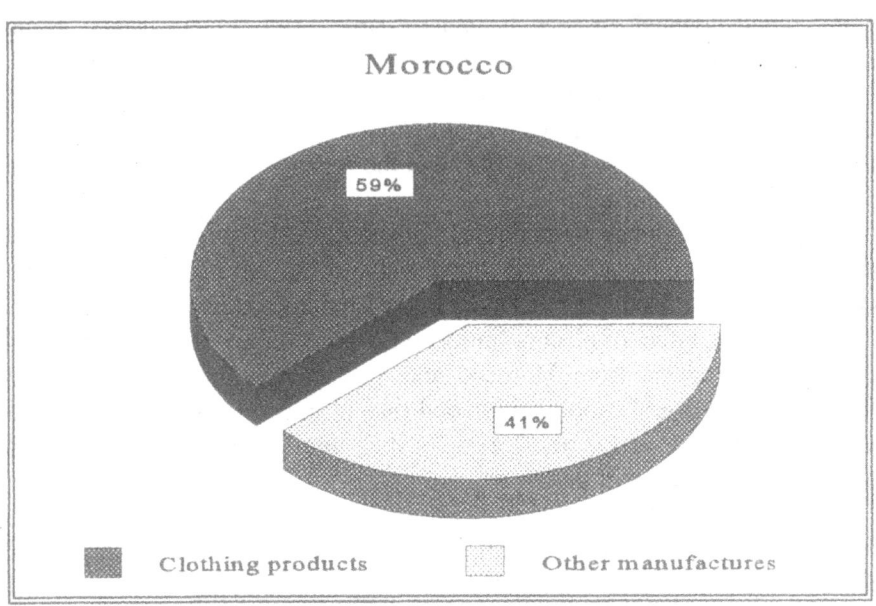

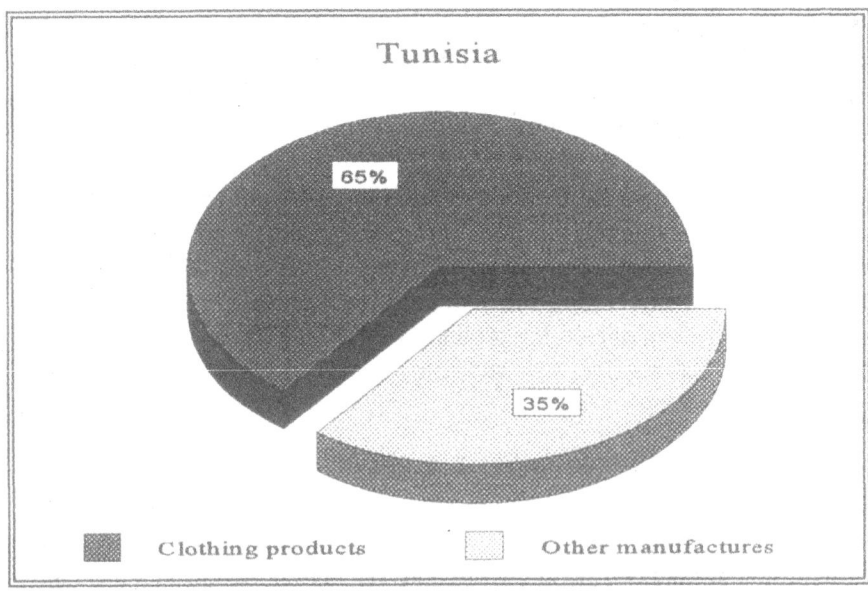

Source: Calculations based on date derived from Eurostat, *External Trade Monthly Statistics*, no. 11, 1996.

this to the trade preferences, was to establish what was called global cooperation combining different means of action that would contribute to the economic and social development of the Maghreb countries.[30] The volume of financial aid was determined on a country-by-country basis in a series of four protocols (see table 3.3). It consisted of EC budgetary contributions in the form of grants and highly concessional loans -- the latter were replaced by risk capital starting from the third protocol -- and European Investment Bank (EIB) own-resources loans.

In the period 1976-1996, the EC total financial appropriations to the Maghreb region totalled 2.687 billion Ecu, with Morocco being allocated a bigger share of 41 per cent followed by Algeria 31 per cent and Tunisia 28 per cent. As it can be noticed, the Community had tended to increase the volume of its aid which more than trebled from the first protocol to the fourth one. This was in large part intended to keep pace with inflation rates.[31]

Within the framework of its redirected Mediterranean policy -- adopted by the Council in September 1990 -- the EC made other additional funds available to its Mediterranean partners. Such funds were destined to support, among other things, the programmes of structural adjustment undertaken by these countries. Out of a special package of 300 million Ecu earmarked for this purpose, 175 million Ecu were committed to the Maghreb countries.[32] During the lifetime of the two fishing agreements (1988-1996) with the EC, Morocco also received 689.5 million Ecu as financial compensation for allowing Community boats to use its waters for catches.[33]

By and large, officials at the Commission had expressed satisfaction regarding the financial assistance provided to the Maghreb countries.[34] The exceptional case of Algeria was, nevertheless, singled out in a document from the Commission's Maghreb Unit which pointed to the fact that: 'Contrary to its neighbours, Algeria has derived little benefit from the 1976 cooperation agreement and its instruments, both in terms of trade and cooperation. In twenty years, rare were the projects that experienced a normal implementation.'[35]

The Commission may be correct in making such a general assessment which, in turn, gives insufficient evaluative account of the effect of EC aid. Thus an appreciation of this aid can be attempted by looking into its process of implementation, its sectoral distribution and its relative significance.

First, each financial protocol was normally concluded for a duration of five years. Yet the effective period of application of the protocols did not in reality adhere to this five-yearly framework. The reason is that the period of application was not fixed in relation to the protocols' date of entry but in respect of an expiry date.[36] And since all protocols were subject to delays -- thereby affecting their entry into force -- that meant a reduced period of application

Table 3.3 Financial appropriations under the four protocols, 1976-1996 (in million Ecu)

	Algeria	Morocco	Tunisia	Maghreb (Total)
1st Protocol 1976-1981				
Budget	44	74	54	172
EIB	70	56	41	167
Total	114	130	95	339
2nd Protocol 1981-1986				
Budget	44	109	61	214
EIB	107	90	78	275
Total	151	199	139	489
3rd Protocol 1986-1991				
Budget	56	173	93	322
EIB	183	151	131	465
Total	239	324	224	787
4th Protocol 1991-1996				
Budget	70	218	116	404
EIB	280	220	168	668
Total	350	438	284	1,072
Total Protocols 1976-1996				
Budget	214	574	324	1,112
EIB	640	517	418	1,575
Total	854	1,091	742	2,687

Source: Commission of the European Communities, *Report on Cooperation with the Mediterranean Partners*, COM(97) 371 final, Brussels, 18 July 1997, pp. 36-37.

which in the context of the Maghreb countries was less than four years overall. These delays were mainly associated with cumbersome procedures of which the slowness of the process of negotiation and ratification was a blatant example.

Another salient weakness in the process of implementation was the long delays in the disbursement of funds. At the end of 1995, it is remarkable that even the funds committed under the first generation of protocols were not totally disbursed. This was particularly the case for budget aid whose rate of implementation had been slower than that of the EIB (see table 3.4). The possibility contained in the protocols for uses to be sought for all residual funds at the end of the period of application until they are exhausted might have justified the tardiness in both commitment and disbursement. But this trend seemed to have had an impact on the implementation of projects. A special report by the European Court of Auditors (ECA) found that, in the Maghreb countries, twenty-five projects funded under the first two series of financial protocols from budgetary sources had still not been closed on 31 December 1996.[37]

Delays experienced in the implementation process had therefore impacted upon the effectiveness of Community aid. In terms of aid projects, these delays, according to the ECA report, increased costs in some instances. In other instances it affected results, as with respect to the latter a number of projects could only be partially completed.[38]

As the major administrator of Community aid, the Commission had been held responsible largely for this situation.[39] Alongside this the Maghreb countries had also shown less efficiency in the utilisation of aid, either because of their limited absorptive capacity or because of a lack of interest illustrated by the attitude of Algeria.

Second, sectoral distribution of aid may provide an indication of its effect on the recipient countries. A look at the breakdown of Community financial intervention reveals interesting facts. For all the Maghreb countries, a large proportion of total resources had been devoted to infrastructure projects (roads, railways, ports, telecommunication, power stations, dams, water supply networks, and so on). In Morocco, this sector alone was the single most important consumer of all EC aid. Between 1979-1994, it accounted for more than 44 per cent of all programmable commitments.[40] Similarly, in Algeria both budget resources and EIB loans placed a great deal of emphasis on infrastructure, such as projects related to the energy sector.[41] The biggest proportion of aid to Tunisia, about 76 per cent, was allocated to rural development and infrastructure, with a rather marked predominance of the former (382 million Ecu committed under the four financial protocols).[42]

The concentration of Community aid on infrastructural projects means

88   *From Preferential Status to Partnership*

Table 3.4 Financial implementation of the four protocols at the end of 1995 (value in million Ecu)

		BUDGET						EIB				
	Total	Commitments		Payments		Total	Commitments			Payments		
		Value	% 1	Value	% 2		Value	% 1		Value	% 2	
PROTOCOL 1												
Algeria	44	37	84	32	86	70	70	100		70	100	
Morocco	74	74	100	74	100	56	56	100		56	100	
Tunisia	54	54	100	53.5	99	41	41	100		41	100	
Maghreb	172	165	96	159.5	96	167	167	100		167	100	
PROTOCOL 2												
Algeria	44	32	73	18	56	107	107	100		89	83	
Morocco	109	108	99	100	92	90	90	100		90	100	
Tunisia	61	61	100	61	100	78	78	100		76	97	
Maghreb	214	201	94	179	89	275	275	100		255	93	
PROTOCOL 3												
Algeria	56	56	100	18	32	183	142	77		70	49	
Morocco	173	172	99	136	79	151	151	100		91	60	
Tunisia	93	91	98	77	84	131	131	100		107	81	
Maghreb	322	319	99	231	72	465	424	91		268	63	
PROTOCOL 4												
Algeria	70	47	67	16	34	280	180	64		24	13	
Morocco	218	190	87	50	26	220	220	100		41	18	
Tunisia	116	108	93	48	44	168	168	100		49	29	
Maghreb	404	345	85	114	33	668	568	85		114	20	

Source: Commission of the European Communities. *Report on Cooperation with the Mediterranean Partners*, COM(97) 371 final, Brussels, 18 July 1997, pp. 36-37.

that little attention had been given to other sectors. Naturally, economic infrastructure is instrumental in the process of development; nevertheless, sectors such as industry and agriculture, which have a direct impact on the development of the productive capacity of the Maghreb countries, were the object of decidedly modest funding. The limited support granted to small and medium industries had been short of the initial hope these countries placed on large-scale industrial cooperation with the EC. This under-funding had also adversely affected education and training which are also decisive in the process of development. Although the choice of projects rested with the Maghreb countries, the Community reserved the right of decision concerning the ones it was willing to finance. Aware of this, the Maghreb countries had thus tended to select those projects which were likely to be accepted by the Community.

Last but not least is the relative significance of EC aid destined to the Maghreb countries. Table 3.5 reveals that Community assistance witnessed a steady growth over time, that is quite apparent in the period 1991-1996. Relative to other sources, however, EC assistance, excluding Member States' contribution, was rather small in size. As such it had never consistently been a major factor in the total external aid picture of these countries, representing a proportion of 7 per cent of total net official assistance received between 1979-1996.[43]

In the period under consideration, bilateral aid from Member States to the Maghreb countries was much more substantial, being six times higher than that originating from the Community.[44] Together they (EC and Member States) were the primary source of official aid. For obvious historical reasons, France alone accounted for more than half of the combined EC and Member States' assistance and about a third of the total external aid to the Maghreb region.[45]

The geographical allocation of EC assistance is equally indicative of the modest volume of its financial contribution to the Maghreb. The share received by this region had not exceeded 3.6 per cent of the EC's global aid programme to the developing countries, and was insignificant when compared to the 7.5 billion dollars channelled just to the CEEC during the period 1990-1996.[46]

Notwithstanding Community efforts to increase the volume of its aid, it is not sustainable to argue that this volume was consistent with the claim of contributing to the socio-economic development of the recipient countries. In practice, due to its small size, it proved of very little bearing on these countries' needs. It fell short of investment requirements and the Commission itself acknowledged the fact that the EC financial support merely accounted for an average of 0.025 per cent of the Maghreb countries' total investments.[47] The amount of EC aid, with the inclusion of the Member States' contribution, was not

Table 3.5 Net official development assistance to the Maghreb countries (annual average / million dollars)

	1979-1984	1985-1990	1991-1996
European Community	28	45	211
EC and Member States	361	521	1,072
Total (World)	916	1,070	1,340
% EC aid / Total aid	3.1	4.2	15.7

Source: Calculations based on data derived from the Organisation for Economic Cooperation and Development (OECD), *Geographical Distribution of Financial Flows to Aid Recipients* (Paris: OECD, 1979-1982, 1982-1985, 1986-1989, 1989-1993 and 1992-1996).

even proportionate to their trade imbalances with the Community.

The Migration Issue

Migration from the Maghreb countries to Western Europe and more particularly to France can be traced back to the beginning of the twentieth century. Initially, this emigration was almost exclusively dictated by the needs and interests of France during the 1914-1918 War and in the interwar period. These immigrants were to serve both as conscripts in the French army and workers in French factories and arsenals.

In the aftermath of the Second World War and especially during the 1960s, migration from North Africa to Europe became primarily driven by economic considerations. Alongside the postwar economic boom in Western Europe there was a corresponding need for an expansion of the industrial work force. And because of the chronic labour shortages experienced at the time, European states encouraged migration of workers from the Maghreb and elsewhere. This trend continued until the early 1970s. By 1973-1974, however, the economic recession that resulted from the oil crisis reversed the trend as, with the first alarming signs of rapidly increasing unemployment, measures were taken to halt further immigration of workers.

The European states' decision to stop foreign labour recruitment, however, had no tangible effect on the status of those migrants already established as they tended to stay rather than to return to their countries of origin. In other words, these measures were not only to 'freeze the foreign population in place' but also 'inadvertently accelerated the processes of settlement and family reunification' (Hollifield, 1997, p. 4). In 1976, the number of Maghreb migrant workers in the Community was estimated at 720,000 of which France was hosting almost 90 per cent, not least because of the historical links between this country and the Maghreb region.[48] According to available statistics, their total number as a community amounted to nearly 2.1 million in 1995 (see table 3.6).

The progressive settlement of North African migrant workers in Europe raised the question of their status and treatment along with that of their families in the receiving countries. Improving the socio-economic situation of these migrants had been and continues to be a constant concern for the 'exporting' countries. Obviously, one fundamental reason is to be found in the relatively significant contribution of these workers to the economies of their home countries in terms of flows of remittances, though with varying degrees -- in time and between countries -- as shown in chart 3.3. In the case of Morocco, the contribution in question was explained more clearly by Abdallah Berrada:

> The Moroccan authorities looked favourably on this emigration, which (...) enabled them to benefit from migrants' remittances greatly needed for the equilibrium of Morocco's balance of payments and to finance its investments. Emigration also acted as a labour market regulator: the labour supply was growing out of proportion to demand. The departures of Moroccan workers to Europe were very much appreciated (1994, p. 268).

The provisions of the agreements were mainly concerned with ensuring non-discrimination *vis-à-vis* the Maghreb workers in terms of conditions of employment, remunerations and social security benefits.[49] Their periods of employment in various Member States, or with different employers within a member state, can also be aggregated without losing pensions or other related social benefits.

In fact, these social provisions drew to a large extent on an early proposal from the Commission for an '*Action programme in favour of migrant workers and their families*' that was adopted in a Council resolution in February

Table 3.6 Maghreb migrants in the EC, 1995 (in thousands)

	Algeria	Morocco	Tunisia	Maghreb (Total)
EC (Total)	653.6	1,125	296.8	2,076.0
France	614.2	572.7	206.3	1,393.2
Belgium	10.0	144.0	5.7	159.7
Germany	19.1	82.4	27.4	128.9
Netherlands	0.9	158.7	2.1	161.7
Spain	3.2	63.9	0.4	67.5
Italy	4.5	95.6	50.4	150.5
United Kingdom	4.0	7.0	1.0	12.0

Source: Eurostat, *Statistics in Focus - Population and Social Conditions*, no. 2, 1996, and no. 3, 1998.

1976.[50] The programme stated that:

> In fact, after more than a decade of benefit from migrant labour, the Community finds itself with a large unassimilated group of foreign workers who share almost all the obligations of the society in which they live and work but, more often than not, have a less than equal share in its benefits and rights. This situation is in the long term intolerable, degrading for the migrant and dangerous for the Community (...) One of the basic objectives of an action programme for migrants must be the progressive elimination of all discrimination against them in living and working conditions.[51]

Chart 3.3 Annual remittances of migrants from the Maghreb countries, 1970, 1980 and 1995 (percentage value)

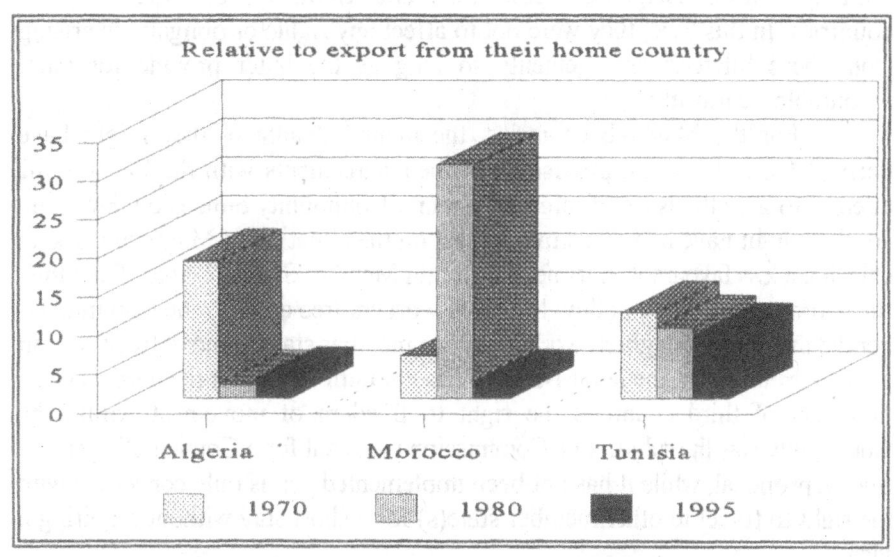

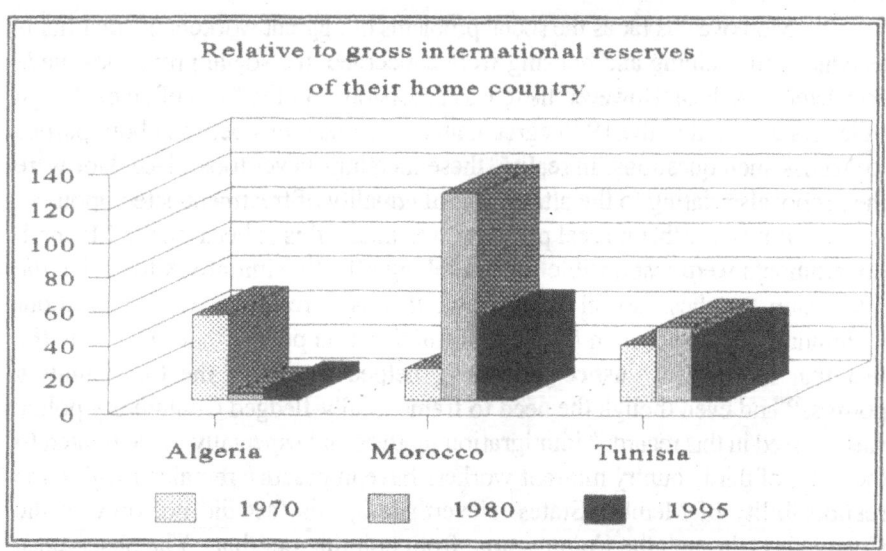

Source: Calculations based on data derived from the World Bank, *World Development Report* (Washington, DC: World Bank, 1995, 1996 and 1997).

The inclusion of these provisions in the agreements was not viewed as a substitute in place of existing bilateral accords between Member States (notably France, Belgium, Netherlands and Germany) and the Maghreb countries. In this case, they were not to affect any rights or obligations arising from these bilateral arrangements so long as the latter provide for more favourable treatment.[52]

For the Maghreb countries, the main 'advantage' they might have derived from the social provisions of their agreements with the EC was the attempt to give the issue of migrant labour a Community dimension. By doing so, this might have had a positive impact on the situation of Maghreb workers enjoying a less favourable treatment in certain Member States.[53] Apart from this, these provisions did not allow Maghreb workers free entry to the Community, nor did they allow Maghreb workers in one member state to move freely within the Community. On the latter issue, it was not until 1995 that the need to grant nationals of third countries the right to freedom of movement within the Community was the subject of a Commission proposal for a Council Directive.[54] Such a proposal, while it has not been implemented yet, is only concerned with the right to travel to other member state(s) for a short stay without requiring a visa.

Moreover, as far as the social problems of migrant workers in such fields as education, training and housing were concerned, the social provisions made no reference to them. However, there was provision -- in the form of an exchange of letters annexed to the 1976 agreements -- for meetings between both parties to discuss such questions. In reality, these meetings never took place. Nor were the proposals relating to the attainment of equality of treatment acted upon.

If it is true that no real progress was made, this is because the Maghreb governments were responsible for not taking effective initiatives to revive the discussion on these social issues. But it was a result of questions about Community competence in the field of immigration policy. Indeed, despite the fact that a Court of Justice judgement helped to clarify the Community's powers,[55] and even though the need to frame a fully-fledged Community policy was stressed in this regard,[56] immigration matters and especially those related to the status of third-country migrant workers have in practice remained within the responsibility of Member States. Nevertheless, this fact did not prevent the Community, through the Commission, from pointing out that: 'The observance of commitments undertaken in agreements with third countries providing for equal treatment of the workers of these countries in matters of remuneration, working conditions and social security, should be ensured.'[57]

In a similar vein, the Commission, in a number of other documents, drew the attention of Member States to the situation of these workers by making proposals and recommendations aimed at promoting their economic and social integration into the host countries.[58]

Bearing in mind that all this had relatively little effect on Member States, it seems worth considering, albeit briefly, some of the problems encountered by the Maghreb immigrants in France. This country hosts the largest proportion of this population in the whole Community, estimated in 1995 at more than 67 per cent. At different periods of time, attempts were made to improve their living and working conditions, but the result achieved proved less successful than hoped for.[59] That is in part due to the economic and social circumstances of France, characterised in this instance by high unemployment affecting mainly the disadvantaged groups, among them, for the most part, migrants from North Africa.

In fact, the Maghreb workers' place in the French labour market shows that they are highly vulnerable to unemployment relative to other groups. In 1995, they accounted for nearly a third of the total labour force of foreign origin which numbered almost 1.6 million.[60] Within this workforce, there were about 24 per cent unemployed, of which more than a half were of Maghreb origin.[61] In addition, the unemployment rate for French and EC nationals was 10.9 per cent and 10.4 per cent respectively, while for the Maghreb workers it was much higher, standing at 36.2 per cent.[62]

This disadvantaged position in the labour market may indicate the extent to which the stated principle of attaining equality in working conditions, especially in terms of employment opportunities, between Maghreb nationals and those of the Community remains far from being a reality. The Commission is quite right in pointing out that among the causes for such a situation are 'the limited employment and career perspectives open to immigrants and discrimination, generally disguised at the recruitment stage'.[63]

In reaction to economic and social pressures, the French authorities have since 1977 taken measures such as *Aide au retour*, *Aide publique à la réinsertion* and *Réinsertion aidée*, whose ultimate aim has been to encourage return migration by providing financial incentives. However, they had little impact as only a small number of migrant workers were tempted by these measures.[64] The limited prospect for jobs in the country of origin and the attachment of young migrants of the second generation (called the *Beurs*) to the host country where they were born and educated account for the lack of interest in leaving.

In parallel, for French society the question of immigration has become a prominent political issue since 1984, when the *Front National* of Jean-Marie

Le Pen achieved its first success in the municipal elections in the City of Dreux. This extreme-right party bases its programme on a single issue, that is hostility to immigration and claiming *La France aux Français*. Increasingly immigrants, including those from the Maghreb, have come to be seen as taking jobs away from French citizens and draining welfare benefits. The focus has also shifted to the cultural and behavioural differences, targeting particularly Muslims who are accused of being unassimilable and hostile to French republican values.

The mounting anti-Arab/Muslim attitudes and the success of the extreme-right wing in gathering support from large sections of the French electorate led other political parties to advocate tougher policies on immigration to ease social tensions and to limit the drawing power of the *Front National*. This was exemplified over recent years by what has come to be known as *Les Lois Pasqua* designed, among other things, to reform the naturalisation procedure in order to make the acquisition of French citizenship much more restrictive (Costa-Lascoux, 1994, pp. 19-43).

Conclusion

In the second phase of Euro-Maghreb relationship, the EC improved the content of its approach to development cooperation, when judging by the wider range of instruments that were involved. Initially, it was acclaimed by both sides as more responsive to the needs of the Maghreb countries because of its significant advance over the earlier attempt, and because it was reflective of a more active role in Community intervention.

From the preceding analysis, however, it is clear that, taken as a whole, the record of twenty years had been less satisfactory. Indeed, in all three main areas examined -- trade, aid and migration -- there is little evidence which suggests that the Community's enlarged approach had a major beneficial impact on the Maghreb countries, particularly in respect of fulfilling its intended objectives.

The trade component, through its preferential regime, saw its value weakened by certain of its restrictions and by the changing policies of the EC. Consequently, it proved less successful in promoting a balanced trade relationship and the potential increase of manufactured exports of the beneficiaries. Nevertheless, without the preferential treatment, these countries' export performance in the EC market might have been substantially worse. The aid package was certainly an additional source of foreign exchange. But because of its modest volume and its bias against productive investment, it did little to assist the structural transformation in the recipient Maghreb countries. This inadequate level of funding was obvious when compared to these countries' investment needs or to the volume of aid received from other sources. As for migrant labour, the lack of tangible progress made on the issue means that it remained a marginal aspect in the whole approach, despite its economic benefit to the 'exporting' countries.

Although the Community approach should be seen only as a contribution to the effort made by these countries in their development process, it is disappointing to admit that even as such it not only suffered a number of inherent shortcomings but also achieved extremely limited results in practice. And it is this rather poor performance, along with the deterioration of the socio-economic situation in the Maghreb countries since the 1980s, which caused growing concern within the EC. Such concern prompted the EC to formulate a partnership initiative as a response to the implications of the continuing instability in the Maghreb region.

Notes

1. *Bulletin of the European Communities*, no. 4, 1971, pp. 30-38.
2. *Ibid.*, p. 40.
3. *Keesing's Contemporary Archives*, vol. 19, 5-11 February 1973, p. 25713.
4. *Keesing's Contemporary Archives*, vol. 18, 28 October - 4 November 1972, p. 25542.
5. *Bulletin of the European Communities*, no. 6, 1976, p. 62.
6. See Article 8 of the 1976 agreements.
7. *Bulletin of the European Communities*, no. 1, 1976, p. 15.
8. Commission of the European Communities, *The Europe-South Dialogue* (Luxembourg: Office for Official Publications of the European Communities, 1989), p. 48.
9. In 34 articles and 9 annexes, Protocol no. 2 (annexed to the 1976 agreements) defines the concept of 'originating products' as well as the methods to administer these rules.
10. See Article 2 of the Protocol no. 2 annexed to the agreements which identifies the products regarded as 'wholly obtained' in the Maghreb countries.
11. The figures given in this paragraph are the author's calculations based on data from the *UN Yearbook of Industrial Statistics*, vol. 1 (New York: United Nations, 1981, 1983 and 1991).
12. See Article 1(2) of the Protocol no. 2.
13. Article 35 of the 1976 agreements.
14. Article 36(3b) of the 1976 agreements.
15. Tariff reductions for principal exports were as follows: 100 per cent for tinned sardines, 80 per cent for wine and citrus fruit, 55 per cent for fruit salad, 30-60 per cent for fresh fruit and vegetables, and 30 per cent for tomato concentrate.
16. For the Mediterranean region, the adjustment the Community was to make in order to maintain the traditional current of exports of its partners in principal products represented 30 per cent of its production of citrus fruit, 3 per cent of olive oil, 1 per cent of tomatoes, and 0.6 per cent of wine; see Colette Cova, 'La politique méditerranéenne des Douzes', *Revue du*

Marché Commun, no. 291, November 1985, p. 526.
17   Concerning the additional protocols with Algeria and Tunisia, see *Official Journal of the European Communities*, no. L 297, 21 October 1987; and with Morocco, no. L 224, 13 August 1988.
18   For a detailed account on the arrangements concluded with the Mediterranean countries, see Jean Raux, 'Le maintien des échanges traditionnels de produits agricoles entre la CEE élargie et les pays méditerranéens', *Revue Trimestrielle de Droit Européen*, vol. 23, no. 4, October-December 1987, pp. 633-648.
19   It was estimated that between 1973-1979 more than seven hundred thousand jobs were lost in the European textiles and clothing industry along with the closure of more than four thousand companies; Commission of the European Communities, 'Textiles: The Multi-Fibre Arrangement', *Background Report*, ISEC/B43/80, 11 September 1980, p. 2; see also Gilles Fievet, 'Les accords d'auto-limitation, une nouvelle technique d'accords communautaires', *Revue du Marché Commun*, no. 262, December 1982, p. 598.
20   Cited in the *Middle East Economic Digest*, 20 December 1978, p. 10.
21   *Ibid.*
22   Author's calculations based on data from Eurostat, *External Trade Statistical Yearbook* (Luxembourg: Office for Official Publications of the European Communities, 1986 and 1997).
23   *Ibid.*
24   Author's calculations based on data from the IMF, *Direction of Trade Statistics Yearbook* (Washington, DC: IMF, 1983, 1989, 1991 and 1997).
25   Eurostat, *op.cit.*, and *Statistics in Focus/External Trade*, no. 13, 1996.
26   *Ibid.*
27   Eurostat, *External and Intra-European Union Trade Statistical Yearbook* (Luxembourg: Office for Official Publications of the European Communities, 1997), pp. 36-37.
28   *Ibid.*
29   Author's calculations based on data from Eurostat, *External Trade Monthly Statistics*, no. 11, 1996.
30   Article 1 of the 1st Protocol on technical and financial cooperation annexed to the 1976 agreements.
31   Commission of the European Communities, 'Les Pays du Grand Maghreb et la Communauté Européenne', *Développement - Europe Information*, DE 68, Brussels, January 1991, p. 14.
32   Commission of the European Communities, *Report on Cooperation with the Mediterranean Partners*, COM(97) 371 final, Brussels, 18 July 1997, p. 20.
33   Délégation de la Commission au Maroc, *Maroc-Union Européenne: Bilan 1979-1994*, Rabat, 30 September 1994, p. 20.
34   Author's interview with officials in the Maghreb Unit of the European Commission, Brussels, 4 March 1998.
35   Commission of the European Communities (Maghreb Unit), *Algérie: Etat de la coopération financière*, Brussels, 20 February 1998, p. 1. On the benefits derived by Algeria from its agreement with the EC, a similar assessment was made by officials in charge of EU-Algeria relations at the Algerian embassy in Brussels, in an interview with the author on 4 March 1998.
36   *Official Journal of the European Communities*, no. C 252, 26 September 1991, pp. 3-6.
37   European Court of Auditors, *Special report in respect of bilateral financial and technical cooperation with non-member Mediterranean countries*, *Official Journal of the European Communities*, no. C 98, 31 March 1998, p. 8.

38 *Ibid.*, pp. 13-14.
39 *Ibid.*, p. 14.
40 Délégation de la Commission au Maroc, *op.cit.*, p. 2.
41 See EIB, *Annual Report* (Luxembourg: Office for Official Publications of the European Communities, 1979-1996).
42 Délégation de la Commission en Tunisie, *Coopération Union Européenne - Tunisie: Rapport 1996*, pp. 14-22.
43 Author's calculations based on data from the OECD, *Geographical Distribution of Financial Flows to Aid Recipients* (Paris: OECD, 1979-1982, 1982-1985, 1986-1989, 1989-1993 and 1992-1996).
44 *Ibid.*
45 *Ibid.*
46 *Ibid.*
47 Commission of the European communities, *The Future of Relations between the Community and the Maghreb*, SEC(92) 401 final, Brussels, 30 April 1992, p. 27.
48 European Parliament, 'Report on the cooperation agreements concluded between the EEC and Algeria, Morocco and Tunisia', *Working Documents 1976-77*, no. 307/76, 4 October 1976, p. 27.
49 Only four articles and an exchange of letter were devoted to the complex issue of migration in the 1976 agreements. On the main provisions, see articles 38 and 39 of the 1976 agreements with Algeria and Tunisia and 39 and 40 With Morocco.
50 *Official Journal of the European Communities*, no. C 34, 14 February 1976, p. 2.
51 *Bulletin of the European Communities*, supplement no. 3, 1976, p. 13.
52 See Articles 41 of the 1976 agreements with Algeria and Tunisia and 42 with Morocco.
53 At a hearing in Bonn in 1974, the Committee on Social Affairs, Employment and Education of the European Parliament was informed by the Moroccan trade unions that there were 30.000 Maghreb workers plus their families without any right of social security benefit; see European Parliament, *op.cit.*, p. 28. Furthermore, on 31 January 1991 the Court of Justice, in its Judgement C-18/90, ruled that the provisions of the EC-Morocco cooperation agreement concerning non-discrimination in pay, employment and social security conditions were directly applicable to Member States regulations (a decision also applicable to the agreements with Algeria and Tunisia); see Court of Justice of the European Communities, *Reports of Cases before the Court of Justice and the Court of First Instance*, Luxembourg, no. 1, 1991, pp. 199-229.
54 Commission of the European Communities, *The right of third country nationals to travel in the Community*, COM(95) 346 final, Brussels, 12 July 1995.
55 See Court of Justice of the European Communities Judgement of 9 July 1987, *Reports of Cases before the Court*, Luxembourg, no. 7, 1987, pp. 3203-3258.
56 See for instance the Economic and Social Committee of the European Communities 'Own-opinion on the status of migrant workers from third countries', *Official Journal of the European Communities*, no. C 159, 17 June 1991, pp. 12-15; and its additional opinion on the same issue in its *Bulletin*, no. 8-9, 1991, Brussels, pp. 3-6.
57 Commission of the European Communities, *Immigration and Right of Asylum*, SEC(91) 1855 final, Brussels, 9 October 1991, p. 35.
58 See Commission of the European Communities, *Guidelines for a Community Policy on Migration*, COM(85) 48 final, Brussels, 7 March 1985; *Policies on Immigration and the Social Integration of Migrants in the European Community*, SEC(90) 1813 final, Brussels, 28 September 1990; *Immigration and Right...*, *op.cit.*; and *Immigration and Asylum*

Policies, COM(94) 23 final, Brussels, 23 February 1994.
59 For a recent critical assessment of these attempts, see in particular the article by Catherine Withol de Wenden (a French expert), 'La politique de l'intégration', *Confluence-Méditerranée*, no. 22, Summer 1997, pp. 63-72. For a wider perspective, see for instance, Alec G. Hargreaves, *Immigration, 'race' and ethnicity* (London: Routledge, 1995).
60 OECD, *Trend in International Migration/ Annual Report 1996* (Paris: OECD, 1997), p. 100.
61 Author's calculations based on data from Direction de la Population et des Migrations/ Ministère de l'Aménagement du Territoire (France), de la Ville et de l'Intégration, *Rapport sur l'immigration et la présence étrangère en France 1995-1996*, December 1996, pp. 102-103.
62 OECD, *op.cit.*, p. 101; and Direction de la Population et des Migrations, *op.cit.*, pp. 44-45.
63 Commission of the European Communities, *Immigration and Asylum Policies, op.cit.*, p. 36.
64 Between 1977-1995, only 104,862 Maghreb workers including their families were beneficiaries of return migration programmes. See in this context Salah Mezdour, 'Economie des migrations internationales', *Revue Française des Affaires Sociales*, vol. 47, no. 1, January-March 1993, p. 189; Direction de la Population et des Migrations, *op.cit.*, pp. 29-32 and 94-97; and Charles Condamines, 'Immigration, intégration et politique de coopération', *Le Monde Diplomatique*, no. 529, April 1998, pp. 14-15.

PART THREE
MAGHREB MALAISE SINCE THE 1980s AND EUROPE'S RESPONSE

4 Factors of Instability in the Maghreb

Introduction

From the early 1980s the Maghreb countries entered an era in which they have undergone decisive societal transformations. The relative euphoria associated with some of their earlier socio-economic accomplishments, notably during the 1970s, has since the 1980s given way to a phase of uncertainty revealing the limits of the policies pursued and the challenges lying ahead in the economic, social, and political spheres. It is this situation, with its diverse dimensions and likely knock-on effect beyond the region, that has given the EU cause for concern about the potential instability on its southern flank and the need to re-define its development cooperation policy instruments whose impact, overall, had proved less effective.

This chapter therefore proposes to analyse the scope of this challenging situation by singling out some of its salient features. On the one hand, it examines the Maghreb's economic stagnation or even deterioration with a specific focus on issues of population growth, unemployment and debt that may be seen as aspects, causes or consequences of this situation. On the other hand, it reviews the Maghreb's social and political malaise which has a strong correlation with the economic difficulties.

Facets of Faltering Economies

In the Maghreb, as in other parts of the developing world, the achievement of independence was followed by the primary aim of initiating rapid economic and social development. In this respect, one can distinguish two major phases. The first covered roughly the decades of the 1960s and 1970s and the second started in the early 1980s and continues today. The distinction between these periods mirrors two different tendencies in the economic performance experienced across the Maghreb region. In other words, the cycle of economic expansion was to be followed by contraction, that is from boom to bust (Page, 1998, pp.133-134).

During the 1970s, in particular, the Maghreb countries succeeded in expanding growth through high levels of public spending financed by means of rising revenues from oil and phosphate exports and relatively easy access to foreign borrowing. This provided the governments concerned with substantial resources and latitude to intervene extensively in economic activities. Significant economic growth certainly did take place. This can be seen, for instance, from these countries' GDP which grew at the rate of over 6.3 per cent per year from 1965 to 1980.[1] The performance in question was also attributable to a considerable investment programme where the gross domestic investment averaged an annual growth rate of 10.6 per cent over the same period, though the extent of this varied between individual countries, being very noticeable in Algeria (15.9 per cent) and Morocco (11.4 per cent) and less so in Tunisia (4.6 per cent).[2]

Thus until the closing years of the 1970s, the region performed relatively well, corresponding to what was described as 'the golden age' for all Maghreb countries.[3] In contrast, the beginning of the 1980s ushered in a period of economic difficulties resulting from, among other things, unfavourable external conditions -- including a prolonged worsening of the terms of trade of primary commodities exports -- and inadequate earlier domestic policies. Also this period was to coincide with the adoption and implementation of reform programmes to restructure the economy which inevitably affected the prospects for resuming growth on the scale enjoyed before. If Tunisia and to a lesser degree Morocco have made some progress, such a slow recovery, however, remains fragile and unsustainable.

Certain aspects, causes or consequences of the economic difficulties can be discerned in the rapid population growth, increasing numbers of jobless, and financial constraints with the external debt being an outstanding example.

Demographic Trends

The population of the Maghreb countries which numbered more than 65.5 million in 1997, will exceed 87 million by 2015 (see table 4.1). These figures, which assume continued population increase, have become an issue of major concern not only for the governments concerned but also for many west European countries for whom they conjure up images of armies of young discontented and unemployed people seeking shelter and jobs in Europe.[4] Overall, this 'explosive' demography is the outcome of a combination of factors.

All the countries concerned witnessed in their post-colonial era a relatively substantial improvement in 'welfare' provision especially in terms of access to adequate health care and other social services. As a direct corollary, the

Table 4.1 Demographic profile of the Maghreb countries

	Algeria	Morocco	Tunisia	Maghreb (Total)
Total population (millions)				
1975	16.0	17.3	4.2	37.5
1997	29.4	26.9	8.8	65.1
2015	41.2	34.8	9.8	85.8
Age structure of population (%)				
0 - 14 years				
1991	43.1	40.7	37.0	40.3
2025	27.0	24.6	23.3	24.9
15 - 64 years				
1991	53.5	57.5	60.2	57.0
2025	67.4	68.7	68.5	68.2
Annual population growth rate (%)				
1975-1997	2.8	2.0	2.2	2.3
1997-2015	1.9	1.4	1.3	1.5

Source United Nations, *World Population Prospects* (New York: United Nations, 1993) and World Bank, *World Development Indicators 2000* (Washington, DC: World Bank, 2000).

Maghreb countries were to experience a bigger rate of population growth which, by being in the average range of 2.3 per cent during the period 1975-1997, was much higher than that of all developing countries (2.0 per cent) and of the EU (0.4 per cent).[5] This rapidly growing demography is characterised by a significantly high proportion of young population.

Another explanatory factor behind this demographic situation is to be found in the attitudes and population policies of the governments concerned. Following independence, few serious attempts were made to tackle high birth rates because continued population growth was thought necessary for the future staffing of the developing economies (Spencer, 1993, p.19). Tunisia was the first country in the region to have initiated a 'population policy' in 1963 consequent on the state's action to improve the women's status in society. The Personal Status Code, elaborated for this purpose, provided an impetus to family planning. While between 1990-1998 birth control was practised by 60 per cent of couples, this rate remains, nevertheless, far smaller in poorer areas and among uneducated women.[6] Algeria adopted its *Programme national en vue de maitrîser la croissance démographique* in 1983. This delay was more or less justified by ideological considerations and the late President Boumediene was often quoted as saying 'the best contraceptive is development' and rejected as a form of neo-colonialism any international warnings about the dangers of population growth (Chevallier and Kessler, quoted in Spencer, 1993, p. 19). In Morocco, family planning, timidly initiated in 1967, was to become forthright ten years later. These birth control programmes seem to have produced some effect since in both Algeria and Morocco nearly 60 per cent of married women were using contraceptives during 1990-1998.[7] However, it is still the case that changes in attitudes towards family planning continue to evolve at a slow pace. With varying degrees, this is partly due to shortcomings in the governments' action in this area. Moreover, besides religious considerations and lack of education as serious hurdles, there is the long held traditional perception, though less prevalent today, according to which: 'Large families are a source of prestige and unpaid work' (Bensalah Alaoui, 1993, p. 166).

With these trends in population growth likely to remain stable or decline moderately over the coming decades, the Maghreb countries are finding it -- and will continue to find it -- difficult to meet the various rising needs of their population. One of the most urgent and challenging problems being faced and likely to remain so, in this context, is that of unemployment.

The Unemployment Challenge

These demographic trends are, to a certain degree, responsible for increasing levels of unemployment among the labour force in the Maghreb countries. After two decades marked by a relative equilibrium on the labour market and stabilisation of unemployment at lower rates,[8] the 1980s inaugurated, in contrast, a reversal of these tendencies. In fact, since then notes an observer: 'The creation of jobs stagnates in industry, decreases in agriculture, while the administration, which used to be one of the major sources of jobs, revises its programmes in a downward direction' (Bouzidi, 1991, p. 61).

In the face of an economic crisis characterised, among other things, by shrinking financial resources, the Maghreb countries have found themselves unable to maintain and continue their investment efforts undertaken in the early post-independence decades. This has resulted in a disequilibrium in the labour market where the quantity of jobs created can no longer keep pace with the additional supply of labour. The constraint placed on the labour market to generate enough jobs, exacerbated by mounting demographic pressure, has given rise to higher rates of unemployment. This amounts to a major challenge that the governments concerned cannot afford to ignore. As table 4.2 indicates, the Maghreb region as a whole will continue to experience an increase in the economically active population despite the forecasted trend towards a slight decline in both Algeria and Tunisia for the coming years.

From 1967 to the mid-1980s and owing to its massive investment programme especially in the industrial sector, Algeria managed to achieve high levels of job creation relative to the growth of its economically active population. Indeed, whereas the average rate of job creation increased by 4.6 per cent a year, that of the active population grew by 3.2 per cent (Abdoun, 1989, p. 31). From 1986 onwards, however, this trend in job creation could no longer be sustained because of a decline in investments consequent on and subsequent to the deterioration of the country's economy. With an additional supply of labour estimated at between 250,000 to 300,000 per year on average since then, it has become very difficult for the authorities to cope with this situation. In addition, the process of economic restructuring has made hundreds of thousands of the labour force redundant and is continuing to exert pressure for lay-offs.[9] The seriousness of this problem is well-illustrated in the rate of unemployment which has tended to increase drastically despite the contribution of the informal sector in absorbing many of the unemployed (more than 67,000 per annum over the period 1990-1996). While according to official sources this rate rose from 17.8 per cent in 1990 to an all-time high proportion of 28.3 at the end of 1998, other

Table 4.2 The growth of the labour force in the Maghreb countries

	Total labour force (millions)			Average annual growth (%)	
	1980	1998	2010	1980-1998	1998-2010
Algeria	5.0	10.0	15.0	3.9	3.4
Morocco	7.0	11.0	15.0	2.4	2.5
Tunisia	2.0	5.0	5.0	2.9	2.2
Maghreb	14.0	22.0	35.0	3.0	2.7

Source: World Bank, *World Development Indicators 2000* (Washington, DC: World Bank, 2000), pp. 45-48.

estimates go further and consider that as much as 40 per cent of Algeria's work force is either unemployed or underemployed.[10]

Prior to the 1980s, Morocco experienced a more-or-less stable situation in the employment sector. Its economically active population passed from 3.7 million in 1971 to 5.4 million in 1982 (Bouzidi, 1991, p. 79). The unemployment rate at these two dates was officially put at 8.6 per cent and 10.7 per cent. This was achievable partly because of the importance of the informal sector in absorbing a fair proportion of the unemployed (Lahlou, 1991, pp. 492-494). By the early 1980s, the economic crisis affecting the country led to the adoption of a series of reform measures. The programme of economic liberalisation and privatisation initiated since then has not brought an improvement to the employment situation. Indeed, while the government figures put urban unemployment at 17.5 per cent, the trade unions claim it is closer to 23 per cent.[11] The estimated 200,000 new jobs created annually are insufficient to absorb the 300,000 new entrants to the labour market every year.[12] Thus the tendency to increasing levels of unemployment is expected to persist.

In Tunisia, the better economic performance accomplished in the areas of growth and investment, particularly during the 1970s, was accompanied by favourable conditions for the creation of employment. The labour force, which amounted to 1.1 million in 1966, attained 1.8 million in 1980 (Bouzidi, 1991, p. 79). At the latter date the unemployment rate was estimated at about 10 per cent. However, just as in neighbouring countries, the economic difficulties experienced, particularly from the mid-1980s onwards, have adversely affected the country's ability to manage the employment situation. Government statistics put the number of jobless at around 395,000, whereas the Tunisian trade union organisation considers it to be over 500,000.[13]

A striking feature worth emphasizing is that the unemployment problem tends to affect mostly young people and increasingly those with a certain level of educational attainment. Algerian government estimates showed that over a total of 2.2 million unemployed in 1996, there was more than 80 per cent who are under 30 years of age.[14] Within this proportion, the number of those with an educational level has been steadily growing. In 1996, about 80,000 university graduates were job seekers according to a report released by the Algerian think-tank, the *Conseil National Economique et Social*.[15] In Morocco, young unemployed graduates represented 33 per cent of all unemployed people in 1998.[16] In Tunisia, about half of the unemployed are under the age of 25,[17] with rising incidence on those possessing at least a secondary school education whose proportion was about one-third of the total unemployed population during 1994-1997.[18]

This state of rising unemployment led the governments concerned to pay particular attention to the generation of more new jobs with the aim of bringing down these increasing unemployment levels. An early report commissioned by the *Ministère des Affaires Sociales* in Algeria considered a 20 per cent rate of unemployment by 2000 as 'a level consistent with the imperative of social stability'.[19] In terms of employment generation, the 1993 national plan set an objective of 774,000 jobs to be created over the period 1993-1997.[20] Further the government set up the *Agence Nationale de Soutien à l'Emploi des Jeunes* in 1996 with a budget of the order of 3 billion dinars per year to support self-employment in particular.[21] The institution a few years ago of the *Conseil National de la Jeunesse et de l'Avenir* in Morocco is a component of this strategy to deal with the problem of youth unemployment.[22] In part the task is also entrusted to the *Fonds de Solidarité Nationale* created in 1992 in Tunisia. This country's 1997-2001 development plan aims to generate 320,000 new jobs against an expected additional demand of 350,000.[23]

Contingent on economic performance, these measures put forward to tackle the unemployment problem have, in most cases, been based on overoptimistic forecasts. Their targets have been and will surely continue, therefore, to prove difficult to attain in practice. In Algeria, for instance, it has been estimated that the labour market needs to generate between 200,000 to 300,000 new jobs per year simply to keep the unemployment rate stable, while, to bring it down, would require the creation of more than 700,000 new jobs every year.[24] Hence the issue of unemployment represents a real challenge which is most likely to be accentuated by recent developments in the Maghreb countries' relations with the EU. As a result of the free trade agreement signed with the Union, more companies in Tunisia have already begun to shed staff as they are seeking to improve productivity and competitiveness under the industrial modernisation programme.[25]

While years ago emigration, as a safety valve, helped more or less to make the tension between the supply and demand for jobs less explosive, this is no longer the case. The unemployment situation may well be exacerbated by the introduction of restrictions on migratory flows in the former recipient countries particularly in the Community. Against a background of rising xenophobic sentiment in Europe, the present and future direction of EU policy points towards much more tightened measures.

Debt Burden

Like many other developing countries, the Maghreb governments are facing a difficult time in managing their foreign debt. According to the World Bank estimates, the region's external debt rose from 32.6 billion dollars at the end of 1980 to 61.6 billion dollars at the end of 1997 (see table 4.3). This state of growing indebtedness has come to impose severe strain on their economy and made any prospect for betterment difficult to predict.

In all Maghreb countries there was an embarkation on strategies of development designed to achieve accelerated and sustained economic growth. These, in a context of limited domestic financial resources, made the recourse to external sources unavoidable. The investment programmes that ensued from such choices were, to a certain extent, undertaken with the aim of boosting and expanding their exports in areas such as phosphates in Morocco and hydrocarbons in Algeria. Parallel to this was also the investment effort directed to the development of human resources in terms of health, education and so forth. In resorting to international borrowing, the Maghreb governments expected that world demand for their exports would remain high and that interest rates would remain low for the foreseeable future. In other words, prospects for increasing export revenues would make it possible for them to honour their debt

Table 4.3 External debt indicators in the Maghreb countries

	Algeria				Morocco				Tunisia			
	1980	1986	1993	1997	1980	1986	1993	1997	1980	1986	1993	1997
Total external debt (million dollars)	19,365	22,634	25,757	30,921	9,710	17,889	21,430	19,321	3,527	5,943	8,701	11,323
Total debt service (million dollars)	4,084	5,145	9,146	4,420	1,413	1,810	2,614	3,082	545	876	1,350	1,413
Total external debt/ GNP (%)	47.1	36.4	57.0	73.0	53.3	109.7	81.7	58.0	41.6	70.6	59.9	63.0
Total debt service/Export of goods and services (%)	27.4	56.3	77.0	30.0	32.4	36.4	30.7	27.0	13.9	28.2	20.2	16.0

Source: World Bank, *World Debt Tables* (Washington, DC: World Bank, 1995 and 1996) and *Global Development Finance 1999* (Washington, DC: World Bank, 1999).

commitments. As a result of the world economic recession, however, these expectations were to suffer a blow which caused their terms of trade to deteriorate and thus their export earnings to decline. In addition, this situation was accompanied by tight monetary policy in the international financial markets, leading to higher rates of interest.[26]

Beyond these considerations, another plausible explanation for the aggravation of the debt crisis lies in the use made of borrowed capital (Bouzidi, 1991, p. 117). First, it served to finance massive investment projects which were either slow or inefficient in generating a surplus that would have made possible the servicing of the debt. Second, a significant part of this capital was diverted to consumption. Over the period 1974-1984, for instance, the proportion allocated to this purpose was estimated at 28 per cent in Algeria, 56 per cent in Morocco, and 42 per cent in Tunisia.

In consequence of these factors, the debt problem has become much more difficult and expensive to manage. The severity of this situation is reflected in the levels of certain ratios that offer various measures of the cost, or capacity for servicing the external debt. Algeria's debt service obligation in 1993, 9.2 billion dollars, was equal to more than 35 per cent of its total debt (it was 21 per cent at the end of 1980). With a total debt standing at almost 26 billion dollars in 1993, it represented about three-fifths of GNP. The debt service equalled more than three-fourths of the value of exported goods and services. This debt ratio was boosted by higher debt service obligations and lower export earnings. Aware of its increasing inability to honour its debt commitments, Algeria made a bold break with its longstanding opposition to debt rescheduling, considered until then as giving 'external bodies a lever with which they could influence the country's economic policy' (Niblock, 1993, p. 73). By doing so, Algeria signed an arrangement with IMF in April 1994 which envisaged a stand-by loan of 625 million dollars and a contingency financing of 375 million dollars.[27] Subsequently, the Paris Club, made up of major holders of Algeria's external public debt, agreed to a reduction in repayment of 5 billion dollars out of 8.5 billion dollars due over the period 1994-1995.[28] The three-year deal agreed a year later with the IMF paved the way for a second rescheduling of the debt in July 1995. This involved a fifteen-year rescheduling of some 5.3 billion dollars in principal payments due over the 1995-1997 period.[29] On 27 June 1996 there was the conclusion of an agreement with the London Club of commercial creditors to reschedule 3.2 billion dollars.[30] This may have provided a breathing-space for the economy, particularly on the financial side, as only a relative proportion of total exports earnings will be diverted to the debt repayment.[31]

Morocco's total external debt rose sharply from 9.7 billion dollars at the end of 1980 to nearly 19.3 billion dollars at the end of 1997. After many reschedulings, of which the last was in 1992, as well as the Saudi and other Gulf creditors debt write-off (3.6 billion dollars) in reward for its pro-coalition and anti-Iraq stance during the 1990-1991 Gulf crisis, Morocco has relatively managed to commit itself to a comparatively strict adherence to its debt-servicing obligations.[32] This has been possible as the ratio of total external debt to GNP fell from 110 per cent in 1986 to 58 per cent in 1997 while debt service was reduced from 36 per cent to 27 per cent.

Tunisia's external debt passed from 3.5 billion dollars at the end of 1980 to nearly 11.4 billion dollars at the end of 1997. As a percentage of GNP, external debt represented 63 per cent in 1997, down from a high of almost 71 per cent in 1986. Similarly the debt service ratio fell from a peak of 28 per cent in 1986 to a more or less manageable level of 16 per cent in 1997. Whereas the bulk of the debt is long-term debt owed to official creditors, the proportion of short-term debt has recently tended to rise -- particularly following the launching of a series of Samurai bonds --[33] and whose effect may place constraints on Tunisia's financial situation.

All in all, the rescheduling process, by alleviating debt-repayment obligations through new terms of reimbursement, may have provided the Maghreb countries with some room for manoeuvre in reorganising their financial situation. Being a temporary relief, however, it remains of little impact if one considers the continued rising volume or build-up of external debt (total debt stock) incurred by these countries. Morocco is a case in point since this country's total foreign debt more than doubled between 1980-1997, despite negotiating several rescheduling packages.[34] This may be the reason which led the government in recent years to adopt a more active strategy designed to alleviate the overall debt burden reflected in debt conversion deals already concluded with France, Spain and Italy.[35]

Moreover, this process of rescheduling has been conditioned by the implementation of a series of economic reforms under the IMF-determined new economic orthodoxy. Intended to generate future economic growth at a higher rate, these reforms have led to the imposition of austerity measures being felt in terms of decreasing employment opportunities and deteriorating living standards. This fact has added more frustration in a social environment that has come to represent over the years a potential threat to the existing order.

Social and Political Environment

The dismal performance of the Maghreb economies has been accompanied by a gradual disengagement of the state from its ambitious commitments to a policy of social justice and equity for its population. The inability to fulfil the society's growing expectations has triggered off the social dissent which has caused a great loss of confidence in state-society relations and thus progressively undermined the relatively sustained domestic stability in the Maghreb states. In a context of economic hardship, this challenge has, to a large extent, compelled the ruling elites to undertake political reforms with a view to redressing the situation.

An Uneasy State-Society Relationship

The post-independence era witnessed an active role assumed by the state in the societies of the Maghreb. This involvement placed the state at the centre of national integration and economic development and from which the population expected everything that had been inaccessible under colonialism (Hermassi, 1985, p. 158). Confronted with colonial legacies, economic backwardness and social desegregation, the state emerged as the principal actor behind the necessary transformations in the Maghreb. In Algeria, notes M'hammed Boukhobza:

> Because of ideological orientations and the fragile situation (...) during the recovery of independence, the weight of the public sector and the state's intervention in all spheres of activity have become a day-to-day reality. As a result, all expectations and ambitions are permanently turned towards the places and persons that represent the structures and institutions of the state. Further the political message spread by the authorities explicitly tackles all aspects of life by making the state liable *vis-à-vis* the society for, among other things, employment, education, health care, requirements of modern life or housing (1991, p. 34).

In a similar way, David Seddon remarks that:

> Whether the dominant political ideology of government was liberal, socialist or Islamic, a form of social contract between state and people was forged, in which the state was identified as the guarantor of basic welfare as well as the promoter of economic and social development (1993, pp. 92-93).

As such this role was institutionalised and reinforced through the monopoly of a single-party system in Algeria and Tunisia. Both the (FLN) and the *Néo-Destour* (renamed the *Parti Socialiste Destourien* in 1964 -PSD) dispensed patronage and were symbols of independence (Hermassi and Vandewalle, 1993, p. 21). In Morocco, the monarchy which was already the legitimate symbol of resistance during colonisation, allowed the formation of political parties on which it was able to retain control in a kind of patron-client relationship (Leveau, 1993, p. 252). Throughout the region, the early years of independence saw the rulers centralising and consolidating their power while eliminating opponents. This monopolisation of power was justified by the exigencies of nation-building and made possible by a certain social consensus which in itself was favoured and sustained by the promotion of a 'distributive social policy'. On the whole, this process of *étatisation*, by which the state came to dominate the society as provider was, in some way, the result of a certain implicit contract 'under which the populace gave up its right to independent political activity in return for the state's provision of social welfare' (Brumberg, 1990, p. 120).

Up to the end of the 1970s, such an implicit social contract between the state and civil society was preserved despite certain signs of contestation. Imbued with religious, historical and revolutionary legitimacy and benefiting from important economic windfalls, Maghreb rulers were able to broaden and consolidate their social basis. Policies such as the famous *Triptyque Révolutionnaire* (industrial, agrarian, and cultural revolutions) in Algeria or the *Marocanisation* in Morocco launched in 1973, can all be considered among the fundamental instruments intended to attain this objective.

Since the 1980s, however, events were to prove that the social consensus experienced during the first decades following independence can no longer be ensured. The environment that made possible the appropriation by the state of the functions of patronage and social welfare together with control over large sectors of the national economy has substantially changed. The earlier assertion that: 'The state could create -- or recreate -- national societies was heard less often and its role as a catalyst in transforming society no longer taken as self-evident' (Hermassi and Vandewalle, 1993, p. 22). At the root of this disenchantment has been the poor results of the economic policies which laid bare the shortcomings of both the state intervention and the state management. Furthermore, its role as a welfare state has been affected as a result.

In fact, the diminishing ability to subsidise food, provide services, or create enough jobs for an increasing unemployed labour force are illustrative of a changing pattern in the role assumed hitherto by the state. The shift in the role of the state or, perhaps more accurately, the state's gradual retreat, stems from its incapacity to continue delivering the goods that had previously maintained and consolidated its social patronage. Such a process has not been occurring without adverse effects on an already fragile social consensus that has come to characterise Maghreb societies since the 1980s. Most of the population regarded this relative disengagement as a betrayal of earlier ambitious social promises to which the state had committed itself. This failure to honour its social commitments is seen to have led 'to belittle the state's symbolic importance within the collective consciousness' (Boukhobza, 1991, p. 34).

For a decade, all the Maghreb countries experienced a number of shocks as an expression of widespread social discontent (Algeria, 1988 -- Morocco, 1984, 1988, 1990 -- Tunisia, 1984, 1988). Called 'bread riots' or 'street politics', the extent of this public disaffection mirrored the widening gap that has come to separate civil society from the state. It is evident, in this context, that there has been a great loss of confidence by ordinary people in the Maghreb in the state-society relationship which, as a consequence, has seriously compromised the process that legitimatised and sustained state policies for decades. Therefore, it comes as no surprise that: 'The contestation in the Maghreb in recent years has amply demonstrated the difficulties the state currently faces in maintaining its claim to be the sole legitimate representative of each country's political community' (Hermassi and Vandewalle, 1993, p. 36).

In an attempt to accommodate to this constraining environment, ruling elites have responded with a series of economic and political reforms. It should be made clear, however, that measures of economic liberalisation which were devised to remedy deepening economic dislocation have had the negative by-product of contributing at the same time to the exacerbation of existing social tensions. And it is this harsh reality with austerity measures, synonymous of still greater popular sacrifice and its eventual undermining effect upon the regimes, that has led these elites to introduce, with varying degrees of depth, sincerity and success, certain reforms in the political sphere. As pointed out by Robert Wood:

> The austerity demands imposed on Third World countries have been so devastating in their social consequences that it is unclear whether most governments can continue to implement them without some form of new 'social contract' with the rest of society - a contract almost sure to involve the expansion of political rights as a trade-off for economic concessions (1985, p. 326).

The Difficult Process of Political Liberalisation

In Algeria the October 1988 riots, described as the most violent social upheaval since independence, were followed by a series of political reforms. In retrospect these reforms appeared as a political watershed. They led to the liberalisation of the political system and the legalisation of a wide spectrum of political parties. This opening up of the political system was formalised with the adoption of a new constitution on 23 February 1989. Among the latter's most significant innovations was the abandonment of the 'revolutionary socialist options' despite the irreversible commitment to socialism of the previous constitution.[36] It ended the FLN's monopoly of political power by completely separating it from the state.[37] More unrestricted freedoms of expression, association and organisation as well as the right to form *des associations à caractère politique* were recognised. Later, a law passed on 5 July 1989 legalised the establishment of political parties thus ending twenty-seven years of single-party system.

With these constitutional and political transformations, Algeria seemed, at the time, to be an interesting and promising experience in the transition from autocratic to democratic rule. The multiparty elections -- municipal and provincial elections in June 1990 and the first round of legislative elections in December 1991 -- resulted in a political stalemate. The ramifications of this impasse were visible by the beginning of 1992. President Benjedid resigned and a provisional council, the *Haut Comité d'Etat*, was established afterwards to run the state affairs over a transitional period (January 1992-January 1994). Since then the country has been witnessing the escalation of violence believed to have caused not only considerable damage to many socio-economic infrastructures but also the loss of thousands of lives.

Subsequent attempts made by the regime to engage in a national dialogue with other political forces with a view to ending the cycle of violence and restoring some stability proved unsuccessful. This failure in the search for a solution to the crisis had above all demonstrated the difficult task of conciliating the various, or perhaps more accurately, divergent positions not only within the opposition itself but between the latter and government as well. The terms set by the government to prepare the grounds for a transitional period, in which most opposition parties would be involved, were met with scepticism and even distrust. Similarly, little resulted from the government's official reaction to the *'Plateforme pour une Solution Politique et Pacifique de la Crise Algérienne'* endorsed by a number of opposition parties in their Rome meeting on 13 January 1995.

Perhaps a positive move started with the holding of the first-ever multiparty presidential elections in November 1995 which saw Liamine Zeroual elected as president. Although boycotted by certain opposition parties, these elections gave President Zeroual the mandate to revive national dialogue with all political groups, with the aim of restoring stability and preparing for the legislative and local elections. But prior to this, new amendments to the 1989 constitution were introduced after the referendum of 28 November 1996. They were mainly concerned with the creation of a second chamber in the national assembly, the law on political parties, the electoral law, and the redefinition of the president prerogatives. And as scheduled, both elections took place in June and October 1997 and were officially hailed as the last step in the democratisation process. The argument of the major opposition parties, which this time participated to these elections, was that the process of elections had, to a certain extent, disadvantaged them *vis-à-vis* the *Rassemblement National Démocratique* that won the biggest number of seats.

Nearly three years after his election, President Zeroual announced his retirement from power. This move to step down from office was motivated by what he considered being the need 'to accelerate the democratisation process and strengthen the institutions of the state'.[38] New presidential elections were organised in April 1999. Abdelaziz Bouteflika, former Foreign Affairs Minister, became president after winning 73.8 per cent of the vote.

Although it is quite early to make anything but a tentative judgement about the new leadership, one can at this stage point to two important waves of change. First, in contrast to the isolation that characterised the country over previous years, the new ruling team seems quite resolved to a more assertive presence of Algeria on the international scene. Second, on the domestic front, the peace plan, the *Concorde Civile*, approved through a national referendum on 16 September 1999, can be seen as a first step towards improved stability and security.

These changes and recent commitments made by the new leadership to accelerate reforms contain within them a potential to move Algeria away from its predicament. Of course, this will depend in part on the political forces/parties abandoning their narrowly-focused partisan interests in favour of seeking a much more active and constructive involvement in the development of a democratic culture capable of bringing about tolerance and stability to the country. For the time being, one can argue that the changes underway may provide a positive beginning and an encouraging sign for further and greater participation in the country's socio-economic and political life.

In Tunisia, meanwhile, the removal of Habib Bourguiba and Zine el-Abidine Ben Ali's assumption of power in November 1987 were hailed as inaugurating a 'new era' in Tunisian politics. Indeed, one of the top priorities to which the new leadership committed himself was to bring democracy back to Tunisia (Bessis, 1991, p. 387). Among a series of important reforms, and which enjoyed greater popular support, were greater freedom for the press, the release of political prisoners, the abolishing of the life-time term for the presidency, the legalisation of several political parties, and the revival and rejuvenation of the ruling party (PSD) which then became the *Rassemblement Constitutionnel Démocratique* (RCD). At an early point, these preliminary changes restored a certain confidence in a political system that came to face serious domestic challenges, some of which could have not only endangered its stability but even its survival, especially during the last years of Bourguiba's rule.

However, the initial enthusiasm that accompanied these transformations was not to last long. The process of political reform proved to have mainly benefited the ruling party (RCD) and enabled President Ben Ali to consolidate his power. The continuing hegemony of the RCD was confirmed in the successive elections held to date. For instance, all the seats in both the legislative and local elections of 1989 and 1990 respectively went to this party. It was only after a change in the electoral law in 1992 that some political parties from the opposition timidly made their first-ever entry into both the national assembly and the municipal councils following respectively the legislative elections of March 1994 and the local elections of May 1995.[39] But with a divided and weak opposition, this entry, especially in the parliament, did not signal the mounting of a serious challenge to the ruling party which:

> After such a victory will be much more tempted than in the past to strengthen its hold over the country's political life, and that the regime uses the parliament merely as a democratic decor, a façade existing for the benefit of international public opinion, but one that modifies in no way the manner in which power is exercised in the country (Denoeux, 1994, p. 1994).

Not surprising, then, was the re-election of President Ben Ali in both presidential elections of March 1994 and October 1999. While previous presidential elections consisted of a single candidate, those of October 1999 saw for the first time the participation of other opposition political parties.[40] Even if for certain observers this participation may be seen as some form of political openness, it does not constitute a rupture, however, with the dominant political order. For it is still the case that there is no true public debate about the country's major problems: neither the media, political parties, trade unions, nor the civil society in general enjoy any autonomy (Denoeux, 1999, p. 37).

It seems quite clear that in Tunisia the transition has moved only from an exclusive model of single party rule to a dominant party rule. The gulf grows wider between the regime's democratic rhetoric and a personalised government whose major preoccupation has been so far confined to what it views as a struggle to maintain and preserve the country's stability. Therefore, in the name of such stability, the regime has been forceful not only in its wave of oppression, but also in stifling all forms of opposition as well.[41] A case in point was the arrest of Mohamed Moada, the leader of the main opposition party in the national assembly, *Mouvement des Démocrates Socialistes*, in October 1995 because of his outspoken criticism of the lack of political freedom in Tunisia.[42] A resolution on human rights in Tunisia adopted by the European Parliament on 23 May 1996 came to denounce this situation and called on the government to alter its policy towards the democratic opposition and honour its international human rights commitments.[43]

Of the three Maghreb countries, Morocco seems to have been the least shaken by events that have prompted change in the region. Although there was a certain degree of political opposition, no fundamental change had taken place prior to 1990. It was more or less the Gulf War of 1990-1991 which signalled the threat stemming from the existing gap between the regime on the one side, and the opposition on the other. Indeed, while the government sided with the US-coalition in liberating Kuwait, the opposition was able to mobilise Moroccan opinion in support of Iraq. This event did not go unnoticed as some reform measures were undertaken afterwards.

Despite being boycotted by the main political parties, the 1992 amendments to the constitution were viewed as a success if one considers, of course, the turn-out of 97.25 per cent of the eleven million voters claimed by the government and a 99.80 per cent approval rate. Besides provisions safeguarding human rights,[44] these constitutional changes provided for the strengthening of the position of both prime minister and parliament. Rather than being part of the royal prerogative, future governments would normally reflect the political composition of the parliament, with the majority party being able to select its own cabinet for royal approval. The parliament also acquired the right to pass a vote of confidence on the programme proposed by the new government on coming into office (Joffé, 1994, pp 212-213).

The organisation of the delayed legislative elections in November 1993 was also another major event as they took place nine years after previous ones. The victory of the main opposition represented by the *Koutla* (referred to as the democratic bloc),[45] enabled it to emerge as the largest political grouping in the newly-elected parliament. This success by the opposition was viewed as constituting a victory for the monarchy in its search for a new kind of political consensus based on the involvement and cooperation of the major part of the opposition. However, the attainment of this goal proved difficult in practice.

Yet the *Koutla* objected to participating in the formation of a government in which the king reserved the right to name key ministers. Apparently, the frustration of this group had to do with the fact that the constitutional changes adopted had in no case affected the functioning of the system in which the king had remained the powerful and central personage. The monarchy, though tempted by the need for change, found the attempt to combine democracy with strong royal prerogatives very difficult. Thus it was not until other amendments were made to the constitution in September 1996 -- such as the change to the electoral system and making the government directly responsible before the parliament -- that the *Koutla* bloc agreed to participate in new elections that were held in November 1997. The formation of a new government in early 1998, while it brought the opposition back into the political mainstream, cannot offer a definitive guarantee for a democratic transition for two main reasons.

First, the elections produced what a keen observer called: 'A fragmented political landscape which does not bode well for the composition of a strong government' (Daoud, 1997, p. 108). For the *Koutla* group, this is most likely to limit its margins for manoeuvre in a government of coalition that includes in its composition pro-monarchy parties from the *Wifaq* (national entente bloc) and the Centre.[46] In other words, any attempt from the first group that may affect the established political order will certainly be resisted by the second bloc. Second, with a participation rate of the order of 58.3 per cent, that is not including the 8.5 per cent spoilt ballot papers, these elections showed that it was the lowest turnout ever registered. This may be indicative of the degree of the public disaffection not only in relation to the political process but also in relation to the opposition, represented by the *Koutla* bloc.

The succession of Mohamed VI to the throne after his father's death in 1999 had initially been heralded as a starting point for change in Morocco. Indeed, the new monarch embarked on a series of reforms in the various spheres of the state apparatus, signalling a clear willingness to depart from previous regime. This move, if welcomed by a large part of the society and many of Morocco's partners, is however giving the impression of a monarchy that wants to retain its hold on power by continuing to play a decisive role in the running of the country's public affairs. This is a role which, in a constitutional monarchy, should normally be within the responsibility of the government, being in this case criticised for its inertia (Daoud and Abderrahim, 2000, p. 14).

All in all, what appears to characterise the Maghreb in the light of the preceding review of recent political developments is that, at the present conjuncture, the region is, with varying degrees, at a critical stage in its move towards democratic rule. In this context, two features can be adduced to account for the difficult process of transition.

In the first place, the regimes, under domestic and external pressures, did introduce a number of measures aimed at a greater opening in the political systems. Initially this resulted in relatively more political rights and freedoms setting parameters for a possible transition to democracy. In practice, however, it has not proven easy to move this process forward. Obviously, one plausible explanation for this is the fact that there is still resistance to change. While the reforms introduced are set to generate their dynamics over time, ruling elites have so far contended themselves with allowing the opposition to participate in politics, not for the sake of change but rather in an attempt to ensure the regimes' survival at a time of rising domestic and external criticism. This accommodation, albeit limited and controlled at this stage, may well signal the beginning for further transformations to follow, as retreat would be quite costly.

Second, political reforms have been concomitant with economic reforms. Yet these have had and continue to have a heavy social cost. Harsh as they have been, these economic reforms may have commanded compliance from both society and political elite to be carried out. Tunisia, as a prominent example, seems to have benefited from a regional and international context that favoured the authoritarian approach of its regime, though increasingly criticised for its human rights practices (Denoeux, 1999, pp. 50-53). The Tunisian regime continues to enjoy large popular support in part because of its socio-economic accomplishments. It is argued that 'most Tunisians generally see limited political freedoms as a price worth paying for the stability and social and economic development Ben Ali's rule has brought'.[47]

Conclusion

The examination of many developments in the Maghreb, notably since the 1980s, has made plain the multi-dimensional crisis being experienced throughout the region. Economic nationalism, which had been a driving force behind orthodox development strategies during more than two decades and which justified in certain periods and instances an excessive dirigisme, lost its importance when major economic problems emerged and more serious dissatisfaction with the regimes became evident and manifest. Indeed, the deleterious results of the economic policies and the increasing scarcity of resources has called into question the state's ability to persist in performing its former social policies. Ruling elites' claims to be the sole representatives of their respective societies have also been challenged.

The attempt being made to redress accumulated economic imbalances through liberalisation programmes means, at least for some time to come, much more austerity. This in turn means that still greater popular sacrifice will have to be endured by the large poor segments of society in particular. In this respect, the Maghreb governments are finding it -- and continue to find it -- very difficult to satisfy the pressing needs of a young and growing population in terms of housing, health care, education and, more importantly, the huge task of creating enough jobs on the scale needed to meet demand.

The socio-economic deficit is compounded by a difficult process of political transition whose manifestation and seriousness differ from one country to another. Although it may be the case in certain instances of a pluralism of façade reflective of a continuing domination and persistent reluctance of the ruling elites or parties to loosen their grip on power, it seems that the wave of change, even slow and gradual, is irreversible, not least because of increasing external pressures. The EU, by concluding new agreements under its partnership initiative, has for the first time as part of these arrangements, emphasised that respect for democratic principles and human rights is a key aspect in future development of its relations with the Maghreb region.

Notes

1 World Bank, *World Development Report 1990* (New York: Oxford University Press, 1990), pp. 180-181.
2 *Ibid.*, pp. 192-193.
3 For more details on the Maghreb countries' economic performance, see for example Karen Pfeifer, 'Between Rocks and Hard Choices: International Finance and Economic Adjustment in North Africa', in Dirk Vandewalle (ed.), *North Africa - Development and Reform in a Changing Global Economy* (New York: St. Martin's Press, 1996), pp. 25-63.
4 *Financial Times*, 25 February 1995.
5 United Nations Development Programme, *Human Development Report 1999* (New York: Oxford University Press, 1999), p. 200.
6 *Ibid.*
7 *Ibid.*, p. 199.
8 During the 1970s, the average of unemployment rate in the Maghreb was within the proportion of 10 per cent of the economic active population.
9 Only between 1994-1997, about 800, 000 jobs were believed to have been lost; a figure reported by *Liberté* (Algiers), 20 April 1998.
10 The Economist Intelligence Unit, *Country Profile - Algeria 1999-2000* (London: EIU,

1999), p. 28.
11 The Economist Intelligence Unit, *Country Profile - Morocco 1999-2000* (London: EIU, 1999), p. 25.
12 *Ibid.*
13 The Economist Intelligence Unit, *Country Profile - Tunisia 1999-2000* (London: EIU, 1999), p. 22.
14 République Algérienne Démocratique et Populaire, *Economie Algérienne - Les Enjeux et les Choix à Moyen Terme 1996-2000*, Algiers, 1996, Appendix 7, p. 12.
15 Conseil National Economique et Social, *Avis Relatif au Plan National Contre le Chômage*, http://www.cnes.dz
16 ArabicNews, 'Employment problem a priority for Morocco', http://www.arabicnews.com/ansub/Daily/day/981214/1998121444.html
17 The Economist Intelligence Unit, *Country Profile Tunisia, op.cit.*, p. 22.
18 World Bank, *World Development Indicators 2000* (Washington, DC: World Bank, 2000), p. 56.
19 Ministère des Affaires Sociales, *Rapport Final de la Commission Nationale pour la Promotion de l'Emploi*, Algiers, December 1989, p. 36.
20 Décret Législatif no. 93-07 du 24 avril 1993 relatif aux objectifs généraux de la période 1993-1997 et portant Plan National 1993, *Journal Officiel de la République Algérienne*, vol. 32, no. 26, 26 April 1993.
21 République Algérienne Démocratique et Populaire (Services du Chef du Gouvernement), *Programme du Gouvernement 1997*, Algiers, July 1997, p. 70.
22 The Economist Intelligence Unit, *Country Profile - Morocco 1995-1996* (London: EIU, 1995), p. 13.
23 Ministry of Economic Development (Tunisia), *9th Development Plan 1997-2001*, http://www.tunisiaonline.com/development/t32.html
24 Conseil National Economique et Social, *op.cit.*
25 The Economist Intelligence Unit, *Country Profile - Tunisia 1997-1998* (London: EIU, 1997), p. 16.
26 For an account on the forms and terms of indebtedness, see Pfeifer, 'Algeria's Implicit Stabilization Program', in Henry J. Barkey (ed.), *The Politics of Economic Reform in the Middle East* (New York: St. Martin's Press, 1992), pp. 159-163.
27 *Financial Times*, 27 May 1994.
28 *Middle East International*, 10 June 1994, p. 15.
29 The Economist Intelligence Unit, *Country Profile - Algeria 1997-1998* (London: EIU, 1997), p. 40.
30 The Economist Intelligence Unit, *Country Profile - Algeria 1999-2000, op.cit.*, p. 46.
31 At the expiry date of the three-year deal with the IMF in April 1998, Algeria's reserves were estimated at 8.8 billion dollars, reported by *Liberté, op.cit.*
32 The Economist Intelligence Unit, *Country Profile - Morocco 1995-1996, op.cit.*, p. 38.
33 The Economist Intelligence Unit, *Country Profile - Tunisia 1999-2000, op.cit.*, p. 37.
34 A similar scenario is predicted for Algeria. According to the government forecasts, the total external debt was 32 billion dollars at the end of 1995 and will reach 40 billion dollars by the end of 2004. Reported by the *Middle East Economic Digest*, vol. 40, no. 18, 3 May 1996, p. 18.
35 The Economist Intelligence Unit, *Country Profile - Morocco 1999-2000, op.cit.*, pp. 38-39.
36 See article 195 of the 1976 Constitution.
37 While the 1976 Constitution devoted nine articles (from 95 to 103) to the FLN, the 1989

Constitution made no reference to it at all.

38 *Keesing's Record of World Events*, vol. 44, no. 9, 1998, p. 42528.

39 Only 19 seats out of 163 in the legislative elections and 6 seats of the 4,090 council seats in the municipal elections went to the opposition parties. For further account on these elections, see Alfred Hermida, 'Tunisia's ruling party to maintain its stranglehold', *The Guardian*, 16 March 1994; Francis Ghilès, 'Tunisians go to the poll tightly muzzled', *Financial Times*, 18 March 1994; and more specifically Guilain Denoeux, 'Tunisie: les élections présidentielles et législatives', *Monde Arabe-Maghreb-Machrek*, no. 145, July-September 1994, pp. 49-72.

40 This follows a constitutional amendment in June 1999 which allows presidents or general secretaries of political parties to stand for presidential elections under certain conditions. The candidate must be leader of the party for at least five years, aged no more than seventy years, and the party represented in the parliament. The participation of two candidates from the opposition was largely symbolic, even if it marked the first ever pluralist presidential elections in Tunisia.

41 The new laws adopted on 22 November 1993 restricted further the fundamental liberties and allowed the internment of prisoners of opinion; see Ramonet, 'Main de fer en Tunisie', *Le Monde Diplomatique*, no. 508, July 1996, p. 1.

42 In a letter addressed to Ben Ali on 21 September 1995, the Leader of the MDS, who initially supported the change in leadership, criticised its subsequent developments as: '*Retour au régime du parti unique hégémonique (...) dans des conditions d'encadrement plus rigide et de quadrillage de la société plus habile et plus systématique que sous le précédent régime*'; quoted from Jacqueline Boucher, 'La société tunisienne privée de parole', *Le Monde Diplomatique*, no. 503, February 1996, p. 11.

43 *Official Journal of the European Communities*, C 166, 10 June 1996, p. 204.

44 Prior to this, King Hassan was reported to have granted amnesty to 2,268 prisoners, among them, his political opponents and military detainees who had allegedly participated in plots against him in 1971 and 1972. Among these was Mohamed Basri, a founder member of the most outspoken opposition party, *Union Socialiste des Forces Populaires* (USFP), who was sentenced three times to death while being in exile in France for 28 years. His return marked a gesture by the authorities towards the Moroccan left.

45 This group represents the left and of which the most influential parties are USFP, *Parti Istiqlal* (PI) and *Parti du Progrès et du Socialisme* (PPS).

46 This bloc is referred to as the right and of which the major parties are *Union Constitutionnelle* (UC), *Rassemblement National des Indépendants* (RNI) and *Mouvement Populaire* (MP).

47 The Economist Intelligence Unit, *Country Profile - Tunisia 1999-2000*, *op.cit.*, p. 5.

5 A Partnership Pact from Europe

Introduction

The limited effect that the Community's development cooperation policy had on the Maghreb countries and the growing signs of instability on its southern borders were among the major factors that have led the EU in recent years to reassess its relationship towards these countries, and towards the Mediterranean region more generally. In an attempt to adapt to these challenges, the EU came up with a new policy initiative. While it does not represent a break with previous policy phases, this initiative, nevertheless, involves certain innovative features.

In addition to its more comprehensive coverage of issues in the political, economic, and socio-cultural areas, the policy approach in question introduces the principle of partnership which is assumed to characterise the relationship and its future development. At the foundation of the whole process is and will remain the gradual establishment of a free trade area between the EU and each of the Maghreb countries. As a central pillar, the free trade zone is expected to be operational after a transitional period which will certainly incur costs and may eventually bring benefits to the Maghreb region.

In dealing with this policy approach and its likely repercussions on the Maghreb countries in particular, this chapter begins with a review that traces the background and reasons behind its formulation. Following that, the chapter analyses the key policy dimensions both in general, and more specifically as embodied in the pacts of association concluded by Morocco and Tunisia. Finally, the trade component of these agreements is investigated along with the costs and benefits associated with the expected liberalisation by the Maghreb countries of their trade *vis-à-vis* the EU.

Formulation and Motives

Before looking more closely at some of the chief concerns that prompted the EU to formulate a new initiative for the Mediterranean, it is worth reviewing the background process that led to its development. A key catalyst was the end of the Cold War which witnessed a shift in the EU's external relations priorities. Down to the end of the 1980s, much of the attention was directed to eastern Europe. The priority given to this part of Europe was met with a growing sense of anxiety by the Union's southern neighbours in the Mediterranean, and particularly the Maghreb countries, who saw it detrimental to their interests with Europe. Nevertheless, their existing problems, heightened by the Gulf War, not only made clear their precarious stability, but precipitated the need for the EU to redirect its efforts towards them as well.

Interestingly, the need to give proper weight to the relations with the Mediterranean originated in the 1992 Lisbon European Council summit conclusions on the likely development of the Common Foreign and Security Policy.[1] The summit was particularly important. For it was agreed that the assessment of major common interests at stake and the definition of issues and areas for joint action should take due account of factors such as the geographical proximity of a given region or country; an important interest in the political and economic stability of a region or country; and the existence of threats to the security interests of the Union.[2] In accordance with this, the Council stressed that: 'The southern and eastern shores of the Mediterranean as well as the Middle East are geographical areas in relations to which the Union has strong interests both in terms of security and social stability.'[3]

Also more important was the major role played by the EU southern Member States, most notably France, Spain and Italy, which had brought pressure to bear on their partners in the Union to shift the focus onto the Mediterranean region in an attempt to redress the balance already weighted towards the immediate eastern neighbours.[4] By way of illustration, Alain Juppé, French Prime Minister from 1995 to 1997, was reported to have cautioned that: 'It is good of course to focus on the problems of eastern Europe, but we must not neglect what is happening on our southern frontiers.'[5] This assertion, while recognising the fact that the EU's geographical balance had been tilting to the East, insisted on the need for comparable attention in respect of the Mediterranean area. Arguably, the interests and intentions of certain Member States such as the United Kingdom and particularly Germany, which used its presidency of the EU to put in place the building blocks of this 'eastern strategy',[6] might not have necessarily converged with those of the southern Member States.

For their part, the southern Member States used their consecutive tenure of the Union's presidency, from January 1995 to June 1996, with the support of the Commission via its former Spanish Commissioner, Manuel Marin, in charge of policy on the Mediterranean, to promote and finalise the new Mediterranean initiative.[7] Under the French presidency, it was adopted and an allocation of EU funds totalling 4,685 million Ecu for the period 1995-1999 was agreed.[8] Likewise, Spain hosted the planned Euro-Mediterranean conference which was hailed by the then Spanish Prime Minister, Felipe Gonzales, as 'the culmination of an ancient aspiration and the start of a new relationship'.[9]

The partnership deal -- which was initially forged to take account of the Maghreb countries' interests -- influenced wider Mediterranean policy. This occurred not least because of the transformed prospects for Middle East peace.[10] The June 1994 summit of EU leaders in Corfu mandated the Council, together with the Commission, to assess:

> The policy of the European Union in the Mediterranean region and possible initiatives to strengthen this policy in the short and medium term, bearing in mind the possibility of convening a conference attended by the European Union and its Mediterranean partners.[11]

In response, the Commission, in a communication to the Council in October 1994, made a proposal for a new Euro-Mediterranean partnership which is considered to mark the inauguration of a new phase of relations.[12]

At the Essen summit in December 1994, the European Council supported the Commission's view of the Mediterranean region as an area of strategic importance. The Council stated that: 'Peace, stability and prosperity in the region are amongst the highest priorities of Europe.'[13] It endorsed the proposal for a new partnership deal and requested the Commission to forward specific proposals in early 1995 for its implementation.[14] These proposals were revealed in a second document and formally approved during the Cannes summit in June 1995.[15] The final conclusions of the summit acknowledged that:

> The European Union is resolved to establish a lasting pattern of relations with other Mediterranean countries in a spirit of partnership. An ambitious policy of cooperation to the south forms a counterpart to the policy of openness to the east and gives the European Union's external action its geopolitical coherence.[16]

The proposals for the implementation of the Euro-Mediterranean partnership later served as the EU's position during the Euro-Mediterranean conference held in Barcelona in November 1995. It was endorsed by the two parties in a Final Declaration and a Work Programme.[17]

This deal is primarily designed as a response to European concerns over the implications of instability in the Mediterranean region. Those sources of instability in the Maghreb countries examined in the previous chapter -- which are more or less common to other parts of the Mediterranean -- have been perceived as presenting potential security threats to Europe. They were explicitly echoed by the European Commission which stated that:

> Most Mediterranean countries are facing political instability, rapid population growth, large movement of population and high unemployment. These problems, especially in the case of the Maghreb countries, are also our problems - such is their influence on the region's security and the potential migratory pressure on the Community.[18]

Notwithstanding the alarming comments made in 1995 by former North Atlantic Treaty Organisation (NATO) Secretary-General, Willy Claes, about Islam becoming the most important challenge to face the West after the end of the Cold War,[19] there seems little or no plausible scenario that might encompass a direct military intervention from the neighbouring countries of the EU. However, this does not exclude a wary eye on terrorist activity and conventional and non-conventional weapons proliferation (Mortimer, 1994, pp. 107-109). A dialogue between NATO and certain Mediterranean countries (Egypt, Morocco, Tunisia, Israel, Mauritania, and Algeria which joined only recently) was initiated in 1995 to promote understanding and confidence-building in the region.

Effects stemming from the region's economic, social, and political difficulties have therefore become a primary focus of attention inasmuch as they are viewed as affecting the Union's security interests. The prevailing perception, particularly amongst the EU southern Member States, has been that the potential impact of a situation of the sort could more likely weaken European export markets, threaten existing energy supplies, and lead to flows of migrants which the EU is categorically and resolutely unwilling to admit.

Trade relations with the Mediterranean are of significant importance to the EU. The Mediterranean remains one of the main destinations for European products. It took around 9.3 per cent and 12 per cent of total extra-EU exports in 1995 and 1998 respectively.[20] Moreover, the Union continues to enjoy a remarkable trade surplus with this region, estimated at 13.7 billion Ecu and 29.5 billion Ecu over the same periods.[21]

Thus for obvious reasons -- such as those to do with the need to preserve and even enhance this trading position in the Mediterranean Basin -- the Union is now championing the formation of a Euro-Mediterranean economic area. This would have as its centrepiece the establishment of the largest free trade area in the world. The shift from a one-way system of preferences to a reciprocal system of preferences, as embodied in the partnership agreements, is therefore aimed at promoting greater penetration of neighbouring countries' markets by European products and eventually investment. The benefits of access to an adjacent consumer market are spelt out:

> The Mediterranean neighbours, from Morocco to Turkey, represent the southern part of the European Union's future economic and social environment. With a rapidly growing population of presently some 200 million people, these countries represent as important an export market potential as eastern Europe. It is of vital political and economic importance for the European Union to develop this relationship into a closer economic symbiosis.[22]

This seems obvious if one takes into account the growing economic interest which the United States had shown in the whole region particularly following the then promising peace process initiated in the Middle East.[23]

By virtue of the fact that the region is a major energy supplier, it is also the case that security of supply must remain a constant concern to the EU. As clearly pointed out by Tim Niblock: 'Oil, oil products and gas constitute strategic goods, the availability of which the European Community needs to be assured' (1996, p. 119). The total energy dependence of the Union on external sources of supply is expected to rise from its current level of 56 per cent to 70 per cent by the year 2020.[24] The Mediterranean countries provide 24 per cent of the total EU energy imports, that is 27 per cent of imports of oil and 32 per cent of natural gas imports.[25] Apart from the supply of oil, there is the growing importance of gas supply from the Maghreb. Besides the existing Transmed pipeline carrying Algerian gas to Italy, via Tunisia, there is also the Maghreb-Europe pipeline, recently completed and now carrying Algerian gas through Morocco to Spain and Portugal.[26] As natural gas is increasing its share from 19 per cent of the EU energy balance today to around 26 per cent by the year 2010, dependence on imports from third countries is projected to rise from almost 40 per cent today to around 60 per cent by 2010, and as high as 75 per cent by 2020.[27] Algeria, as the second biggest supplier after Russia, provided some 24 per cent of EU gas imports in 1994.[28]

Several documents reflect the importance attached to the energy factor. They include the Commission's Green Paper and subsequent White Paper in which security of supply is highlighted as one of the principal pillars of the EU's energy policy.[29] The management of energy dependence was stressed further in the European Parliament resolution which pointed to the necessary creation of a framework for closer cooperation policy matters with, among others, the countries of the Mediterranean region.[30] It is therefore of direct relevance to the

EU to contribute to the stability required in the region, by means of its partnership initiative, as an essential condition for guaranteeing supply. Population growth together with economic development in the Mediterranean suggest that producers in this region could triple their present requirements over the next twenty-five years.[31] This has constituted an additional motive for the EU to seek to enhance its energy relationship in the area. The convening of a Euro-Mediterranean conference on energy issues in Tunisia in March 1995,[32] the results of which later served as an input in the Work Programme of the Barcelona conference, was indicative of the efforts made in this context.[33]

Migration from the Mediterranean, and more particularly from the Maghreb countries, is regarded as one of the most direct security challenge to Europe. Fear of migratory pressures was well expressed by Jacques Poos, Foreign Affairs Minister of Luxembourg, who stated that:

> The immigration from the Mediterranean basin towards the countries of the European Union (...) has serious implications for the social fabric of the EU. These implications might constitute sooner or later a potential for risks that would be dangerous to neglect (1995, p. 14)

That statement is only a recent reminder of the seriousness of an issue that has been and continues to be the object of an extensive debate and policy measures from both the EU and the individual Member States. Although it is still the case that there is no truly common EU immigration policy,[34] policy responses from Europe tend to converge on the principal concern of reducing unwanted migration. This is evidenced by the fact that it features on the first page of the Commission's document on implementing the Euro-Mediterranean strategy. While the document in question does not elaborate on the point, the partnership scheme, in particular its economic dimension, can be seen partly as the materialising of the 1992 Edinburgh European Council conclusions and the Commission's 1994 paper on immigration.[35]

The main thrust of the Council conclusions and the Commission paper is on ways and means to remove what some call the 'push' forces or factors that motivate migration (Martin, p. 243). In its declaration on principles governing external aspects of migration policy, the European Council concluded that migration movements into Member States may be reduced by, inter-alia, encouraging liberal trade and economic cooperation with countries of emigration thereby promoting economic development and increasing prosperity in those countries; and to the same end ensuring the appropriate volume of development aid is effectively used to encourage sustainable social and economic development, in particular to contribute to job creation and the alleviation of poverty in the countries of origin.[36] The Commission paper, which identified the root causes of migration pressures and singled out economic disparities as the most significant ones, stressed the necessary integration of an active migration policy into general development policies and external economic relations of the EU.[37]

Arguably, the EU's partnership strategy, without neglecting to address the politically motivated dimension of migration, does put considerable emphasis on the economic incentives. By attempting to combine most notably a two-pronged policy, trade and aid, the EU intends to promote the improvement of economic conditions in the countries of immigration. This way of tackling the migration issue recalls Lord Ralf Dahrendorf's clear assertion that: 'If we do not want people from the poor countries of our neighbourhood, we have to take the goods which they produce at home',[38] as well as the United States' response to its analogous problem with Mexico through the conclusion of the North American Free Trade Area scheme.

Dimensions of the Partnership

The overall aim of the European initiative is to build a space for dialogue, exchange and cooperation which will ensure peace, stability and economic and social development in the Mediterranean region. As such the multi-dimensional scope of the partnership scheme can be seen in its ambitious coverage of issues that goes beyond the almost exclusively economic basis of previous policy phases. The Barcelona Declaration defined three principal issues which will govern relations between the parties within the framework of the Euro-Mediterranean partnership:

- Political and security partnership aimed at defining a common area of peace and stability;
- Economic and financial partnership, aimed at building a zone of shared prosperity, notably by progressively bringing in free trade;
- Social, cultural and human partnership, which is designed to foster exchanges between civil societies.

The first dimension of the partnership on political and security aspects, having as its main objective the establishment of a zone of peace and stability, is founded upon the adopted declaration of principles which all the parties are expected to promote through an enhanced and regular dialogue. Within each state

(Mediterranean non-member states in particular), this involves reaffirming the importance of respect for human rights and basic freedoms (expression, association for peaceful purposes, conscience, and religion), pluralism and tolerance, and of strengthening of the rule of law and democracy (free and regular elections to governing and representative bodies, independent judiciary, balance of power, and good governance).

Similarly, regional security, seen as an asset to the promotion of stability in the Mediterranean basin, is underscored by pointing to certain principles which must guide relations between parties to the partnership. Among these principles one can cite non-interference in internal affairs; respect for territorial integrity; peaceful settlement of disputes; fighting against terrorism, drug trafficking and organised crime, as well as the commitment to disarmament and adherence to the non-proliferation of weapons of mass destruction. Moreover, with a view to creating an 'area of peace and stability in the Mediterranean', consideration was initially given to the possibility of eventually implementing France's proposal of a 'Euro-Mediterranean Stability Pact'.[39] This Pact, according to former NATO Secretary-General, Javier Solana, 'would be different from that between the EU and CEEC in the sense that with Mediterranean countries it would mean ensuring political and economic stability while with eastern Europe the goal was to settle border and refugee issues'.[40] The proposal, which has changed name to a 'Euro-Mediterranean Charter for Peace and Stability', is at an advanced negotiating stage between the parties concerned as of May 2000.

As for the economic and financial aspects, the objective is to achieve a Euro-Mediterranean economic area. This is to be fashioned by speeding up the pace of sustained socio-economic development; improving people's living conditions through raising employment opportunities and closing the development gap in the Euro-Mediterranean area; and promoting regional cooperation and integration. The main vehicle for progress in these directions will be the gradual introduction of a free trade area by the year 2010. The area is to be established via the new Euro-Mediterranean association agreements (already concluded or under negotiation) and free trade arrangements between the EU's Mediterranean partners themselves. This will involve the progressive removal of tariff and non-tariff barriers on manufactured goods and progressive liberalisation of trade in services and farm produce (as far as various agricultural policies allow).

To promote the gradual development of the free trade area, the EU's Mediterranean partners will undertake to upgrade economic and social structures. The priority is given to modernising the productive sector and creating an institutional and regulatory framework conducive to the promotion and development of local economic forces, particularly within the private sector, and the attraction of foreign investment. Since the whole process entails a substantial increase in financial assistance, the EU, as mentioned before, already earmarked a financial package for the period 1995-1999 for this purpose. This was to be supplemented by loans totalling 3,996 million Ecu from the EIB together with bilateral financial contributions from the Member States of the Union.

A final area within the scope of the partnership policy relates to the social, cultural and human dimension. Here the emphasis is on the general aim of bringing peoples of the Mediterranean region closer together by means of dialogue, exchange and respect among cultures and religions. The underlying philosophy behind this dimension is the promotion of decentralised cooperation between civil societies on either shore of the Mediterranean in areas such as education, vocational training, the media, as well as between trade unions and public and private companies. Along with this cooperation, the parties commit themselves to prevent and fight any phenomenon that may jeopardise mutual understanding, such as terrorism, intolerance, corruption, racism and xenophobia.

It may be argued that the new policy's objectives are nothing if not ambitious. Its chances of success, however, would seem difficult to predict. Beyond the fact that it was agreed by all parties and even regarded by some as providing 'global and coherent answers to the numerous challenges facing the region',[41] this initiative is first and foremost a reflection of the EU's concerns and perception of the Mediterranean region. Being so and taking account of the fragmented concerns of the region, it is most likely to open areas of controversy. These may be expected to prove uneasy to conciliate during the implementation process, especially on sensitive issues of a political, security and even social nature (an example being the obligation for source countries to readmit illegal immigrants). There are also EU constraints stemming not only from budget limits, but also from the degree of commitment of Member States, being in this case primarily motivated by the concrete gains and interests that the whole process may induce.

All this does not mean that the attempt is doomed to failure. There is no doubt that the task ahead is enormous and the prospects will depend on the economic aspects which constitute its vital component. Whatever progress is made on the political and social side, this will contribute to supporting its central economic thesis. While the achievement of the multilateral dimension of the partnership policy is still a long way off, progress is being made on the multi-bilateral front through the conclusion of a number of association agreements between the EU and certain Mediterranean countries.[42] Among these are Morocco and Tunisia.

Essential Features of the Agreements

Formal negotiations on the Euro-Mediterranean agreements with Morocco and Tunisia, which started in early 1994, were concluded in 1995.[43] They are set to replace for an unlimited duration the 1976 cooperation arrangements. While the agreement with Tunisia came into force on 1 March 1998, the one with Morocco entered into force on 1 March 2000, taking much longer during the process of ratification. Their major aim is to develop a relationship based on reciprocity and partnership where respect for democratic principles and human rights is a key aspect. Special emphasis is also placed on regular political and social dialogue intended to contribute to stability and mutual understanding between contracting parties.

In the area of trade, the agreements provide for a free trade zone which will be gradually established over a transitional phase lasting a maximum of twelve years from their entry into force. In the case of industrial products, the Maghreb countries will continue to enjoy free access to the EU for most of their exports of manufactures. Upon the effectiveness of the agreements, the Maghreb countries start removing on a gradual basis those trade restrictions within a twelve-year period. The range of manufactures and timetable for tariff dismantling were worked out in a way that takes account of the sensitive nature of the industrial product/sector. For Tunisia, the tariff liberalisation schedule of industrial products is as follows:

- The first list essentially consists of capital and semi-finished products not produced locally. They represent 12 per cent of imports from the EU and the tariff protection is to be removed as soon the agreement takes effect;
- A second list for which tariff restrictions are to be removed over a five-year period from the entry into effect of the agreement. This list represents 28 per cent of imports and corresponds to products manufactured locally and liable to sustain competition;
- A third list representing 30 per cent of imports is to undergo suppression of tariffs over the full twelve year transition period at a rate of 8 per cent per year;
- A fourth list accounting for 29.5 per cent of imports, whose tariffs will be dismantled starting from the fifth year over a period of eight years;
- A final list of products representing a mere 0.5 per cent is exempted from tariff reductions. This list involves products such as handicrafts and some varieties of textiles and clothing articles.[44]

Similarly, Morocco has equally committed itself to gradually dismantling all existing trade restrictions standing in the way of industrial products coming from the EU. This process takes place as indicated below:

- A first list of products for which tariffs and other duties are to be removed with the entry into force of the agreement. They are basically capital goods not produced locally;
- A second list of goods for which all tariffs are to be lifted over a period of three years from the entry into effect of the agreement. These products mainly consist of industrial raw materials not produced locally and of spare parts;
- A final list of 'sensitive' products manufactured locally, whose tariffs will be removed starting from the fourth year over a period of nine years at a rate of 10 per cent per year (Zaim, 1999, p. 51).

For agricultural products, the existing preferential regime is maintained. It is accompanied by limited improvements in access for certain products especially via increased tariff quotas. Under a special clause contained in the agreements, both the EU and the Maghreb countries will undertake to examine the trade agricultural situation starting from 2000 with a view to establishing further reciprocal trade liberalisation. And this will depend on the outcome of the multilateral negotiations under the aegis of the WTO which started in Seattle in November 1999.

The parties agree to widen the scope of the agreements to cover a number of other trade-related issues. These include the objective of granting the right of establishment to each others' companies in each others' territories as well as the liberalisation of cross-border supply of services and movement of capital. Equally, the Maghreb countries are required, under the terms of these arrangements, to adapt their regulatory framework to approximate that in the EU in areas such as competition, government procurement and subsidy insofar as these may affect trade between both sides.

Economic and financial cooperation are additional issues covered by these agreements. The prime goal of economic cooperation, which is broadly defined,[45] is to support the Maghreb countries' efforts to restructure their economies. Accordingly, cooperation is to target sectors suffering the effects of internal constraints and difficulties or more particularly those to be affected by the process of EU-Maghreb liberalisation of trade. Special heed is also to be given to measures which may foster economic integration among the Maghreb countries. The methods to be involved within the framework of this cooperation consist of a regular economic dialogue on macro-economic policy, provision of expert services, joint ventures, and assistance with technical, administrative and regulatory matters.

The financial provisions are aimed to contribute to the modernisation of Maghreb countries' economies, encourage private investment, promote job-creating activities and gradually establish a free trade area. In this context, the innovation is that the financial protocols are not renewed. Rather, the amount of financial support, while globally already determined for the Mediterranean region, will depend on the pace of reforms, including the implementation by the Maghreb countries of the objectives of the agreements.

Market Access Conditions

As noted, the establishment of a free trade area between the EU and the Maghreb countries is at the heart of Europe's present Mediterranean strategy. The fundamental condition under which new free trade areas are to be formed, according to Article XXIV of GATT/WTO rules, is that they must cover 'substantially all trade' among members. This GATT/WTO rule, means that reciprocal trade liberalisation should be wider in scope. This is a matter of which the European Commission seems well aware, since it states that: 'It will be harder than ever before to limit the coverage of a free trade agreement. In other words, the exclusion of a major component of bilateral trade would result in the agreement being in contravention of WTO rules.'[46] However, the ambiguity surrounding the wording of WTO rules, that is in not referring to sectors to be included, and the transitional period of time allowed for the full implementation of the free trade area, may together have provided the EU with room for manoeuvre. The argument of the EU in respect of the exclusion of the agricultural sector from immediate complete liberalisation is that:

> GATT Article XXIV has never envisaged that a free trade area or customs union would require entirely free trade in all products between the participant members. It envisaged that the general tests in Article XXIV would be met and that substantially all the trade would be liberalised. Nevertheless, it remains the case that a more restrictive regime in agriculture remains possible in a manner consistent with Article XXIV provided the sector is itself covered and provided there is real liberalisation within that sector over the transitional period.[47]

Hence from the EU perspective, what is at issue is not the immediate formation of an all-embracing free trade area but rather a partial one where some 'sensitive' sectors/products are not part of this process (Langhammer, 1992, pp. 223-227). While only time will tell how quick the liberalisation in those excluded areas is going to proceed, one may, at this stage, question the value of an unbalanced free trade area that has not taken into account one of the partners' comparative advantages, precisely at this difficult transitional phase. Thus it comes as no surprise that differences between both sides were much more evident with respect to their market access conditions.

In the sphere of industrial products, textiles and clothing are the principal manufactures exported by Morocco and Tunisia to the Union. Under the partnership agreements, this group of products was not to benefit from an immediate total liberalisation. Certainly, this has to do with the EU commitment in the Uruguay Round deal. This sector is being gradually integrated into WTO discipline over a ten-year period that started from 1995. For the Maghreb countries a number of existing restrictive measures on their exports of textiles no longer apply because the arrangements concluded to this effect with the EU had expired by the end of 1997. This means that their exports of these products will henceforth enjoy a similar liberal regime as other industrial products.[48] Nevertheless, this does not prevent the EU, as a major importer, from having a considerable flexibility in resorting to protective measures provided for by a 'transitional safeguard mechanism'.[49] Moreover, the progressive trade liberalisation of this sector is very likely to place Maghreb exports in a disadvantaged position *vis-à-vis* other much more competitive suppliers in the European market, especially Asian and eastern European countries.

With regard to farm produce, the EU attitude does not suggest any intention to immediately liberalise trade in this sector. That is why it emerged as the thorniest, most controversial issue during the negotiations, particularly with Morocco and to a certain extent Tunisia. These countries' dissatisfaction had to do with what they considered as the EU's derisory offer. Olive oil is Tunisia's major agricultural export to the Union. Under the new accord, Tunisia wanted its quota for olive oil into the Union to be raised from 46,000 tonnes to 60,000 per year. This product is a key crop for Greece, Italy, Portugal and Spain. Furthermore, the EU as a whole is more than self-sufficient in this respect. Since that is the case, the European Commission made it clear that in view of the surpluses on the EU olive oil market, additional imports would cause problems, particularly with regard to the high amounts of export refunds required to dispose of these imports on the world market.[50] In addition, due to the unyielding stand of the EU southern Member States on this sensitive matter, Tunisia's export quota, under the agreement concluded, had initially been renewed for only four years.[51] Thereafter it will be reviewed according to conditions prevailing in the

Union's market. Though at this stage Tunisia seems more or less satisfied with this outcome, the Moroccan reaction has been cooler.

Disputes over agricultural products, and later fishing, made the agreement's conclusion difficult to finalise. Morocco's expectations appeared frustrated because of the EU reluctance to include farm produce in the free trade arrangement. This was underlined by the European negotiator, Juan Prat, who reportedly said that: 'The Commission is well-aware that such an offer may not come up to Morocco's expectations. However, the economic situation in the agricultural sector requires us to take a prudent approach.'[52]

The situation was further complicated by Morocco's setting new conditions for the renewal of a fishing scheme it has with the EU. Its insistence on halving a previously-agreed level of catches in its waters on the ground of being overfished, along with an obligation to load catches in Moroccan ports, was described by the EU side as 'clearly out of proportion and unacceptable'.[53]

Such a dispute was related to Morocco's dissatisfaction regarding agricultural exports. Its intransigent attitude might have been intended as leverage to secure better terms for its farm products. Commenting earlier on this issue, a Moroccan official pointed out that: 'Our main exports to the European Community, and the most difficulties we have in trade with the European Community are agricultural products. On this particular point we have been disappointed.'[54] Thus without the compromise achieved, Moroccan fruit and vegetable exports, as an important component in the trade relations with the Union, could have faced uncertainty.[55] The socio-economic importance of this sector is such that it provides an estimated half million jobs and the livelihood of three million people. It is clearly of vital importance to Morocco's social stability.

The fact that there has been no significant trade liberalisation in agriculture reflects first and foremost the sensitive nature of this sector. It is a sector which continues to be sheltered under the EU's CAP. Moreover the progress made in the last Uruguay Round as regards this sector was only concerned with a minimum access commitment. In other words, for importing countries like the EU, this was defined as either the existing level, because of special arrangements for instance, or a modestly higher level of current imports until the scheduled negotiations for further liberalisation to be initiated under WTO from 2000 (Inggo, 1995, p. 45).

Overall, for the Maghreb countries market access conditions in the association agreements fail to equate with a substantial achievement for their exports. By and large, they reflect the confirmation of previous concessions. The 1976 accords already offered them free access for nearly all their manufactured exports. In this context, the only improvement was the gradual elimination of the remaining restrictions on textiles and clothing, though in a more competitive environment. As for agricultural products, limited improvements in market access have been granted and are for the most part concerned with increased quota for certain specific products. For the EU the new concessions granted to Morocco and Tunisia in this sector will have a financial impact on its budget, that is potential customs revenue losses, estimated at about 18 million Ecu over the period 1996-2000.[56] Whatever the concessions made and the cost incurred by the EU, the Moroccans in particular remain unsatisfied. As their King's advisor, André Azoulay, stated: 'Morocco will not accept for much longer that agriculture remains excluded from free trade with the European Union.'[57]

Potential Costs and Benefits

It is not the case here to give extensive and in-depth analysis of the costs and benefits associated with the establishment of free trade between the EU and the Maghreb countries because the agreements concluded are still at an early phase of implementation. It is a matter of several years before any thorough and consolidated assessment of their effective impact can be made. Therefore, the purpose is only to briefly address a number of apparent effects that are more likely to be experienced by the Maghreb countries.

Potential Costs

The free trade area, to be phased in over twelve years, will undoubtedly set the Maghreb countries a difficult challenge.[58] Previously, these countries benefited from non-reciprocal preferences in their trade relations with the EU. With the present partnership agreements they are required to gradually and unilaterally open up their respective markets to European products. This process of liberalisation in its adverse effects will be felt in terms of a fall of tax duties, deterioration of the balance of payments, contraction and displacement of a significant part of the industrial sector, and a loss of jobs.

First, a corollary of trade liberalisation is the potential loss of tax duties consequent on the lifting of existing trade barriers. As table 5.1 reveals, the import duties account for a much higher share of the Maghreb countries total revenue. This compares with other countries such as Egypt and Mexico where on average the share of import duties in total revenue does not exceed 10 per cent and 5 per cent respectively. As European products will be granted a preferential

Table 5.1 Share of trade taxes in the Maghreb countries' revenue, selected years (1990, 1993 and 1996)

	1990	1993	1996
Morocco			
Total revenue (million dirhams)	56,635	78,653	--
of which			
Total trade taxes (million dirhams)	10,026	12,483	--
Import duties (%)	17.4	15.9	--
Export duties (%)	0.3	0.00	--
Tunisia			
Total revenue (million dinars)	3,325.8	4,442.1	5,670.1
of which			
Total trade taxes (million dinars)	932	1,239.1	1,449.9
Import duties (%)	27.4	27.4	25.0
Export duties (%)	0.3	0.3	0.1

Source: Calculations based on data derived from the IMF, *Government Finance Statistics Yearbook* (Washington, DC: IMF, 1999), pp. 283 and 408.

treatment through a gradual lowering of tariffs, this means for the Maghreb economies the shrinking of a significant source of revenue. With the EU, as their major trading partner, accounting for the bulk of their total imports, the fiscal cost associated with free trade is inevitably expected to be greater.[59] According to certain estimates the revenue loss is equivalent to 3 percent of Morocco's GDP and 6 per cent of Tunisia's GDP (Bensidoun and Chevallier, 1996, p. 90).

Given the significant reliance on trade taxes, particularly import duties, as a source of revenue for the government concerned, this new situation will lead them to tighten their budget control through either of the two policy measures --

curbing public expenditure or increasing indirect taxation -- to offset this fiscal loss (Kebabjian, 1995, p. 90). The first measure amounting to a reduced government public services, would prove risky since it may exacerbate the already social hardship being experienced in these societies. Though the second measure has a social cost, it seems to be the one that is now being contemplated. Morocco has given no indication how it will deal with this problem. But Tunisia, which started implementing a programme of tax reform since 1987, has made clear the need to mobilise alternative sources, primarily by targeting domestically-based taxes. For instance, value-added tax is to be extended to all sectors, having taken on board an earlier recommendation made by the World Bank. The latter estimated that an elimination of exemptions and the move towards a uniform value-added tax rate could lower its current average rate and the revenue welfare would be even greater than the benefits from tariff reductions under the free trade agreement with the EU.[60] As for the tax rebates (incentives) which aim to encourage investment and the development of new industries, they will instead, according to the government policy, last for a limited period of time.[61] However, such a policy measure may act, paradoxically, as a disincentive to the very investment needed by Tunisia over this transitional phase.

Second, as trade liberalisation takes place with the removal of quantitative and tariff restrictions, it is expected that this will lead to an increase in overall consumption levels in the Maghreb countries. Besides a rise in capital goods imports resulting from the need for further investment to be induced by the agreements, consumers will also be increasingly inclined to purchase imported products rather than local ones. The plausible explanation for this is that the local manufacturing sector does not either meet the needs of the domestic market or cannot face up to stiff competition in terms of quality and prices. In both cases, the increase in imports is likely, at least for some time, to affect the Maghreb countries' balance of payment adversely, particularly when the prospects for an expansion of their exports are dimmed in the immediate future. They already benefit from a preferential treatment for their existing exports into the EU market and expanding their range of manufactured products will depend on raising new investments in the export sector. Fear stemming from such competition has already been taken seriously. The Tunisian president was reported to have himself called on Tunisians to consume local products; an appeal justified on the basis that: 'If you buy a local product, you contribute to the preservation of a job in Tunisia, when, on the contrary, you buy an imported product, you contribute to the maintenance of a job in a foreign country.'[62]

Third, a transitional cost stems from the impact trade liberalisation will have on protected industries of the Maghreb countries in the face of increased exposure to EU competition and the need to adjust to it. Indeed, with industries at an early stage of development and under high levels of protection, ranging on average between 35 per cent to 43 per cent of tariff protection for Morocco and Tunisia, it would be a painful exercise to adapt to this new competitive environment. Following a preliminary diagnosis, it was estimated that at least one-third of Tunisia's manufacturing sector (about 6,000 companies) will disappear whatever the level and nature of support provided.[63] The textiles would be the first to be threatened as 45 per cent of it would find it even harder to face up to competition as a result of multilateral liberalisation in this sector (Grimaud, 1996, p. 344).

A more-or-less similar scenario is predicted for Moroccan industries where the establishment of a free trade zone will result in the emergence of four categories of companies.[64] The first category concerns those companies which will find no difficulty in withstanding competition and might even benefit from liberalised trade with Europe. The second one relates to those that would require specific measures of restructuring at an initial phase. The third category are those companies which, without punctual and sufficient support, run the risk of bankruptcy. A final category consists of companies that are condemned to disappear. Textiles, knitwear and processing sectors would be the most likely to suffer from an opening of the market to international competition.[65]

Because of these competitive pressures associated with an open trading regime vis-à-vis the EU, Morocco and Tunisia will require a huge effort to bring their infrastructure into line with those of Europe. The need to adapt to this new situation has become a high priority for these countries. In recent years, programmes of upgrading local companies, known as 'La mise à niveau', have been elaborated and are being implemented. In the first phase, 1996-2000, Tunisia -- the country that first started this programme -- has estimated the financial cost at 2.5 billion dollars, of which 60 per cent will go into modernising companies, and the remaining 40 per cent into infrastructure and improving the business environment.[66] Over a similar period, the Moroccan Ministry of Trade and Industry has also identified those measures deemed necessary to restructure domestic industries and improve their environment (see tables 5.2 and 5.3). The corresponding financial resources needed to implement this programme of restructuring have been estimated at a cost of more than 45 billion dirhams (more than 5 billion dollars).

In this regard and in addition to other sources of funding such as the EIB, individual Member States and international bodies, the EU, within its 1995-1999 Meda financial package, pledged to provide support.[67] As of January 1999, the available figures show an EU total commitment of 476.3 million Ecu to

Table 5.2 Cost of the overall adjustment measures (million dirhams)

Sectors and measures	Amount
Basic infrastructure	18,000
Promotion of European investment	7,000
Support to exports	660
Assistance to SMIs	40
Financing of handicraft and commercial activities	200
Protection of environment	500
Development of technical infrastructure	652
Development of technical standards	384
Funds for the *'mise à niveau'* activities	18,000
Support to professional associations	110
Total	45,546

Source: Ministère de l'Industrie, du Commerce et de l'Artisanat (Morocco), *Programme de Mise à Niveau*; published in *L'Economiste* (Rabat), 22 February 1996, p. 21.

Morocco and 289.5 million Ecu to Tunisia, and the payment made represented only 14.9 per cent and 37.6 per cent respectively.[68] As initially made clear by Brussels, it is on the speed up and progress of reforms in these countries that the

Table 5.3 Cost of industrial restructuring by sector (million dirhams)

	Organisation and management	Equipment	Total
Textiles, clothing and leather	970	4,550	5,520
Chemical industry	1,160	4,032	5,162
Food-processing	865	1,920	2,785
Mechanical and metal industry	521	2,996	3,517
Electrical and electronic industry	249	790	1,039
Total	3,765	14,288	18,023

Source: Ministère de l'Industrie, du Commerce et de l'Artisanat (Morocco), *Programme de Mise à Niveau*; published in *L'Economiste* (Rabat), 22 February 1996, p. 21.

funding is made available. Recent experience, as corroborated by these figures, indicates that it is not quite the case. The delays in the disbursement of funds -- also a salient feature of previous financial protocols -- even if they have to do with the limited absorptive capacity of the recipient countries, they are also caused by cumbersome procedures on the part of the donor.[69] The end result is that this adversely affects the pace of reforms required in preparation for the full establishment of the free trade area. Aware of this the EU, under its planned Meda II for the period 2000-2004, seemed to have committed itself to a more efficient approach towards the use and disbursement of its financial assistance.

In addition to those delays, there is the level of assistance that remains very modest when compared to that provided either to Spain and Portugal to prepare their accession or to the prospective members in eastern Europe. The Tunisian former Foreign Affairs Minister, Said Ben Mustapha, reportedly said that: 'The funding for Meda I was woefully insufficient to cover national needs and meet the objectives of economic transition and socio-economic equilibrium.'[70] The issue of insufficient assistance may also have been among the reasons that led the EU trade counsellors to consider Morocco unlikely to be ready for the planned free trade area, in what was quoted to be a confidential report tabled officially before the Council of Ministers on 14 September 1999.[71]

Fourth, the liberalisation of trade and the necessary reforms required will also have a social cost.[72] As the process of upgrading local industries along with their environment takes place, more job losses are predicted. For the Maghreb countries one policy option, among others, likely to be contemplated to improve the competitiveness of their industrial companies is the reduction of labour costs. This policy option will not only make opportunities for job creation, at least in the short and medium term, less likely, but will also contribute to the exacerbation of the existing unemployment problem (discussed in Chapter Four). To minimise the effect this might have on their fragile social stability, the countries concerned will have to devise measures to provide assistance and opportunities for possible retraining of the displaced workforce. In this instance, more resources will be required with an attendant additional burden on their economies.

Expected Benefits

Although the establishment of a free trade zone will certainly entail transitional costs for the Maghreb countries, it is also expected that this process is likely to have a positive impact on their economies. The anchoring of these economies into the European economic space, while promising very limited welfare gains in the immediate future, might be beneficial in the long run. Enhancing policy reform, attracting significant foreign direct investment as well as promoting regional integration are among the objectives the countries concerned aspire to achieve through their partnership agreements with the EU.

First, at different periods of time, the Maghreb countries have launched programmes of economic reforms. Yet the progress made until now is not sufficient and hence much needs to be done to deepen and sustain those reforms. For instance, further reforms of their banking system, public sector, tax and business regulations all ought to be coordinated with trade liberalisation. Entering a phase of free trade with the EU, while motivated by securing -- and even the prospects for improving -- access to the European market, also involves the benefits of locking in policy reforms undertaken by the Maghreb countries. Thus liberalising trade *vis-à-vis* a major trading bloc (EU) can have a positive effect for the Moroccan and Tunisian governments by enhancing the credibility of their packages of domestic reforms (Collier and Gunning, 1995, pp. 395-398). Because of the binding nature of the association agreements and the explicit conditionality attached to their implementation (access to EU financial and other forms of support), the countries concerned are left with no other alternative than to continue on this path.

Locking in of reforms at this stage is, indeed, essential. With the EU becoming a policy reforms anchor, any attempt at reversing them would seem rather difficult, not least because of the high cost that might be incurred by the Maghreb countries as a consequence. Not only is there a possibility of EU retaliation for failing to abide by the association agreements, but also there is a risk of losing that element of credibility, something which would prove difficult to regain in the future. All this would, in principle, reinforce the process of reforms by making it sustainable. Thus an irreversible commitment to economic changes, with an enhanced credibility through the linkage to Europe, is likely to foster a favourable investment climate, in particular foreign investment.

Second, as experience with other integration arrangements suggests an important motive behind the formation of free trade areas, particularly for participating countries such as those of the Maghreb, is the expected substantial increase of foreign capital inflow, primarily in the form of direct foreign investment. This almost characteristically brings additional resources -- technology, management know-how and access to export markets -- that are desperately needed (Bergsman and Shen, 1995, p. 6). Therefore, their participation in the new Euro-Mediterranean scheme is meant to provide a positive signal or even a powerful incentive to potential foreign investors. For some time to come, the importance of foreign financing promises to be extremely decisive in smoothing their transitional process. Given their financial constraints, inward investment will provide capital that has the advantage of reducing the reliance on aid -- becoming in any case much more difficult to obtain -- and of not generating new debt. This would obviously relieve the Maghreb countries from the pressures of servicing increasing levels of external borrowings.

Despite the efforts made over recent years to attract foreign direct investment (see chart 5.1), the Maghreb has, compared with other regions, remained one of the less attractive ones. By way of illustration, with a global foreign net direct investment flow to the developing countries estimated at about 180 billion US dollars in 1998, their share -- Morocco and Tunisia -- was 0.54 per cent.[73] With this in mind, these countries are placing high hopes on their partnership deal with Europe. The targeted growth rate of 8 per cent a year expected by Morocco from the agreement is based in large part on attracting foreign direct investment.[74] Equally for Tunisia, it is argued that unless it can

Chart 5.1 Flows of net foreign direct investment to the Maghreb countries, 1990-1998

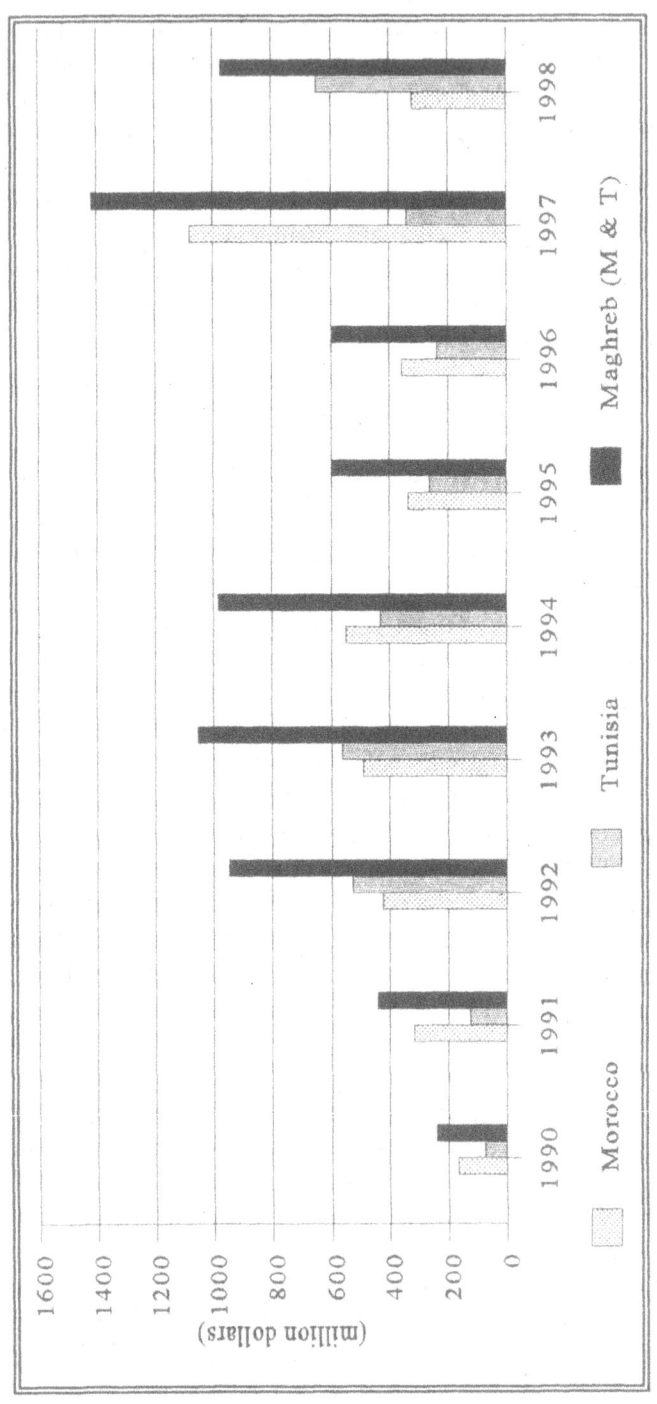

Source: Based on data derived from the IMF, *Balance of Payments Statistics Yearbook 1999*, Part II (Washington, DC: IMF, 1999), p. 64.

attract at least one billion US dollars of new foreign direct investment per year in all sectors, then its free trade deal with the EU will be detrimental to its economy.[75]

However, any tangible achievement in this direction will depend, to an extent, on the progress to be made regarding the issue of the right of establishment as stipulated by the agreements. As already mentioned, this right is defined as an objective and its realisation is to be decided by both sides. In the absence of a target date and a well-defined policy action for its materialisation, the provision for reciprocal free entry and national treatment to their companies in their respective territories is likely to have a restrictive effect to be felt mainly by the Maghreb countries. Moreover, any potential foreign investment may also be determined by the so-called 'hub-spoke' effect. In other words, establishing a free trade area with the EU, while at the same time maintaining high levels of trade barriers among them, may lead foreign investors to locate their business in the 'hub' (the EU) which offers them access to all the 'spokes' (the Maghreb countries) rather than the other way around where they only have access to the domestic market within which they decide to invest. Thus to become a more attractive location for investment, requires greater integration of their respective economies in a larger market.

Last but not least, there is the fact that the present partnership arrangements aim to promote closer intra-regional linkages particularly between the Maghreb countries, and more generally between all the EU's partners in the Mediterranean. In addition to the bilateral free trade areas the Union is in the process of developing with these countries, the latter are also expected to foster intra-regional trade by setting up free trade areas between themselves. The Barcelona Declaration pointed to this issue by stating that: 'Cooperation on a voluntary basis, particularly with a view to developing trade between the partners themselves, is a key factor in promoting the creation of a free trade area.' In the Maghreb, where the institutional framework already exists, this may impart a renewed momentum for the countries concerned to revitalise their moribund grouping, the UMA.[76]

The intra-regional dimension is given a special impetus chiefly through the rules of origin which are to determine the access to the European market. As the agreements provide for cumulation of the rules of origin between the Maghreb countries, this may be instrumental in promoting intra-trade and developing the potential for closer intra-industry links. A provision of the kind was also included in previous trade and cooperation agreements, but seemed not to have had any effect in practice. Perhaps an initial move by these countries would be to fully implement existing agreements on free movement of industrial and agricultural products as a first step towards reviving their free trade area which was originally planned for 1990. The effect of which could lead to an increased intra-Maghreb trade that is still very small in size, accounting on average for a mere 2 per cent share of their total external trade.

It should be noted that since its inception the Euro-Mediterranean process has established regular ministerial meetings, working groups, and other mechanisms of consultation and cooperation between the EU and its partners on areas such as transportation, industry, energy, environment, and private sector investment. Overall, this could contribute to the development of regional integration, especially among the Mediterranean partners of the EU. But it seems that there is no consistency between the importance given to such an issue and the financial means dedicated to it. For example, only 11 per cent of the whole Meda I went to regional projects or activities.[77]

Conclusion

The aim of the EU in launching its partnership initiative is to promote stability and prosperity within its southern neighbours. This latest attempt, to judge by its content, is, indeed, wide-ranging in the coverage of issues. It is ambitious in nature. But like previous policy approaches, trade remains the key dimension on which hinges, to a large extent, the present and the future of the relationship. Moreover, the partnership plan marks a shift from a relatively favoured position, that is from one of a preferential status, towards a relationship based, albeit progressively, on reciprocal treatment. This point is especially central with regard to trade links.

For the Maghreb countries, the association arrangements and most notably their trade component do not represent a significant improvement to their previous status in the relationship. Apart from modest concessions granted to their exports, it seems as if the former regime has been maintained. This suggests not an increased access but rather a security of access against a background of growing liberalisation. Parallel to this is the fact that the gradual establishment of a free trade zone will result, this time, in a unilateral dismantling of their barriers to trade with the EU. Such a liberalisation constitutes a real challenge to their respective economies notably over the transitional period prior to the full implementation of reciprocal free trade. The cost of adjusting to it is significantly higher and would prove difficult to surmount, particularly without a much more assertive role and strong support from the EU. How far the Union is committed to provide this remains, however, to be seen.

Furthermore, the success of the whole operation would require immense efforts from the Maghreb countries at sustaining their domestic reforms, improving their economic environment and transforming their exiguous national markets into an enlarged regional market. These will be a determining factor in easing the transitional phase. For they condition, among other things, the EU's assistance on the one hand, as well as the credibility needed to attract further foreign investments on the other. The benefits the Maghreb countries may reap are not in the immediate future and would therefore depend on the degree of success that will come out of the adjustment process itself.

Notes

1. *Bulletin of the European Communities*, no. 6, 1992, pp. 18-22.
2. *Ibid.*, p. 19.
3. *Ibid.*, p. 20.
4. On the role of Spain, see Richard Gillespie, 'Spanish Protagonismo and the Euro-Med Partnership Initiative', *Mediterranean Politics*, vol. 2, no. 1, Summer 1997, pp. 33-48.
5. Quoted in the *Middle East International*, 27 May 1994, p. 13.
6. *Financial Times*, 20 October 1994.
7. See for instance, *European Report*, no. 2006, 11 January 1995, section V, pp. 5-6, and no. 2009, 21 January 1995, section V, p. 6.
8. This amount is composed of funds from previous financial protocols, that is 1,260 million Ecu, and Meda I programme, that is 3,425 million Ecu.
9. Cited in the *Middle East Economic Digest*, vol. 39, no. 49, 8 December 1995, p. 6.
10. Commission of the European Communities, *The Future of Relations between the Community and the Maghreb*, SEC(92) 401 final, Brussels, 30 April 1992.
11. *Bulletin of the European Union*, no. 6, 1994, p. 13.
12. Commission of the European Communities, *Strengthening the Mediterranean Policy of the European Union: Establishing a Euro-Mediterranean partnership*, COM(94) 427 final, Brussels, 19 October 1994.
13. *Bulletin of the European Union*, supplement no. 2, 1995, p. 29.
14. *Ibid.*, p. 30.
15. Commission of the European Communities, *Strengthening of the Mediterranean Policy of the Union: Proposals for implementing a Euro-Mediterranean partnership*, COM(95) 72 final, Brussels, 8 March 1995.
16. *Bulletin of the European Union*, supplement no. 2, p. 57.
17. On the Barcelona Declaration and the Work Programme, see appendix no. 1.
18. Commission of the European Communities, *From the Single Act to Maastricht - The means to match our ambitions*, COM(92) 2000 final, Brussels, 11 February 1992, p. 17.
19. Quoted in *The Independent*, 8 February 1995.
20. Eurostat, *External and Intra-European Union Trade Statistics Yearbook 1958-1999* (Luxembourg: Office for Official Publications of the European Communities, 1996), pp. 15-17.
21. *Ibid.*

22 Commission of the European Communities, Growth, *Competitiveness, and employment - The challenges and ways forward into the 21st century*, COM(93) 700 final, Brussels, 5 December 1993, p. 23; see also, *The Global Challenge of International Trade: A Market Access Strategy for the European Union*, COM(96) 53 final, Brussels, 14 February 1996, p. 6.
23 An illustration of such interest was the US leading role in the convening of the three Middle East and North Africa economic summits in 1994 in Casablanca (Morocco), 1995 in Amman (Jordan), and a year later in Cairo (Egypt). The American enthusiasm for the creation of a Middle East and North Africa development bank with an initial capital of 5 billion US dollars, was met with a certain reticence on the part of many EU governments. See *Keesing's Record of World Events*, vol. 40, no. 11, 1994, pp. 40305-40306, and vol. 41, no. 10, 1995, p. 40801; and 'Member States against setting up Middle East Bank', *European Report*, no. 2079, 28 October 1995, section V, p. 10.
24 *Official Journal of the European Communities*, vol. 30, no. C 287, 30 October 1995, p. 36.
25 Commission of the European Communities, *Strengthening the Mediterranean Policy of the European Union: Establishing ...*, *op.cit.*, p. 28.
26 Commission of the European Communities, *The Mediterranean Region in 2020 and its Role in the European Energy Network*, MEMO/95/49, Brussels, 27 March 1995, p. 1.
27 Commission of the European Communities, *European Community Gas Supply and Prospects*, COM(95) 478 final, Brussels, 18 October 1995, p. 16.
28 *Ibid.*, p. 7.
29 Commission of the European Communities (Green Paper), *For a European Union energy policy*, COM(94) 659 final, Brussels, 11 January 1995, and (White Paper) *An energy policy for the European Union*, COM(95) 682 final, Brussels, 13 December 1995.
30 *Official Journal of the European Communities*, *op.cit.*, p. 37.
31 Commission of the European Communities, *European Community Gas*, *op.cit.*, p. 43.
32 Commission of the European Communities, *The EU and the Mediterranean countries put their energy act together in Tunis*, IP/95/283, Brussels, 27 March 1995.
33 In this regard, the Euro-Med Energy Forum was set up following the Euro-Mediterranean Conference in Trieste, Italy, in June 1996, and the Action Plan adopted for the period 1998-2000 highlighted security of supply as one of its main objectives.
34 For further discussion of this issue, see for instance, Martin Baldwin-Edwards, 'Immigration and migrants in the Europe of the 1990s', *European access*, no. 3, June 1992, pp. 14-16; Thomas Straubhaar and Klaus F. Zimmermann, 'Towards a European migration policy', *Population Research and Policy Review*, vol. 12, no. 3, 1993, pp. 225-241; Alan Butt Philip, 'European Union Immigration Policy: Phantom, Fantasy of Fact?', *West European Politics*, vol. 17, no. 2, April 1994, pp. 168-191; and David O'Keeffe, 'The Emergence of European Immigration Policy', *European Law Review*, vol. 20, no. 1, 1995, pp. 20-36.
35 On the Edinburgh European Council conclusions, see *Bulletin of the European Communities*, no. 12, 1993, pp. 22-24. As for the Commission Paper, see its Communication, *Immigration and Asylum Policies*, COM(94) 23 final, Brussels, 23 February 1994.
36 *Bulletin of the European Communities*, *op.cit.*, p. 23.
37 Commission of the European Communities, *Immigration ...*, *op.cit.*, pp. 13 and 16.
38 *Financial Times*, 12 December 1991.
39 See interview of French Foreign Affairs Minister, Hervé de Charette, in *Bulletin*

d'Information (published by the French Ministry of Foreign Affairs), no. 229/95, 28 November 1995.
40 *European Report*, no. 2088, 29 November 1995, Section V, p. 9.
41 For a recent account, see George Joffé, 'The Euro-Mediterranean Partnership Initiative: Problems and Prospects', *The Journal of North African Studies*, vol. 3, no. 2, Summer 1998, pp. 247-266.
42 The progress made in bilateral negotiations on the association agreements is given in appendix no. 2.
43 Part of the description that follows in this section is based on the provisions of the association agreements. See Commission of the European Communities, *Proposal for a Decision on the conclusion of a Euro-Mediterranean Agreement establishing an association between the European Communities and their Member States, on the one part, and the Republic of Tunisia, on the other part*, COM(95) 235 final, Brussels, 31 May 1995; and similarly with the Kingdom of Morocco, COM(95) 740 final, Brussels, 20 December 1995.
44 *Maghreb Quarterly Report*, no. 19, September 1995, pp. 72-73.
45 Among these areas, one may cite regional development, industry including industrial standards, investment promotion and protection, agriculture and fisheries, energy, tourism, environment, transport, telecommunications, science and technology, and education and training.
46 Commission of the European Communities, *Commission concludes evaluation of free trade agreements*, Press Releases, IP/95/215, Brussels, 8 March 1995.
47 Commission of the European Communities (DGI), *WTO Aspects of EU Preferential Trade Agreements with Third Countries*, http://europa.eu.int/en/comm/dg01/dg1.htm.
48 *European Report*, no. 2410, 26 May 1999, Section V, p. 3.
49 *European Report*, no. 2163, 5 October 1996, Section V, pp. 2-4.
50 *European Report*, no. 1915, 8 January 1994, Section V, p. 7.
51 This arrangement was extended by one year on the same terms until 31 December 2000; see *Official Journal of the European Communities*, no. L 340, 31 December 1999, pp. 107-108.
52 *Délégation de la Commission des Communautés Européennes au Royaume du Maroc, Lettre d'Information*, no. 115, March 1994, p. 2.
53 *Financial Times*, 28 April 1995.
54 House of Lords/Select Committee on the European Communities, *Eleventh Report* (London: HMSO, 1995), p. 39.
55 It was after lengthy and arduous negotiations that outstanding problems on trade in farm produce were settled between Morocco and the EU. As a result, Morocco managed to obtain some concessions regarding its export quotas and calendars for cut flowers, oranges and tomatoes which initially were opposed by Germany, Italy, Belgium and the Netherlands. For more details, see *European Report*, no. 2084, 15 November 1995, Section V, pp. 13-16.
56 This represents the sum of the figures quoted in the two association agreements.
57 Cited in *Arabies*, no. 114, June 1996, p. 36.
58 The challenge expected from the establishment of a free trade area with the EU was the major point stressed during the author's interview with officials at both the Algerian and Tunisian embassies in Brussels, on 4-5 March 1998.
59 The Tunisian former Minister of Finance stated that 'Our customs receipts, mainly from the EU, are 700 million Tunisian dinars (746 million US dollars) a year, but in the first year of the accord we lose 75 million TD (*80 million US dollars*) of this, a figure which rise progressively'; cited in the *Middle East Economic Digest*, 6 October 1995, p. 25.

60 World Bank, *Tunisia's Global Integration and Sustainable Development - Choices for the 21st Century* (Washington, DC: World Bank, 1996), p. 31; see also European Report, no. 2410, 26 May 1999, Section V, p. 10.
61 *Financial Times*, 28 November 1995.
62 *Arabies*, no. 107, November 1995, p. 34.
63 Cited in House of Lords, *op.cit.*, p. 45.
64 *L'Economiste*, 22 February 1996.
65 European Report, no. 2176, 20 November 1996, Section V, p. 8.
66 *Arabies, op.cit.*, p. 34.
67 Though foreseen for a period of five years, the financial programme started in September 1996 as the necessary legal base was adopted only in July of that year; see Commission of the European Communities, *Annual Report of the Meda Programme 1998*, COM(99) 291 final, Brussels, 22 June 1999, p. 48.
68 Author's calculations based on data from Commission of the European Communities (DGIB), *Exécution de la programmation budgétaire en Méditerranée au 15/01/1999*, http://europa.eu.int/en/comm/dg1b/budget/index.html.
69 See 'The European Union's External Policies and the Mediterranean', speech by Christopher Patten, European Commissioner for External Relations, Cairo 1 April 2000; published in *Euromed Reports*, no. 8, 4 April 2000.
70 Statement made during the third Euro-Mediterranean Conference of foreign ministers, held in Stuttgart on 15-16 April 1999; see European Report, no. 2401, 21 April 1999, Section V, p. 10.
71 European Report, no. 2453, 20 September 1999, Section V, p. 7.
72 For a detailed analysis on the social effect, see Azzam Mahjoub, 'Social Feasibility and Costs of the Free Trade Zone', *The Journal of North African Studies*, vol. 3, no. 2, Summer 1998, pp.121-129.
73 Author's calculations based on data from IMF, *Balance of Payments Statistics Yearbook*, part II (Washington, DC: IMF, 1999), p. 64.
74 *Financial Times*, 19 December 1995.
75 *Arabies, op.cit.*, p. 34; see also *Financial Times*, 28 November 1995.
76 On the issue of reviving regional integration in the Maghreb, see the recent book by F. Oualalou, *Après Barcelona - Le Maghreb est nécessaire* (Casablanca: Editions Toubkal, 1996).
77 European Report, no. 2428, 28 July 1999, Section V, pp. 7-8.

6 Conclusion

Summary

This study set out to investigate the relationship between the EU and the Maghreb countries from its inception to the present time. Its main emphasis has been on the apparent effect the Union's policy, in its different stages and corresponding instruments, has had on the Maghreb countries. The effect in question has been examined in relation to the objectives the policy intended to achieve.

The relationship between the two sides, as this research has revealed, witnessed three major phases. In each period, it has been associated with a new generation of agreements indicating in this context, particularly from a European initiative, a need to upgrade its content. In its original form, it was exclusively confined to trade matters. Then the relationship was significantly improved in a second phase as its scope was expanded to include economic aid and social provisions for the benefit of migrant labour from the Maghreb region. In the third stage, reflecting the present situation at the beginning of 2000, the relationship, while again enlarged to political and socio-cultural dimensions as innovative features, is set to develop, after a transitional period, on *quid pro quo* principles with trade at the centre of the whole process.

After examining the Euro-Maghreb relationship in its successive main phases, one may argue at this stage that its overall outcome was much less than satisfactory, especially with regard to earlier phases. This should not be understood, however, as complete failure. The fact is, if anything, the conclusion of the partnership agreements in 1995 provides evidence of its resilience and an acknowledgment of certain of its beneficial effects particularly to the Maghreb countries, albeit not as expected.

This less than satisfactory result of the EU policy was apparent in those main areas -- that is trade, economic aid and migration -- which, as instruments underlying the Union's intervention, were all considered to be supportive to the Maghreb countries' quest for socio-economic development. In the area of trade, the final value of the preferential treatment granted resided in its prospective effect on the well-being of these countries. In measurable terms, this preferential treatment was expected to promote a well-balanced trade relationship, generate an increase in the exports of the beneficiaries and help boost their trade diversification.

The empirical analysis carried out in this study has demonstrated that the trade relations between the EU and the Maghreb countries featured a decidedly unbalanced pattern. Apart from Algeria, which experienced a trade surplus from the 1980s, it had not been possible for either Morocco or Tunisia to overcome the chronic trade balance deficit that had constantly characterised their trade relations with the Union. A situation of the sort was to a considerable extent linked to their export performance in the European market. If, as indicated, this market had been of crucial importance as a destination for their exports, it was not parallelled by a significant penetration of it. In the aggregate, the increase of exports supposed to be brought about by the preferential trade regime, when measured in terms of share in the market in question, proved to be only minor. Any noticeable market share increase at certain periods of time, was mainly associated with the impact of the energy factor in the exports of the Maghreb countries -- the case of Algeria and to a lesser extent Tunisia. However, although it is a question of a 'dog that did not bark in the night', one must admit that without preferential access their export performance might have been worse, not least because of the CAP and the subsequent southern enlargement of the Union. This held principally true for Morocco and Tunisia.

At the product level, the Maghreb countries did better in the sector of manufacturing than in agricultural produce. The trade preferences appeared to have given an impetus to the industrialisation process as revealed by the changing structure of these countries' exports. An increase in the share of manufactured products in total exports did take place. However, this diversification away from traditional products was mainly confined to a handful of goods, namely textiles and clothing.

By and large, the preferential trade regime had been less effective in relation to the objectives it set out to attain. Besides its inherent limitations through restrictive rules and product exclusion, its value eroded as a result of its generalisation and the multilateral liberalisation. A further obstacle was the contradiction regarding its implementation as illustrated by the imposition of restrictions on the textiles and clothing sector. This represented the start-up process of industrialisation which the preferential regime aimed to support. All that can be said about this preferential access is that, if it maintained some form of trade links and even had some positive effect on the beneficiary countries, it did not give full scope to their export potential where they had a strong comparative advantage.

The second area of EU action was the provision of financial assistance. The amount of aid made available to the Maghreb countries tended to increase from one protocol to another. In practice, this financial transfer proved to have little impact. First, its implementation, which suffered from delays and red tape, affected its effectiveness in certain cases. Second, a major part of this aid had been invested in infrastructure projects that were more likely to be beneficial to the recipient countries. This emphasis on infrastructure meant that the proportion invested in the industrial sector and thus having a direct effect on its productive capacity was relatively low, despite being explicitly encouraged by the agreements. Third, despite increases in the volume of aid, its size met only a small share of Maghreb countries' investment needs, and was a very modest contribution when compared to other sources or even to the Union commitments to other regions such as central and eastern Europe. Finally, apart from France in particular, bilateral aid from other Member States had not increased to any considerable degree as a consequence of the agreements.

The third area covered by the Union policy was the social provisions destined to improve the working and living conditions of Maghreb migrants. In fact, they were never acted upon and therefore remained virtually a dead letter. Increasing domestic employment problems of their own and eventual pressures from Member States had together acted as a constraint on the EU margin for manoeuvre to develop these manpower provisions. With the issue of migrant workers having remained for the most part a matter within the competence of Member States, the situation of these workers was, in certain circumstances, dealt with in a way rather contrary to the stipulations of the agreements. Incentives to encourage their return, discrimination in job opportunities, and lack of a real policy of integration were among the measures, practices and realities that were not well received by the countries of origin, for all these contradicted earlier EU commitments and, as a result, would amount to fewer transfers and an exacerbation of the unemployment situation.

Having summarised the achievements and shortcomings in these sectoral areas, it is worth drawing some general conclusions about EU policy towards the Maghreb region. There is no doubt that the Union had from one phase to another made an effort to improve its policy content and related instruments. Such improvement had certainly enabled the Maghreb countries to derive some benefits/gains even if not as many as hoped for. In some instances aware of the limitations, and especially those inherent in the agreements they concluded with the EU, the deception they expressed afterwards on these grounds was in a way not justified.

Beyond these considerations, however, the EU policy had not been able to create the necessary conditions for the promotion of a stable and reliable environment conducive to development in the Maghreb countries. It was regarded as a source of primary importance to their economic growth, but because of its intrinsic weaknesses compounded by changes that affected its development and execution, it engendered at different periods of time uncertainties as to where these countries had to bear the brunt of all this. If they have hitherto shown no intention of discarding their relationship with the EU, one has to concede that the Community policy had, in its former phases, lost some of its credibility in their eyes.

At the root of this lay a basic inconsistency between its declared main objective of contributing to the socio-economic development of the Maghreb region and the means mobilised to achieve it. The instruments used, trade preferences and financial assistance in particular, had little actual impact. They were not up to the huge task at hand. With their extent and shortcomings, they might have been consistent with a policy that consisted of maintaining the *status quo* at a low price rather than favouring change. Its limited influence was reflected in its essentially 'guided' commercial aspects which, in turn, favoured neither the emergence of a new kind of complementarity of production patterns based on comparative advantages, nor a project of joint development that would have certainly necessitated a much higher level of commitment and involvement from the EU.

The North-South divide in the EU based on different perceptions of interest towards the Maghreb region is what has more likely influenced that degree of involvement of the Union. The policy developed in respect of this North African region, being the outcome of divergent political and economic perspectives, was to prove less responsive to both the needs and capacities of the countries concerned. Lacking a common interest for all EU Member States, the policy had not been able to give the region a high profile in the EU priorities. And it is this missing fundamental element which the European Commission signalled in 1990 (Communication on Redirecting the Community's Mediterranean Policy) by calling for, among other things, the need for a truly global policy in origin towards the Mediterranean area, including the Maghreb region.

The Barcelona process initiated in 1995 along with its partnership agreements apparently seems to have taken certain of the shortcomings of earlier phases of the policy on board. Accordingly, relations with each region are henceforth to be based on its specific needs and capacities. A much more coordinated and global approach from the EU has also been emphasised. The present transitional period, gradually leading to the establishment of a free trade area, is assuredly a test for these commitments.

Implications

There is no doubt that the relationship between the EU and the Maghreb countries is expected to take on, under the present partnership pacts, a different orientation from that of all previous attempts. And it is this phase, with its prominent free market approach to economic development, that the attention ought to focus on. Therefore, the remainder of this section will, in view of the risks it poses to the Maghreb countries, suggest a number of recommendations to smooth the transitional period -- a period which, in turn, is a decisive and determinant phase for the future successful development of the relationship.

First, a fundamental pre-requisite is that a strong and credible assertion of the EU presence in the Maghreb region be forthcoming. The greater emphasis put on the concept of partnership suggests, in principle, a high level of mutual interaction in various spheres between the parties involved. To make it materialise, the EU, as the major actor in the process, needs to show a more active involvement backed by a well-coordinated policy with common and firmly agreed objectives towards the Maghreb countries.

Second, in liberalising their economies, these countries have little choice but to speed up domestic reforms to improve their capacity to adjust to an increasingly competitive environment. The funding package from the EU, both from the budget and the EIB, is insignificant when compared to the high cost resulting from this liberalisation. And if the Union is to ensure a sustained effort to implement the much needed economic reforms and mitigate their social cost, a case exists for granting them additional financial support. Aware of EU budget limits, this could be possible through a much more coordinated action between the Community, its Member States, the EIB and the relevant international financial institutions, and whose ultimate aim should be to target the pressing needs of the region.

Third, under present circumstances the debt problem facing the Maghreb countries, if not properly addressed, is likely to reduce the prospects for success of the proposed partnership. The EU and its Member States, being major holders of this debt (both official and private), could, on the basis of a bold policy, take measures that would help reduce these countries' indebtedness. Among the measures that can be contemplated, one may suggest the possibility of writing off part or all the public or publicly guaranteed debt. Another possibility would be a programme for debt conversion such as debt for development swaps targeting infrastructure, education, health and environment in these countries, and all of which are of course an integral part of the Barcelona process.

Fourth, in view of the acute need for substantial financial resources, the

Maghreb countries may explore the possibility of mobilising migrants' savings. Although remittances have over the years represented a significant source of hard currency for them, their use has for the most part been directed at unproductive spheres (consumption, building of private houses and so forth). A reorientation of these savings towards productive activities now becomes necessary and would require from the countries concerned an effort to set up an incentive framework to motivate interested migrants. This could also be extended to migrant entrepreneurs and businessmen by encouraging them to develop joint ventures with their counterparts in the Maghreb region to serve for instance the local/regional market or niche export markets in the EU or elsewhere. Furthermore by doing so, the prospects for job creation opportunities are raised at a moment when unemployment has reached alarming proportions and become a major challenging issue.

Fifth, whatever the financial support that can be secured, it will not be large enough to meet the inevitable transitional cost in the Maghreb countries. Estimates from the European Commission have suggested a figure of between 50 and 100 billion Euros simply to meet minimal investment needs. Therefore, action needs to be directed at making the region more attractive to foreign direct investment. This has the advantage of not only bringing technology, know-how and generating employment, but also providing capital and thus reducing the scope for external borrowing and indebtedness. In addition to the task for Maghreb countries to improve their business environment, the EU could also do more by taking appropriate measures to assist in this context. This may take the form of an incentive scheme like a jointly-managed Euro-Maghreb agency designed to restore the confidence of private investors, and particularly Europeans, by offering them certain guarantees and assurances against non-commercial risks as well as providing a wide range of services to facilitate their establishment and operation. By way of illustration, foreign direct investment from the EU in the Mediterranean represents only 2 per cent of its global investments in the world according to the conclusions of the Euro-Mediterranean Conference on investment organised in Lisbon in March 2000.

On the European side, one must not lose sight of the fact that certain measures are being undertaken such as the recently established 'Business Centres' in individual Mediterranean partners, encouragement of networking between similar economic entities, co-sponsoring of conferences, management of meetings ('Med Partenariat' and 'Med Interprise') which, overall, are aimed at providing support to private investment.

Sixth, regional cooperation between the Maghreb countries, if revitalised and given impetus, can bring benefits to the region. It is now an established fact that among the conditions that motivate foreign investors to locate in a region is the size of the market. Present exiguous national markets need to be transformed into a large regional market to make it much more attractive. Efforts ought to be directed as a priority at what can be achieved to promote intra-regional cooperation and integration which, if the will to do so exists, will also contribute to lessen tensions and related problems that have until now overshadowed the scope for constructive regional endeavours among these countries.

Seventh, the plan for the progressive free trade area has left aside a key sector -- agriculture. It would be illogical to pretend that the well-being of the Maghreb societies is a priority objective or better served while at the same time excluding their agricultural products. A more active role for the EU in the socio-economic development of these countries, especially over this period of hardship, would normally be consistent with a rather much more liberal European policy towards their exports in the farm sector. The stability sought in the region entails the granting of better market access conditions, not least because of the contribution of this sector to employment as well as the livelihood of a fairly significant part of the population. The negotiations on the agricultural sector planned to start during 2000 are certainly an opportunity for the EU to grant further concessions to the Maghreb countries.

Eighth, certain areas of cooperation have not figured prominently in the Union partnership deals and if given due consideration may have a beneficial effect. Among these is the services sector whose liberalisation remains ill-defined in time. The removal of barriers to cross-border supply of services could prove advantageous to the Maghreb countries and in particular to Tunisia. This country has a greater potential which is reflected not only in the economic importance of the sector in question (accounts for 51 per cent of employment and contributes 50 per cent to GDP) but in the availability of a well-qualified labour force as well.

In short, the aforementioned suggestions are neither exhaustive nor a panacea to the difficulties the Maghreb countries will experience during this transition. These suggestions, formulated much more at a macro-level, have singled out several areas where policy action is deemed necessary. In the final analysis, the hope is that all these would prove helpful in the overall endeavour of both the EU and these countries to manage such a period of change successfully.

Suggestions for Further Investigation

This research has made a modest contribution to the understanding of the development of the Euro-Maghreb relationship. Its merits lie first and foremost in the fact that it has attempted to provide a study with a comprehensive and long-term perspective on this relationship. In other words, all the principal areas covered under the institutionalised relationship have been examined over a longer period of time. This being so, at least two suggestions emerge from this work as for the direction of future studies on this topic.

First, possible future research may find it propitious to use an alternative approach which, while ranging over the long term, would this time be selective. It could involve, for instance, the investigation of selected aspects of the relationship by looking in greater depth into specific areas such as trade, economic aid or even the migration issue.

Second, the present study has dealt with the third phase of the Euro-Maghreb relationship in a provisional and tentative way mainly because it corresponds to the recently concluded agreements that need time to reveal their results. Some of the issues raised by this study at this stage could serve as a starting point for further research on the effectiveness of the present EU free market approach to the economic development of the Maghreb countries, as opposed to development cooperation operated under previous phases.

All in all, these propositions, if taken into consideration in future research, would certainly make a notable contribution to the literature on the Euro-Maghreb relationship.

The ultimate hope is that this study, through its modest contribution to the theme, has offered some new and valuable ideas which may contribute to the improvement of the relationship between both parties and make it much more effective in assisting the socio-economic development of the Maghreb countries and therefore facilitating their anchoring in the European economic space.

Appendix One

Barcelona Euro-Mediterranean Conference (27-28 November 1995) - Declaration and Work Programme
DN: DOC/95/7
Date: 1995-12-04

Barcelona Declaration adopted at the Euro-Mediterranean Conference (27 and 28 November 1995)

The Council of the European Union, represented by its President, Mr Javier SOLANA, Minister for Foreign Affairs of Spain;
The European Commission, represented by Mr Manuel MARIN, Vice-President;
Germany, represented by Mr Klaus KINKEL, Vice-Chancellor and Minister for Foreign Affairs;
Algeria, represented by Mohamed Salah DEMBRI, Minister for Foreign Affairs;
Austria, represented by Mrs Benita FERRERO-WALDNER, State Secretary, Ministry of Foreign Affairs;
Belgium, represented by Mr Erik DERYCKE, Minister for Foreign Affairs;
Cyprus, represented by Mr Alecos MICHAELIDES, Minister for Foreign Affairs;
Denmark, represented by Mr Ole Loensmann POULSEN, State Secretary, Ministry of Foreign Affairs;
Egypt, represented by Mr Amr MOUSSA, Minister for Foreign Affairs;
Spain, represented by Mr Carlos WESTTENDORP, State Secretary for Relations with the European Community;
Finland, represented by Mrs Tarja HALONEN, Minister for Foreign Affairs;
France, represented by Mr Hervé de CHARETTE, Minister for Foreign Affairs;
Greece, represented by Mr Károlos PAPOULIAS, Minister for Foreign Affairs;
Ireland, represented by Mr Dick SPRING, Deputy Prime Minister and Minister for Foreign Affairs;
Israel, represented by Mr Ehud BARAK, Minister for Foreign Affairs;
Italy, represented by Mrs Susanna AGNELLI, Minister for Foreign Affairs;
Jordan, represented by Mr Abdel-Karim KABARITI, Minister for Foreign Affairs;
Lebanon, represented by Mr Fares BOUEZ, Minister for Foreign Affairs;

Luxembourg, represented by Mr Jacques F. POOS, Deputy Prime Minister and Minister for Foreign Affairs;
Malta, represented by Prof. Guido DE MARCO, Deputy Prime Minister and Minister for Foreign Affairs;
Morocco, represented by Mr Abdellatif FILALI, Prime Minister and Minister for Foreign Affairs;
the Netherlands, represented by Mr Hans van MIERLO, Deputy Prime Minister and Minister for Foreign Affairs;
Portugal, represented by Mr Jaime GAMA, Minister for Foreign Affairs;
the United Kingdom, represented by Mr Malcolm RIFKIND QC MP, Secretary of State for Foreign and Commonwealth Affairs;
Syria, represented by Mr Farouk AL-SHARAA, Minister for Foreign Affairs;
Sweden, represented by Mrs Lena HJELM-WALLEN, Minister for Foreign Affairs;
Tunisia, represented by Mr Habib Ben YAHIA, Minister for Foreign Affairs;
Turkey, represented by Mr Deniz BAYKAL, Deputy Prime Minister and Minister for Foreign Affairs;
the Palestinian Authority, represented by Mr Yassir ARAFAT, President of the Palestinian Authority;
taking part in the Euro-Mediterranean Conference in Barcelona:

- stressing the strategic importance of the Mediterranean and moved by the will to give their future relations a new dimension, based on comprehensive cooperation and solidarity, in keeping with the privileged nature of the links forged by neighbourhood and history;
- aware that the new political, economic and social issues on both sides of the Mediterranean constitute common challenges calling for a coordinated overall response;
- resolved to establish to that end a multilateral and lasting framework of relations based on a spirit of partnership, with due regard for the characteristics, values and distinguishing features peculiar to each of the participants;
- regarding this multilateral framework as the counterpart to a strengthening of bilateral relations which it is important to safeguard, while laying stress on their specific nature;
- stressing that this Euro-Mediterranean initiative is not intended to replace the other activities and initiatives undertaken in the interests of the peace, stability and development of the region, but that it will contribute to their success. The participants support the realisation of a just, comprehensive

and lasting peace settlement in the Middle East based on the relevant United Nations Security Council resolutions and principles mentioned in the letter of invitation to the Madrid Middle East Peace Conference, including the principle land for peace, with all that this implies;
- convinced that the general objective of turning the Mediterranean basin into an area of dialogue, exchange and cooperation guaranteeing peace, stability and prosperity requires a strengthening of democracy and respect for human rights, sustainable and balanced economic and social development, measures to combat poverty and promotion of greater understanding between cultures, which are all essential aspects of partnership,

hereby agree to establish a comprehensive partnership among the participants -- the Euro-Mediterranean Partnership -- through strengthened political dialogue on a regular basis, the development of economic and financial cooperation and greater emphasis on the social and human dimension; these being the three aspects of the Euro-Mediterranean Partnership.

Political and Security Partnership:
Establishing a Common Area of Peace and Stability

The participants express their conviction that the peace, stability and security of the Mediterranean region are a common asset which they pledge to promote and strengthen by all means at their disposal. To this end they agree to conduct a strengthened political dialogue at regular intervals, based on observance of essential principles of international law, and reaffirm a number of common objectives in matters of internal and external stability.

In this spirit they undertake in the following declaration of principles to:

- act in accordance with the United Nations Charter and the Universal Declaration of Human Rights, as well as other obligations under international law, in particular those arising out of regional and international instruments to which they are party;
- develop the rule of law and democracy in their political systems, while recognising in this framework the right of each of them to choose and freely develop its own political, socio-cultural, economic and judicial system;
- respect human rights and fundamental freedoms and guarantee the effective legitimate exercise of such rights and freedoms, including freedom of expression, freedom of association for peaceful purposes and freedom of

thought, conscience and religion, both individually and together with other members of the same group, without any discrimination on grounds of race, nationality, language, religion or sex;
- give favourable consideration, through dialogue between the parties, to exchanges of information on matters relating to human rights, fundamental freedoms, racism and xenophobia;
- respect and ensure respect for diversity and pluralism in their societies, promote tolerance between different groups in society and combat manifestations of intolerance, racism and xenophobia. The participants stress the importance of proper education in the matter of human rights and fundamental freedoms;
- respect their sovereign equality and all rights inherent in their sovereignty, and fulfil in good faith the obligations they have assumed under international law;
- respect the equal rights of peoples and their right to self-determination, acting at all times in conformity with the purposes and principles of the Charter of the United Nations and with the relevant norms of international law, including those relating to territorial integrity of States, as reflected in agreements between relevant parties;
- refrain, in accordance with the rules of international law, from any direct or indirect intervention in the internal affairs of another partner;
- respect the territorial integrity and unity of each of the other partners;
- settle their disputes by peaceful means, call upon all participants to renounce recourse to the threat or use of force against the territorial integrity of another participant, including the acquisition of territory by force, and reaffirm the right to fully exercise sovereignty by legitimate means in accordance with the UN Charter and international law;
- strengthen their cooperation in preventing and combatting terrorism, in particular by ratifying and applying the international instruments they have signed, by acceding to such instruments and by taking any other appropriate measure;
- fight together against the expansion and diversification of organised crime and combat the drugs problem in all its aspects;
- promote regional security by acting, inter-alia, in favour of nuclear, chemical and biological non-proliferation through adherence to and compliance with a combination of international and regional non-proliferation regimes, and arms control and disarmament agreements such as NPT, CWC, BWC, CTBT and/or regional arrangements such as weapons free zones including their verification regimes, as well as by fulfilling in good faith their

commitments under arms control, disarmament and non-proliferation conventions.

The parties shall pursue a mutually and effectively verifiable Middle East Zone free of nuclear weapons of mass destruction, nuclear, chemical and biological, and their delivery systems.

- Furthermore the parties will consider practical steps to prevent the proliferation of nuclear, chemical and biological weapons as well as excessive accumulation of conventional arms.
- Refrain from developing military capacity beyond their legitimate defence requirements, at the same time reaffirming their resolve to achieve the same degree of security and mutual confidence with the lowest possible levels of troops and weaponry and adherence to CCW.
- Promote conditions likely to develop good-neighbourly relations among themselves and support processes aimed at stability, security, prosperity and regional and sub-regional cooperation.
- Consider any confidence and security-building measures that could be taken between the parties with a view to the creation of an 'area of peace and stability in the Mediterranean', including the long term possibility of establishing a Euro-Mediterranean pact to that end.

Economic and Financial Partnership:
Creating an Area of Shared Prosperity

The participants emphasise the importance they attach to sustainable and balanced economic and social development with a view to achieving their objective of creating an area of shared prosperity.

The partners acknowledge the difficulties that the question of debt can create for the economic development of the countries of the Mediterranean region. They agree, in view of the importance of their relations, to continue the dialogue in order to achieve progress in the competent fora.

Noting that the partners have to take up common challenges, albeit to varying degrees, the participants set themselves the following long term objectives:

- acceleration of the pace of sustainable socio-economic development;
- improvement of the living conditions of their populations, increase in the

employment level and reduction in the development gap in the Euro-Mediterranean region;
- encouragement of regional cooperation and integration.

With a view to achieving these objectives, the participants agree to establish an economic and financial partnership which, taking into account the different degrees of development, will be based on:

- the progressive establishment of a free trade area;
- the implementation of appropriate economic cooperation and concerted action in the relevant areas;
- a substantial increase in the European Union's financial assistance to its partners.

Free Trade Area

The free trade area will be established through the new Euro-Mediterranean Agreements and free trade agreements between partners of the European Union. The parties have set 2010 as the target date for the gradual establishment of this area which will cover most trade with due observance of the obligations resulting from WTO.

With a view to developing gradual free trade in this area: tariff and non-tariff barriers to trade in manufactured products will be progressively eliminated in accordance with timetables to be negotiated between the partners; taking as a starting point traditional trade flows, and as far as the various agricultural policies allow and with due respect to the results achieved within the GATT negotiations, trade in agricultural products will be progressively liberalised through reciprocal preferential access among the parties; trade in services including right of establishment will be progressively liberalised having due regard to the GATS agreement.

The participants decide to facilitate the progressive establishment of this free trade area through:

- the adoption of suitable measures as regard rules of origin, certification, protection of intellectual and industrial property rights and competition;
- the pursuit and the development of policies based on the principles of market economy and the integration of their economies taking into account their respective needs and levels of development;
- the adjustment and modernisation of economic and social structures, giving

priority to the promotion and development of the private sector, to the upgrading of the productive sector and to the establishment of an appropriate institutional and regulatory framework for a market economy. They will likewise endeavour to mitigate the negative social consequences which may result from this adjustment, by promoting programmes for the benefit of the neediest populations;
- the promotion of mechanisms to foster transfers of technology.

Economic Cooperation and Concerted Action

Cooperation will be developed in particular in the areas listed below and in this respect the participants:

- acknowledge that economic development must be supported both by internal savings, the basis of investment, and by direct foreign investment. They stress the importance of creating an environment conducive to investment, in particular by the progressive elimination of obstacles to such investment which could lead to the transfer of technology and increase production and exports;
- affirm that regional cooperation on a voluntary basis, particularly with a view to developing trade between the partners themselves, is a key factor in promoting the creation of a free trade area;
- encourage enterprises to enter into agreements with each other and undertake to promote such cooperation and industrial modernisation by providing a favourable environment and regulatory framework. They consider it necessary to adopt and to implement a technical support programme for SMEs;
- emphasise their interdependence with regard to the environment, which necessitates a regional approach and increased cooperation, as well as better coordination of existing multilateral programmes, while confirming their attachment to the Barcelona Convention and the Mediterranean Action Plan. They recognise the importance of reconciling economic development with environmental protection, of integrating environmental concerns into the relevant aspects of economic policy and of mitigating the negative environmental consequences which may result. They undertake to establish a short and medium-term priority action programme, including in connection with combatting desertification, and to concentrate appropriate technical and financial support on those actions;
- recognise the key role of women in development and undertake to promote

their active participation in economic and social life and in the creation of employment;
- stress the importance of the conservation and rational management of fish stocks and of the improvement of cooperation on research into stocks, including aquaculture, and undertake to facilitate scientific training and research and to envisage creating joint instruments;
- acknowledge the pivotal role of the energy sector in the economic Euro-Mediterranean Partnership and decide to strengthen cooperation and intensify dialogue in the field of energy policies. They also decide to create the appropriate framework conditions for investments and the activities of energy companies, cooperating in creating the conditions enabling such companies to extend energy networks and promote link-ups;
- recognise that water supply together with suitable management and development of resources are priority issues for all Mediterranean partners and that cooperation should be developed in these areas;
- agree to cooperate in modernising and restructuring agriculture and in promoting integrated rural development. This cooperation will focus in particular on technical assistance and training, on support for policies implemented by the partners to diversify production, on the reduction of food dependency and on the promotion of environment-friendly agriculture. They also agree to cooperate in the eradication of illicit crops and the development of any regions affected.

The participants also agree to cooperate in other areas and, to that effect:

- stress the importance of developing and improving infrastructures, including through the establishment of an efficient transport system, the development of information technologies and the modernisation of telecommunications. They agree to draw up a programme of priorities for that purpose;
- undertake to encourage cooperation between local authorities and in support of regional planning;
- recognising that science and technology have a significant influence on socio-economic development, agree to strengthen scientific research capacity and development, contribute to the training of scientific and technical staff and promote participation in joint research projects based on the creation of scientific networks;
- agree to promote cooperation on statistics in order to harmonise methods and exchange data.

Financial Cooperation

The participants consider that the creation of a free trade area and the success of the Euro-Mediterranean Partnership require a substantial increase in financial assistance, which must above all encourage sustainable indigenous development and the mobilisation of economic operators. They note in this connection that:

- the Cannes European Council agreed to set aside ECU 4,685 million for this financial assistance in the form of available Community budget funds for the period 1995-1999. This will be supplemented by EIB assistance in the form of increased loans and the bilateral financial contribution from Member States;
- effective financial cooperation managed in the framework of a multiannual programme taking into account the special characteristics of each of the partners is necessary;
- sound macro-economic management is of fundamental importance in ensuring the success of the partnership. To this end they agree to promote dialogue on their respective economic policies and on the method of optimising financial cooperation.

Partnership in Social, Cultural and Human Affairs:
Developing Human Resources, Promoting Understanding between Cultures and Exchanges between Civil Societies

The participants recognise that the traditions of culture and civilisation throughout the Mediterranean region, dialogue between these cultures and exchanges at human, scientific and technological level are an essential factor in bringing their peoples closer, promoting understanding between them and improving their perception of each other.

In this spirit, the participants agree to establish a partnership in social, cultural and human affairs. To this end:

- they reaffirm that dialogue and respect between cultures and religions are a necessary pre-condition for bringing the peoples closer. In this connection they stress the importance of the role the mass media can play in the reciprocal recognition and understanding of cultures as a source of mutual enrichment;
- they stress the essential nature of the development of human resources, both

as regards the education and training of young people in particular and in the area of culture. They express their intent to promote cultural exchanges and knowledge of other languages, respecting the cultural identity of each partner, and to implement a lasting policy of educational and cultural programmes; in this context, the partners undertake to adopt measures to facilitate human exchanges, in particular by improving administrative procedures;
- they underline the importance of the health sector for sustainable development and express their intention of promoting the effective participation of the community in operations to improve health and well-being;
- they recognise the importance of social development which, in their view, must go hand in hand with any economic development. They attach particular importance to the respect for fundamental social rights, including the right to development;
- they recognise the essential contribution civil society can make in the process of development of the Euro-Mediterranean Partnership and as an essential factor for greater understanding and closeness between peoples;
- they accordingly agree to strengthen and/or introduce the necessary instruments of decentralised cooperation to encourage exchanges between those active in development within the framework of national laws: leaders of political and civil society, the cultural and religious world, universities, the research community, the media, organisations, the trade unions and public and private enterprises;
- on this basis, they recognise the importance of encouraging contacts and exchanges between young people in the context of programmes for decentralised cooperation;
- they will encourage actions of support for democratic institutions and for the strengthening of the rule of law and civil society;
- they recognise that current population trends represent a priority challenge which must be counterbalanced by appropriate policies to accelerate economic take-off;
- they acknowledge the importance of the role played by migration in their relationships. They agree to strengthen their cooperation to reduce migratory pressures, among other things through vocational training programmes and programmes of assistance for job creation. They undertake to guarantee protection of all the rights recognised under existing legislation of migrants legally resident in their respective territories;
- in the area of illegal immigration they decide to establish closer cooperation.

In this context, the partners, aware of their responsibility for readmission, agree to adopt the relevant provisions and measures, by means of bilateral agreements or arrangements, in order to readmit their nationals who are in an illegal situation. To that end, the Member States of the European Union take citizens to mean nationals of the Member States, as defined for Community purposes;
- they agree to strengthen cooperation by means of various measures to prevent terrorism and fight it more effectively together;
- by the same token they consider it necessary to fight jointly and effectively against drug trafficking, international crime and corruption;
- they underline the importance of waging a determined campaign against racism, xenophobia and intolerance and agree to cooperate to that end.

Follow-up to the Conference

The participants:

- considering that the Barcelona Conference provides the basis for a process, which is open and should develop;
- reaffirming their will to establish a partnership based on the principles and objectives defined in this Declaration;
- resolved to give practical expression to this Euro-Mediterranean Partnership;
- convinced that, in order to achieve this objective, it is necessary to continue the comprehensive dialogue thus initiated and to carry out a series of specific actions;

hereby adopt the attached work programme:

The Ministers for Foreign Affairs will meet periodically in order to monitor the application of this Declaration and define actions enabling the objectives of the partnership to be achieved.

The various activities will be followed by ad hoc thematic meetings of ministers, senior officials and experts, exchanges of experience and information, contacts between those active in civil society and by any other appropriate means.
    Contacts between parliamentarians, regional authorities, local authorities and the social partners will be encouraged.

A 'Euro-Mediterranean Committee for the Barcelona process' at senior-official level, consisting of the European Union Troika and one representative of each Mediterranean partner, will hold regular meetings to prepare the meeting of the Ministers for Foreign Affairs, take stock of and evaluate the follow-up to the Barcelona process and all its components and update the work programme.

Appropriate preparatory and follow-up work for the meetings resulting from the Barcelona work programme and from the conclusions of the 'Euro-Mediterranean Committee for the Barcelona process' will be undertaken by the Commission departments.

The next meeting of the Ministers for foreign Affairs will be held in the first semester of 1997 in one of the twelve Mediterranean partners of the European Union, to be determined through further consultations.

Work programme

Introduction

The aim of this programme is to implement the objectives of the Barcelona Declaration, and to respect its principles, through regional and multilateral actions. It is complementary both to the bilateral cooperation, implemented in particular under the agreements between the EU and its Mediterranean partners, and to the cooperation already existing in other multilateral fora.

The preparation and the follow-up to the various actions will be implemented in accordance with the principles and mechanisms set out in the Barcelona Declaration.

The priority actions for further cooperation are listed below. This does not exclude Euro-Mediterranean cooperation being extended to other actions if the partners so agree.

The actions may apply to States, their local and regional authorities as well as actors of their civil society.

With the agreement of the participants, other countries or organisations may be involved in the actions contained in the Work programme. The implementation must take place in a flexible and transparent way.

With the agreement of the participants, future Euro-Mediterranean cooperation will take account, as appropriate, of the opinions and recommendations resulting from the relevant discussions held at various levels in the region.

The implementation of the programme should start as soon as practical after the Barcelona Conference. It will be reviewed at the next Euro-Mediterranean Conference on the basis of a report to be prepared by the European Commission departments, particularly on the basis of reports from the various meetings and Groups mentioned below, and approved by the 'Euro-Mediterranean Committee for the Barcelona process' set up by the Barcelona Declaration.

**Political and Security Partnership:
Establishing a Common Area of Peace and Stability**

With a view to contributing to the objective of progressively creating a zone of peace, stability and sccurity in the Mediterranean, senior officials will meet periodically, starting within the first quarter of 1996. They will:

- conduct a political dialogue to examine the most appropriate means and methods of implementing the principles adopted by the Barcelona Declaration, and
- submit practical proposals in due time for the next Euro-Mediterranean Meeting of Foreign Ministers.

Foreign policy institutes in the Euro-Mediterranean region will be encouraged to establish a network for more intensive cooperation which could become operational as of 1996.

Economic and Financial Partnership: Building a Zone of Shared Prosperity

Meetings will take place periodically at the level of Ministers, officials or experts, as appropriate, to promote cooperation in the following areas. These meetings may be supplemented, where appropriate, by conferences or seminars involving the private sector likewise.

The establishment of a free trade area in accordance with the principles contained in the Barcelona Declaration is an essential element of the Euro-Mediterranean Partnership.

Cooperation will focus on practical measures to facilitate the establishment of free trade as well as its consequences, including:

- harmonising rules and procedures in the customs field, with a view in particular to the progressive introduction of cumulation of origin; in the meantime, favourable consideration will be given, where appropriate, to finding ad hoc solutions in particular cases;
- harmonisation of standards, including meetings arranged by the European Standards Organisations;
- elimination of unwarranted technical barriers to trade in agricultural products and adoption of relevant measures related to plan-health and veterinary rules as well as other legislation on foodstuffs;
- cooperation among statistics organisations with a view to providing reliable data on a harmonised basis;
- possibilities for regional and sub-regional cooperation (without prejudice to initiatives taken in other existing fora).

Investment

The object of cooperation will be to help create a climate favourable to the removal of obstacles to investment, by giving greater thought to the definition of such obstacles and to means, including in the banking sector, of promoting such investment.

Industry

Industrial modernisation and increased competitiveness will be key factors for the success of the Euro-Mediterranean partnership. In this context, the private sector will play a more important role in the economic development of the region and the creation of employment. Cooperation will focus on:

- the adaptation of the industrial fabric to the changing international environment, in particular to the emergence of the information society;
- the framework for and the preparation of the modernisation and restructuring of existing enterprises, especially in the public sector, including privatisation;
- the use of international or European standards and the upgrading of conformity testing, certification, accreditation and quality standards.

Particular attention will be paid to means of encouraging cooperation among SMEs and creating the conditions for their development, including the possibility of organising workshops, taking account of experience acquired under MED-INVEST and inside the European Union.

Agriculture

While pointing out that such matters are covered under bilateral relations in the main, cooperation in this area will focus on:

- support for policies implemented by them to diversify production;
- reduction of food dependency;
- promotion of environment-friendly agriculture;
- closer relations between businesses, groups and organisations representing trade and professions in the partner States on a voluntary basis;
- support for privatisation;
- technical assistance and training;

- harmonisation of plan-health and veterinary standards;
- integrated rural development, including improvement of basic services and development of associated economic activities;
- cooperation among rural regions, exchange of experience and know-how concerning rural development;
- development of regions affected by the eradication of illicit crops.

Transport

Efficient interoperable transport links between the EU and its Mediterranean partners, and among the partners themselves, as well as free access to the market for services in international maritime transport, are essential to the development of trade patterns and the smooth operation of the Euro-Mediterranean Partnership.

The Transport Ministers of Western Mediterranean countries met twice in 1995 and, following the Regional Conference for the Development of Maritime Transport in the Mediterranean, the Mediterranean Waterborne Transport Working Group adopted a multiannual programme.

Cooperation will focus on:

- development of an efficient Trans-Mediterranean multimodal combined sea and air transport system, through the improvement and modernisation of ports and airports, the suppression of unwarranted restrictions, the simplification of procedures, the improvement of maritime and air safety, the harmonisation of environmental standards at a high level including more efficient monitoring of maritime pollution, and the development of harmonised traffic management systems;
- development of east-west land links on the southern and eastern shores of the Mediterranean, and
- connection of Mediterranean transport networks to the Trans-European Network in order to ensure their interoperability.

Energy

A high-level Conference was held in Tunisia in 1995 with a follow-up meeting in Athens and an Energy Conference in Madrid on 20 November 1995.

With a view to creating appropriate conditions for investment in and activities by energy companies, future cooperation will focus, inter alia, on:

- fostering the association of Mediterranean countries with the Treaty on the European Energy Charter;
- energy planning;
- encouraging producer-consumer dialogue;
- oil and gas exploration, refining, transportation, distribution, and regional and trans-regional trade;
- coal production and handling;
- generation and transmission of power and interconnection and development of networks;
- energy efficiency;
- new and renewable sources of energy;
- energy-related environmental issues;
- development of joint research programmes;
- training and information activities in the energy sector.

Telecommunications and Information Technology

With a view to developing a modern, efficient telecommunications network, cooperation will focus on:

- information and telecommunications infrastructures (minimum regulatory framework, standards, conformity testing, network interoperability, etc.);
- regional infrastructures including links with European networks;
- access to services, and
- new services in priority fields of application.

Intensification of Euro-Mediterranean exchanges and access to the nascent information society will be facilitated by more efficient information and communications infrastructures.

A regional conference is planned for 1996 with the aim of paving the way for pilot projects to show the concrete benefit of the information society.

Regional Planning

Cooperation will focus on:

- defining a regional planning strategy for the Euro-Mediterranean area commensurate with the countries' requirements and special features;
- promoting cross-border cooperation in areas of mutual interest.

Tourism

The Ministers for Tourism, meeting in Casablanca, adopted the Mediterranean Tourism Charter in 1995. The cooperation actions to be initiated will relate in particular to information, promotion and training.

Environment

Cooperation will focus on:

- assessing environmental problems in the Mediterranean region and defining, where appropriate, the initiatives to be taken;
- making proposals to establish and subsequently update a short and medium-term priority environmental action programme for intervention coordinated by the European Commission and supplemented by long term actions; it should include among the main areas for action, the following: integrated management of water, soil and coastal areas; management of waste; preventing and combatting air pollution and pollution in the Mediterranean sea; natural heritage, landscapes and site conservation and management; Mediterranean forest protection, conservation and restoration, in particular through the prevention and control of erosion, soil degradation, forest fires and combatting desertification; transfer of Community experience in financing techniques, legislation and environmental monitoring; integration of environmental concerns in all policies;
- setting up a regular dialogue to monitor the implementation of the action programme;
- reinforcing regional and sub-regional cooperation and strengthening coordination with the Mediterranean Action Plan;
- stimulating coordination of investments from various sources, and implementation of relevant international conventions;
- promoting the adoption and implementation of legislation and regulatory measures when required, especially preventive measures and appropriate high standards.

Science and Technology

Cooperation will focus on:

- promoting research and development and tackling the problem of the

widening gap in scientific achievement, taking account of the principle of mutual advantage;
- stepping up exchanges of experience in the scientific sectors and policies which might best enable the Mediterranean partners to reduce the gap between them and their European neighbours and to promote the transfer of technology;
- helping train scientific and technical staff by increasing participation in joint research projects.

Following the Ministerial meeting at Sophia Antipolis in March 1995, a Monitoring Committee was set up; this Committee will meet for the first time immediately after Barcelona conference. It will focus on making recommendations for the joint implementation of the policy priorities agreed at Ministerial level.

Water

The Mediterranean Water Charter was adopted in Rome in 1992.
Water is a priority issue for all the Mediterranean partners and will gain in importance as water scarcity becomes more pressing. The purpose of cooperation in this area will be as follows:

- to take stock of the situation taking into account current and future needs;
- to identify ways of reinforcing regional cooperation;
- to make proposals for rationalising the planning and management of water resources, where appropriate on a joint basis;
- to contribute towards the creation of new sources of water.

Fisheries

In view of the importance of conservation and rational management of Mediterranean fish stocks, cooperation in the framework of the General Fisheries Council for the Mediterranean will be reinforced.
Following the Ministerial Fisheries Conference held in Heraklion in 1994, appropriate follow-up action will be taken in the legal sphere through meetings to take place in 1996.
Cooperation will be improved on research into fish stocks, including aquaculture, as well as into training and scientific research.

Social, Cultural and Human Partnership:
Developing Human Resources, Promoting Understanding between Cultures and Exchanges between Civil Societies

Development of Human Resources

The Euro-Mediterranean partnership must contribute to enhancing educational levels throughout the region, whilst laying special emphasis on the Mediterranean partners. To this end, a regular dialogue on educational policies will take place, initially focusing on vocational training, technology in education, the universities and other higher education establishments and research. In this context as well as in other areas, particular attention will be paid to the role of women. The Euro-Arab Business School in Granada and the European Foundation in Turin will also contribute to this cooperation.

A meeting of representatives of the vocational training sector (policy makers, academics, trainers, etc) will be organised with the aim of sharing modern management approaches.

A meeting will be held of representatives of universities and higher education establishments. The European Commission will strengthen its ongoing MED-Campus programme.

A meeting will also be called on the subject of technology in education.

Municipalities and Regions

Municipalities and regional authorities need to be closely involved in the operation of the Euro-Mediterranean Partnership. City and regional representatives will be encouraged to meet each year to take stock of their common challenges and exchange experiences. This will be organised by the European Commission and will take account of previous experience.

Dialogue between Cultures and Civilisations

Given the importance of improving mutual understanding by promoting cultural exchanges and knowledge of languages, officials and experts will meet in order to make concrete proposals for action, inter alia, in the following fields: cultural and creative heritage, cultural and artistic events, co-productions (theatre and cinema), translations and other means of cultural dissemination, training.

Greater understanding among the major religions present in the Euro-Mediterranean region will facilitate greater mutual tolerance and cooperation.

Support will be given to periodic meetings of representatives of religions and religious institutions as well as theologians, academics and others concerned, with the aim of breaking down prejudice, ignorance and fanaticism and fostering cooperation at grass-roots level. The conference held in Stockholm (15-17/06/1995) and Toledo (4-7/11/1995) may serve as examples in this context.

Media

Close interaction between the media will work in favour of better cultural understanding. The European Union will actively promote such interaction, in particular through the ongoing MED-Media programme. An annual meeting of representatives of the media will be organised in this context.

Youth

Youth exchanges should be the means to prepare future generations for a closer cooperation between the Euro-Mediterranean partners. A Euro-Mediterranean youth exchange programme should therefore be established based on experience acquired in Europe and taking account of the partners' needs; this programme should take account of the importance of vocational training, particularly for those without qualifications, and of the training of organisers and social workers in the youth field. The European Commission will make the necessary proposals before the next meeting of Euro-Mediterranean Foreign Ministers.

Exchanges between Civil Societies

Senior officials will meet periodically to discuss measures likely to facilitate human exchanges resulting from the Euro-Mediterranean Partnership, especially those involving officials, scientists, academics, businessmen, students and sportsmen, including the improvement and simplification of administrative obstacles might exist.

Social Development

The Euro-Mediterranean partnership must contribute to improving the living and working conditions and increasing the employment level of the population in the Mediterranean partner States, in particular of women and the neediest strata of the population. In this context, the partners attach particular importance to the respect and promotion of basic social rights. To that end, actors in social policies will meet periodically at the appropriate level.

Health

The partners agree to concentrate cooperation in this area on:

- action on raising awareness, information and prevention;
- development of public health services, in particular health care, primary health centres, maternal and child health care services, family planning, epidemiological supervision systems and measures to control communicable diseases;
- training of health and health-administration personnel;
- medical cooperation in the event of natural disasters.

Migration

Given the importance of the issue of migration for Euro-Mediterranean relations, meetings will be encouraged in order to make proposals concerning migration flows and pressures. These meetings will take account of experience acquired, inter alia, under the MED-Migration programme, particularly as regards improving the living conditions of migrants legally established in the Union.

Terrorism, Drug Trafficking, Organised Crime

Fighting terrorism will have to be a priority for all the parties. To that end, officials will meet periodically with the aim of strengthening cooperation among police, judicial and other authorities. In this context, consideration will be given, in particular, to stepping up exchanges of information and improving extradition procedures.

Officials will meet periodically to discuss measures which can be taken to improve cooperation among police, judicial, customs, administrative and other authorities in order to combat, in particular, drug trafficking and organised crime, including smuggling.

All these meetings will be organised with due regard for the need for a differentiated approach that takes into account the diversity of the situation in each country.

Illegal Immigration

Officials will meet periodically to discuss practical measures which can be taken to improve cooperation among police, judicial, customs, administrative and other authorities in order to combat illegal immigration.

These meetings will be organised with due regard for the need for a differentiated approach that takes into account the diversity of the situation in each country.

Institutional Contacts

Euro-Parliamentary Dialogue

An Inter-Parliamentary Conference on Security and Cooperation in the Mediterranean was held in Valletta from 1 to 4 November 1995. The European Parliament is invited to take the initiative with other parliaments concerning the future Euro-Mediterranean Parliamentary Dialogue, which could enable the elected representatives of the partners to exchange ideas on a wide range of issues.

Other Institutional Contacts

Regular contacts among other European organs, in particular the Economic and Social Committee of the European Community, and their Mediterranean counterparts, would contribute to a better understanding of the major issues relevant in the Euro-Mediterranean Partnership.

To this end, the Economic and Social Committee is invited to take the initiative in establishing links with its Mediterranean counterparts and equivalent bodies. In this context, a Euro-Mediterranean meeting of Economic and Social Committees and equivalent bodies will take place in Madrid on 12 and 13 December.

Appendix Two

Progress of Negotiations on Euro-Mediterranean Association Agreements

Partner	Conclusion of Negotiations	Signature of Agreement	Entry into Force
Tunisia	June 1995	July 1995	March 1998
Israel	September 1995	November 1995	June 2000
Morocco	November 1995	February 1996	March 2000
Palestinian Authority	December 1996	February 1997	July 1997
Jordan	April 1997	November 1997	--
Egypt	Negotiations concluded in June 1999	--	--
Lebanon	Negotiations in progress	--	--
Algeria	Negotiations in progress	--	--
Syria	Negotiations in progress	--	--

Source: Commission of the European Communities, External Relations DG (Unit F.1), March 2000.

Bibliography

Abdoun, R. (1989), 'Crise économique et satisfaction des besoins sociaux', *Revue du CREAD*, no. 17, January-March.
Africa Research Bulletin (1993), Political, Social and Cultural Series, vol. 30, no. 1.
Aghrout, A. (1990), *South-South Cooperation with Special Reference to the Maghreb Countries*, MPhil thesis, University of Salford.
Aghrout, A. (1992), 'Africa's Experiences with Regional Cooperation and Integration: Assessing some groupings', *Africa*, vol. 48, no. 4, December.
Aghrout, A. and Geddes, A. (1996), 'The Maghreb and the European Union: From development cooperation to partnership?', *International Politics*, vol. 33, no. 3, September.
Aghrout, A. and Sutton, K. (1990), 'Regional Economic Union in the Maghreb', *The Journal of Modern African Studies*, vol. 28, no. 1, March.
Alaoui, M. (1994), *La Coopération entre l'Union Européenne et les Pays du Maghreb*, Editions Nathan, Paris.
Alker, H.R. et al (1974), *Analysing Global Interdependence*, Center for International Studies (MIT), Cambridge, Massachusetts.
Andresen, H. (1977), 'Le Maghreb dans la politique communautaire d'aide au développement', in Institut d'Etudes Européennes, *Les Relations du Maroc et de la Communauté Européenne*, Université Libre de Bruxelles, Brussels.
Annuaire de l'Afrique du Nord (1963), vol. 2.
Annuaire de l'Afrique du Nord (1969), vol. 8.
Arabies (1995), no. 107, November.
Arabies (1996), no. 114, June.
Asante, S.K.B. (1981), 'The Lomé Convention: Towards Perpetuation of Dependence or Promotion of Interdependence?', *Third World Quarterly*, vol. 3, no. 4, October.
Asante, S.K.B. (1986), 'Africa and Europe: Collective Dependence or Interdependence', in Sesay, A. (ed.), *Africa and Europe: From partition to interdependence or dependence?*, Croom Helm, London.
Baldwin, D.A. (1980), 'Interdependence and Power: A Conceptual Analysis', *International Organization*, vol. 34, no. 4, Autumn.
Baldwin-Edwards, M. (1992), 'Immigration and migrants in the Europe of the

1990s', *European Access*, no. 3, June.
Bensalah Alaoui, A. (1993), 'Partenariat et accord de libre-échange', in Vasconcelos, A. (ed.), *Européens et Maghrébins - Une solidarité obligée*, Editions Karthala, Paris.
Bensidoun, I. and Chevallier, A. (1996), *Europe-Méditerranée: Le pari de l'ouverture*, Economica, Paris.
Bergsman, J. and Shen, X. (1995), 'Foreign Direct Investment in Developing Countries: Progress and Problems', *Finance and Development*, vol. 32, no. 4, December.
Berrada, A. (1994), 'Migration, structural change and economic development', in OECD, *Migration and Development - New Partnership for Cooperation*, OECD, Paris.
Bessis, S. (1991), 'La vie politique tunisienne: Autoritarisme moue ou démocratie musclée', in Lacoste, C. and Lacoste, Y. (eds), *L'Etat du Maghreb*, La Découverte, Paris.
Boucher, J. (1996), 'La société tunisienne privée de parole', *Le Monde Diplomatique*, no. 503, February.
Boukhobza, M. (1991), *Octobre 88 - Evolution ou Rupture?*, Editions Bouchène, Algiers.
Bourrinet, J. (1993), The Implications of EC Commercial Policy on Developing Countries, in McAleese, D. et al (eds), *Africa and the Community after 1992*, World Bank, Washington, DC.
Bouzidi, A. (1991), *Panorama des Economies Maghrébines Contemporaines*, Editions ENAG, Algiers.
Brumberg, D. (1990), 'An Arab Path to Democracy', *Journal of Democracy*, vol. 1, no. 4, Fall.
Bulletin of the European Communities/ European Union (various issues).
Cable, V. (1990), '1992 and its Implications for Developing Countries', in Siebert, H. (ed.), *The Completion of the Internal Market*, Mohr, Tubingen.
Caporaso, J. (1978), 'Dependence and Dependency in the Global system: A Structural and Behavioural Analysis', *International Organization*, vol. 32, no. 1, Winter.
Cherkaoui, A. (1987), 'Entre les deux rives de la Méditerranée', *Futuribles*, March.
Chevallier, A. and Kessler, V. (1989), *Economies en développement et défis démographiques*, Calmann-Lévy, Paris.
Church, C.H. and Phinnemore, D. (1994), *European Union and European Community: A Handbook and Commentary on the Post Maastricht*

Treaties, Harvester Wheatsheaf, Hertfordshire.
Collier, P. and Gunning, J. W. (1995), 'Trade Policy and Regional Integration: Implications for Relations between Europe and Africa', *The World Economy*, vol. 18, no. 3, May.
Commission of the European Communities (1980), 'Textiles: The Multi-Fibre Arrangement', *Background Report*, ISEC/B43/80, Brussels, 11 September.
Commission of the European Communities (1985), *Guidelines for a Community Policy on Migration*, COM(85) 48 final, Brussels, 7 March.
Commission of the European Communities (1989), *The Euro-South Dialogue*, Office for Official Publications of the European Communities, Luxembourg.
Commission of the European Communities (1990), *Policies on Immigration and the Social Integration of Migrants in the European Community*, SEC(90) 1813 final, Brussels, 28 September.
Commission of the European Communities (1991), 'Les Pays du Grand Maghreb et la Communauté Européenne', *Développement-Europe Information*, DE 68, Brussels, January.
Commission of the European Communities (1991), *Immigration and Right of Asylum*, SEC(91) 1855 final, Brussels, 9 October.
Commission of the European Communities (1992), *From the Single Act to Maastricht: The Means to Match our Ambitions*, COM(92) 2000 final, Brussels, 11 February.
Commission of the European Communities (1992), *The Future of Relations between the Community and the Maghreb*, SEC(92) 401 final, Brussels, 30 April.
Commission of the European Communities (1993), *Growth, competitiveness, and employment - The challenges and ways forward into 21st century*, COM(93) 700 final, Brussels, 5 December.
Commission of the European Communities (1994), *For a European Union energy policy*, COM(94) 659 final, Brussels, 11 January.
Commission of the European Communities (1994), *Immigration and Asylum Policies*, COM(94) 23 final, Brussels, 23 February.
Commission of the European Communities (1994), *Strengthening the Mediterranean Policy of the European Union: Establishing a Euro-Mediterranean partnership*, COM(94) 427 final, Brussels, 19 October.
Commission of the European Communities (1995), *Strengthening of the Mediterranean Policy of the Union. Proposals for implementing a Euro-Mediterranean partnership*, COM(95), 72 final, Brussels, 8 March.

Commission of the European Communities (1995), *Commission concludes evaluation of free trade agreements*, IP/95/215, Brussels, 8 March.

Commission of the European Communities (1995)EC, *The Mediterranean Region in 2020 and its Role in the European Energy Network*, MEMO/95/49, Brussels, 27 March.

Commission of the European Communities (1995), *The EU and the Mediterranean countries put their energy act together in Tunis*, IP/95/283, Brussels, 27 March.

Commission of the European Communities (1995), *Complementarity between the Community's development cooperation policy and the policies of Member States*, COM(95) 160 final, Brussels, 3 May.

Commission of the European Communities (1995), *Proposal for a decision on the conclusion of a Euro-Mediterranean Agreement establishing an association between the European Communities and their Member States, on the one part, and the Republic of Tunisia, on the other part*, COM(95) 235 final, Brussels, 31 May.

Commission of the European Communities (1995), *The right of third country to travel in the Community*, COM(95) 346 final, Brussels, 12 July.

Commission of the European Communities (1995), *European Community Gas Supply and Prospects*, COM(95) 478 final, Brussels, 18 October.

Commission of the European Communities (1995), *An energy policy for the European Union*, COM(95) 682 final, Brussels, 13 December.

Commission of the European Communities (1995), *Proposal for a decision on the conclusion of a Euro-Mediterranean Agreement establishing an association between the European Communities and their Member States, on the one part, and the Kingdom of Morocco, on the other part*, COM(95) 740 final, Brussels, 20 December.

Commission of the European Communities (1996), *The Global Challenge of International Trade: A Market Access Strategy for the European Union*, COM(96) 53 final, Brussels, 14 February.

Commission of the European Communities (1997), *Report on Cooperation With Mediterranean Partners*, COM(97) 371 final, Brussels, 18 July.

Commission of the European Communities/ Maghreb Unit (1998), *Algérie: Etat de la coopération financière*, Brussels, 20 February.

Commission of the European Communities (1999), *Annual Report of the Meda Programme 1998*, COM(99) 291 final, Brussels, 22 June.

Commission of the European Communities (DGIB), *Exécution de la Programmation Budgétaire en Méditerranée au 15/01/1999*, http://europa.eu.int/en/comm/dg1b/budget/index.html

Commission of the European Communities (DGI), *WTO Aspects of EU Preferential Trade Agreements with the Third Countries*, http://europa.eu.int/en/comm/dg01/dg1.htm

Commission of the European Communities (various years), *General Report on the Activities of the Community*.

Condamines, C. (1998), 'Immigration, intégration et politique de coopération', *Le Monde Diplomatique*, no. 529, April.

Conseil National Economique et Social, *Avis Relatif au Plan National contre le Chômage*, http://www.cnes.dz

Constitutions (1976 and 1989), Algiers.

Costa-Lascoux, J. (1994), 'Les Lois "Pasqua": une nouvelle politique de l'immigration', *Monde Arabe-Maghreb-Machrek*, no. 144, April-June.

Court of Justice of the European Communities (1987), *Reports of Cases before the Court of Justice and the Court of First Instance*, no. 7, Office for Official Publications of the European Communities, Luxembourg.

Court of Justice of the European Communities (1991), *Reports of Cases before the Court of Justice and the Court of First Instance*, no. 1, Office for Official Publications of the European Communities, Luxembourg.

Cova, C. (1985), 'La politique méditerranéenne des Douze', *Revue du Marché Commun*, no. 291, November.

Daoud, Z. (1997), 'Maroc: Les élections de 1997', *Monde Arabe-Maghreb-Machrek*, no. 158, October-December.

Daoud, Z. and Abderrahim, K. (2000), 'Activisme du Monarque, Immobilisme du Gouvernement - Le Maroc change t-il vraiment?', *Le Monde Diplomatique*, no. 551, February.

Davenport, M. and Page, S. (1991), *Europe 1992: 1992 and the Developing World*, Overseas Development Institute, London.

Délégation de la Commission Européenne au Maroc (1994), *Lettre d'Information*, no. 115, Rabat, March.

Délégation de la Commission Européenne au Maroc (1994), *Maroc-Union Européenne: Bilan 1979-1994*, Rabat, 30 September.

Délégation de la Commission Européenne en Tunisie (1996), *Coopération Union Européenne - Tunisie: Rapport 1996*, Tunis.

Denoeux, G. (1994), 'Tunisie: les élections présidentielles et législatives', *Monde Arabe-Maghreb-Machrek*, no. 145, July-September.

Denoeux, G. (1999), 'La Tunisie de Ben Ali et ses paradoxes', *Monde Arabe-Maghreb-Machrek*, no. 166, October-December.

Direction de la Population et des Migrations/ Ministère de l'Aménagement du Territoire, de la Ville et de l'intégration (1996), *Rapport sur*

l'immigration et la présence étrangère en France 1995-1996, Paris, December.
Duchêne, F. and Holmes, P. (1984), *The European Community and the Mediterranean Basin*, Office For Official Publications of the European Communities, Brussels.
Dupouy, A. (1979), 'Statut juridique de la coopération entre l'Algérie et la CEE', *Revue Algérienne des Sciences Juridiques, Economiques et Politiques*, vol. 16, no. 1, March.
Dusan, S. (1974), *Current Problems of Economic Integration*, UNCTAD, New York.
Eberhardt, R. (1989), 'The European Community and the Maghreb: prospects for cooperation in the decades ahead', Paper presented at the *Conference on North Africa and the EEC*, School of Oriental and African Studies, London, 10 February.
Economist Intelligence Unit (1995), *Country Profile - Morocco 1995-1996*, The Economist Intelligence Unit, London.
Economist Intelligence Unit (1997), *Country Profile - Tunisia 1997-1998*, The Economist Intelligence Unit, London.
Economist Intelligence Unit (1997), *Country Profile - Algeria 1997-1998*, The Economist Intelligence Unit, London.
Economist Intelligence Unit (1997), *Country Profile - Tunisia 1997-1998*, The Economist Intelligence Unit, London.
Economist Intelligence Unit (1999), *Country Profile - Algeria 1999-2000*, The Economist Intelligence Unit, London.
Economist Intelligence Unit (1999), *Country Profile - Morocco 1999-2000*, The Economist Intelligence Unit, London.
Economist Intelligence Unit (1999), *Country Profile - Tunisia 1999-2000*, The Economist Intelligence Unit, London.
EIB (various years), *Annual Report*, Office for Official Publications of the European Communities, Luxembourg.
El-Meloukhi, R. (1989), *La Politique Française de Coopération avec les Etats du Maghreb 1955-1987*, Editions Toubkal, Casablanca.
Etudes Internationales (1993), vol. 48.
Etudes Maghrébines (1965), no. 4, April.
European Economy (1996), no. 6.
European Parliament (1976), 'Report on the cooperation agreements concluded between the EEC and Algeria, Morocco and Tunisia', *Working Documents*, no. 307/76, 4 October.
European Report (various issues).

Euromed Reports (2000), no. 8, April.
Eurostat (various years).
Evans, G. and Newham, J. (1990), *Dictionary of World Politics - A Reference Guide to Concepts, Ideas and Institutions*, Harvester Wheatsheaf, London.
Evans, P. and Walsh, J. (1994), *The EIU Guide to the New GATT*, The Economist Intelligence Unit, London.
Faini, R. et al (1995), 'A Primer on the MFA Maze', *The World Economy*, vol. 18, no. 1, January.
Fievet, G. (1982), 'Les accords d'auto-limitation, une nouvelle technique d'accords communautaires', *Revue du Marché Commun*, no. 262, December.
Final Declaration of the 7th Conference of the Maghreb Economic Ministers (1975), Algiers, 23 May.
Flory, M. (1966), 'La succession d'Etat aux traités', *Annuaire de l'Afrique du Nord*, vol. 5.
GATT (1991), *Trade Policy Review: The European Community*, vol. 1, GATT, Geneva.
Ghozali, S.A. (1986), 'Maghreb-CEE: Enjeux et Perspectives', *Revue Algérienne des Relations Internationales*, no. 2.
Gillespie, R. (1997), 'Spanish Protagonismo and the Euro-Med Partnership Initiative', *Mediterranean Politics*, vol. 2, no. 1, Summer.
Gilpin, R. (1987), *The Political Economy of International Relations*, Princeton University Press, New Jersey.
Green, R.H. (1976), 'The Lomé Convention: Updated Dependence or Departure towards Collective Self-Reliance?', *African Review*, vol. 6, no. 1.
Grilli, E.R. (1993), *The European Community and the Developing Countries*, Cambridge University Press, Cambridge.
Grimaud, N. (1996), 'Le Maghreb et le partenariat euro-méditerranéen', *Revue des Affaires Européennes*, vol. 6, no. 4.
Gruhn, I. (1976), 'The Lomé Convention: Inching towards Interdependence', *International Organization*, vol. 30.
Habeeb, W.M. (1988), *Negotiations - How Weak Nations Bargain with Strong Nations*, Johns Hopkins University Press, Baltimore.
Habeeb, W.M. (1993), 'The Maghribi States and the European Community', in Zartman, W.I. and Habeeb, W.M. (eds), *Polity and Society in Contemporary North Africa*, Westview Press, Boulder, Colorado.
Hamill, J. (1989), *Mediterranean Textiles and Clothing*, The Economist Intelligence Unit, London.

Hargreaves, A.G. (1995), *Immigration, 'race' and ethnicity*, Routledge, London.

Hermassi, E. (1985), 'States and Regimes in the Maghreb', in Barakat, H. (ed.), *Contemporary North Africa - Issues of Development and Integration*, Croom Helm, London.

Hermassi, E. and Vandewalle, D. (1993), 'The Second Stage of State Building', in Zartman, W.I. and Habeeb, W.M. (eds), *op.cit.*

Hine, R.C. (1985), *The Political Economy of European Trade: An Introduction to the Trade Policies of the EEC*, Wheatsheaf Books Ltd, Sussex.

Hollifield, J.F. (1997), 'Ideas, Institutions, and Civil Society: On the Limits of Immigration Control in Europe', Paper prepared for the *Workshop on Immigration Control in Europe*, University of Bologna/Italy, April.

Hopkins, M. (1989), *Tunisia to 1993 - Steering for Stability*, The Economist Intelligence Unit, London.

House of Lords/ Select Committee on the European Communities (1995), *Eleventh Report*, HMSO, London.

IMF (1997), *International Financial Statistics Yearbook 1997*, IMF, Washington, DC.

IMF (1999), *Government Finance Statistics Yearbook 1999*, IMF, Washington, DC.

IMF (1999), *Balance of Payments Statistics Yearbook 1999*, IMF, Washington, DC.

IMF (various years), *Direction of Trade Statistics Yearbook*, IMF, Washington, DC.

Inggo, M. D. (1995), 'Agricultural liberalisation in the Uruguay Round', *Finance and Development*, vol. 32, no. 2, September.

Izam, M. (1993), 'European Integration and Latin American Trade', *CEPAL Review*, no. 51, December.

Joffé, G. (1994), 'Relations between the Middle East and the West', *The Middle East Journal*, vol. 48, no. 2, Spring.

Joffé, G. (1994), 'Elections and Reform in Morocco', *Mediterranean Politics*, vol. 1, no. 1.

Joffé, G. (1998), 'The Euro-Mediterranean Partnership Initiative: Problems and Prospects', *The Journal of North African Studies*, vol. 3, no. 2, Summer.

Journal of Common Market Studies (1990), special issue, vol. 29, no. 2.

Journal of Development Planning (1991), special issue, vol. 21-22.

Journal Officiel des Communautés Européennes (1962), vol. 5.

Journal Officiel des Communautés Européennes (1969), vol. 12, no. L 197 and L 198, 8 August.

Journal Officiel de la République Algérienne (1993), vol. 32, no. 26, 26 April.
Kahler, M. (1982), 'Europe and its "Privileged Partners" in Africa and the Middle East', *Journal of Common Market Studies*, vol. 21, no. 1-2.
Kebabjian, G. (1995), 'Eléments d'une prospective euro-méditerranéenne', in Bistofli, R. (ed.), *Euro-Méditerranée: Une région à construire*, Publisud, Paris.
Keesing's Contemporary Archives (1972), vol. 18, 28 October - 4 November.
Keesing's Contemporary Archives (1973), vol. 19, 5-11 February.
Keesing's Record of World Events (1994), vol. 40, no. 11.
Keesing's Record of World Events (1995), vol. 41, no. 10.
Keesing's Record of World Events (1998), vol. 44, no. 9.
Keohane, R.O. and Nye, J.S. (1977), *Power and Interdependence: World Politics in Transition*, Little Brown, Boston.
Khader, B. (1992), *Le Grand Maghreb et L'Europe - Enjeux et Perspectives*, Editions Publisud, Paris.
Lahlou, M., 'Le travail des enfants, un phénomène essentiellement marocain', in Lacoste, C. and Lacoste, Y. (eds), *op.cit.*
Lall, S. (1975), 'Is Dependence a Useful Concept in Analysing Underdevelopment', *World Development*, vol. 3, no. 11-12, November-December.
Langhammer, R.J. (1992), 'The Developing Countries and Regionalism', *Journal of Common Market Studies*, vol. 30, no. 2, June.
Leveau, R. (1993), 'Reflections on the State in the Maghreb', in Joffé, G. (ed.), *North Africa: Nation, State and Region*, Routledge, London.
Maghreb-Etudes et Documents (1968), no. 26, March-April.
Maghreb-Etudes et Documents (1972), no. 49, January-February.
Maghreb Quarterly Report (1995), no. 19, September.
Mahjoub, A. (1998), 'Social Feasibility and Costs of the Free Trade Zone', *The Journal of North African Studies*, vol. 3, no. 2, Summer.
Mameri, A. (1968), 'L'Adhésion de l'Algérie à la Communauté Européenne', *Revue Algérienne des Sciences Juridiques, Economiques et Politiques*, vol. 5, no. 2, June.
Martin, G. (1982), *The Political Economy of African-European Relations from Yaoundé I to Lomé II, 1963-1980: A Case Study in Neo-Colonialism and Dependency*, PhD dissertation, Indiana University.
Martin, P.L. (1994), 'Reducing emigration pressure: What role can foreign aid play?', in Bohning, W.R. and Schloeter, M.L. (eds), *Aid in Place of Migration*, ILO, Geneva.
McAleese, D. (1993), 'The Community's external trade policy', in Mayes, D.G.

(ed.), *The External Implications of European Integration*, Harvester Wheatsheaf, Hertfordshire.

Mezdour, S. (1992), 'Economie des migrations internationales', *Revue Française des Affaires Sociales*, vol. 47, no. 1, January-March.

Middle East Economic Digest (1978), 20 December.

Middle East Economic Digest (1995), 6 October.

Middle East Economic Digest (1995), 8 December.

Middle East Economic Digest (1996), 3 May.

Middle East International (1993), 5 March.

Middle East International (1994), 10 June.

Middle East International (1994), 27 May.

Ministère des Affaires Etrangères/ France (1995), *Bulletin d'Information*, no. 229/95, Paris, 28 November.

Ministère des Affaires Sociales (1989), *Rapport Final de la Commission Nationale pour la Promotion de l'Emploi*, Algiers, December.

Ministère de l'Industrie, du Commerce et de l'Artisanat/ Morocco (1996), *Programme de Mise à Niveau*; published in *L'Economiste*, 22 February.

Ministry of Economic Development, 9th *Development Plan 1997-2001*, http://www.tunisiaonline.com/development/t32.html

Mokaddem, B. (1987), *L'Unité du Maghreb Arabe*, Doctorat d'Etat, University of Clermont-Ferrand.

Mortimer, E. (1994), 'Europe and the Mediterranean: The Security Dimension', in Ludlow, P. (ed.), *Europe and the Mediterranean*, Brassey's for Centre for European Policy Studies, London.

Mortimer, R. (1993), 'Regionalism and Geopolitics in the Maghreb', *Middle East Report*, September-October.

Muzikar, J. (1967), *Les perspectives de l'intégration des pays du Maghreb*, Centre Européen Universitaire, Nancy.

Niblock, T. (1993), 'International and Domestic Factors in the Economic Liberalization Process in Arab Countries', in Niblock, T. and Murphy, E. (eds), *Economic and Political Liberalization in the Middle East*, British Academic Press, London.

Niblock, T. (1996), 'North-South Socio-Economic Relations in the Mediterranean', in Aliboni, R., Joffé, G. and Niblock, T. (eds), *Security Challenges in the Mediterranean*, Frank Cass, London.

OECD (various years), *Geographical Distribution of Financial Flows to Aid Recipients*, OECD, Paris.

OECD (1997), *Trend in International Migration/ Annual Report 1996*, OECD, Paris.

Official Journal of the European Communities (1976), no. C 34, 14 February.
Official Journal of the European Communities (1987), no. L 297, 21 October.
Official Journal of the European Communities (1988), no. L 224, 13 August.
Official Journal of the European Communities (1991), no. C 159, 17 June.
Official Journal of the European Communities (1991), no. C 252, 26 September.
Official Journal of the European Communities (1995), no. C 88, 10 April.
Official Journal of the European Communities (1995), no. C 287, 30 October.
Official Journal of the European Communities (1996), no. C 166, 10 June.
Official Journal of the European Communities (1998), no. C 98, 31 March.
Official Journal of the European Communities (1999), no. L 340, 31 December.
O'Keeffe, D. (1995), 'The Emergence of European Immigration Policy', *European Law Review*, vol. 20, no. 1.
Oualalou, F. (1969), *L'Assistance Etrangère Face au Développement Economique du Maroc*, Editions Maghrébines, Casablanca.
Oualalou, F. (1989), 'La problématique de la coopération maghrébine face au dynamisme de la Communauté européenne', *Cahiers du CERMAC*, no. 66-67.
Oualalou, F. (1996), *Après Barcelona - Le Maghreb est nécessaire*, Editions Toubkal, Casablanca.
Page, J. (1998), 'From Boom to Bust - and Back? The Crisis of Growth in the Middle East and North Africa', in Shafik, N. (ed.), *Prospects for Middle Eastern and North African Economies*, Macmillan Press Limited and St. Martin's Press, London and New York.
Pellerin, M. (1966), 'La Communauté Economique Européenne et les Etats du Maghreb', *Le Mois en Afrique*, September.
Pfeifer, K. (1992), 'Algeria's Implicit Stabilization Program', in Barkey, H.J. (ed.), *The Politics of Economic Reform in the Middle East*, St. Martin's Press, New York.
Pfeifer, K. (1996), 'Between Rocks and Hard Choices: International Finance and Economic Adjustment in North Africa', in Vandewalle, D. (ed.), *North Africa - Development and Reform in a Changing Global Economy*, St. Martin's Press, New York.
Pickles, D. (1973), *The Government and Politics of France*, Methuen, London.
Philip, A.B. (1994), 'European Union Immigration Policy: Phantom, Fantasy or Fact?', *West European Politics*, vol. 17, no. 2, April.
Poos, J.F. (1995), 'Paramètres pour la stabilité en Europe', *Studia Diplomatica*, vol. 48, no. 4.

Protocol of Tunis (1964), Tunis, 1 October.
Protocol of Tripoli (1965), Tripoli, 26 May.
Ramonet, I. (1996), 'Main de fer en Tunisie', *Le Monde Diplomatique*, no. 508, July.
Raux, J. (1987), 'Le maintien des échanges traditionnels de produits agricoles entre la CEE élargie et les pays méditerranéens', *Revue Trimestrielle de Droit Européen*, vol. 23, no. 4, October-December.
Ravenhill, J. (1979), 'Regional Integration and Development in Africa: Lessons from East African Community', *Commonwealth Journal of Comparative Politics*, vol. 17, no. 3, November.
Ravenhill, J. (1985), *Collective Clientelism -The Lomé Conventions and North-South Relations*, Columbia University Press, New York.
République Algérienne Démocratique et Populaire (1996), *Economie Algérienne - Les Enjeux et les Choix à Moyen Terme 1996-2000*, Algiers.
République Algérienne Démocratique et Populaire (Services du Chef du Gouvernement) (1997), *Programme du Gouvernement 1997*, Algiers.
Reuter, P. (1965), *Droit International Public*, Presse Universitaire Française, Paris.
Revue du Marché Commun (1969), July-August.
Revue du Marché Commun (1971), March-April.
Rivlin, B. (1966), 'Problems and Prospects for North African Unity', in Brown, C. (ed.), *State and Society in Independent North Africa*, Middle East Institute, Washington, DC.
Robana, A. (1973), *The Prospects for an Enlarged Economic Community in North Africa - Managing Economic Integration in the Maghreb*, Praeger Publishers, New York.
Rosecrance, R. and Stein, A. (1973), 'Interdependence: Myth or Reality?', *World Politics*, vol. 26, no. 1, October.
Rosecrance, R. et al (1977), 'Whither Interdependence?', *International Organization*, vol. 26, no. 3, Summer.
Santos (Dos), T. (1970), 'The Structure of Dependence', *American Economic Review*, vol. 60.
Seddon, D. (1993), 'Austerity Protests in Response to Economic Liberalisation in the Middle East', in Niblock, T. and Murphy, E. (eds), *op.cit.*
Shaw, T. (1980), *Towards an International Political Economy for the 1980s: From dependence to (inter)dependence*, Centre for Foreign Policy Studies, Dalhousie University, Halifax.
Shlaim, A. and Yannopoulous, G.N. (eds) (1976), *The EEC and the*

Mediterranean Countries, Cambridge University Press, Cambridge.
Siotis, J. (1974), 'The European Economic Community and its Emerging Mediterranean Policy', in Geusau (Alting Von), A.M.F. (ed.), *The External Relations of the European Community*, Saxon House, London.
Slim, H. (1980), *Le Comité Permanent Consultatif et les Institutions de Coopération Maghrébine*, Doctorat d'Etat, University of Tunis.
South Commission (1990), *The Challenge to the South*, Oxford University Press, Oxford.
Spencer, C. (1993), *The Maghreb in the 1990s*, International Institute for Strategic Studies, London.
Stevens, C. (1990), '1992 and its effects on the Maghreb countries and Sub-Saharan Africa', *Journal of Common Market Studies*, vol. 29, no. 2.
Straubhaar, T. and Zimmerman, K.F. (1993), 'Towards a European migration policy', *Population Research and Policy Review*, vol. 12, no. 3.
Sutton, K. (1972), 'Political Association and Maghreb Economic Development', *The Journal of Modern African Studies*, vol. 10, no. 2.
Talha, L. (1993), 'Relations Europe-Maghreb: La Question des Investissements Directs', *Revue Tiers Monde*, vol. 34, no. 136, October-December.
Taylor, R. (1980), 'Implications for the Southern Mediterranean Countries of the Second Enlargement of the European Community', *Development-Europe Information*, Brussels, June.
Treaties establishing the European Communities (1987), Luxembourg.
Treaty establishing the UMA (1989), Marrakech, 17 February.
Tsoukalis, L. (1997), *The New European Economy Revisited*, Oxford University Press, Oxford.
UN (various years), *Yearbook of Industrial Statistics*, vol. 1, UN, New York.
UN (1993), *World Population Prospects*, UN, New York.
UNCTAD (1990 and 1991), *Trade and Development Report*, UNCTAD, Geneva.
UNDP (1999), *Human Development Report 1999*, Oxford University Press, New York.
UNECA (1964), *Industrial Coordination Mission to Algeria, Libya, Morocco, and Tunisia*, UN Document E/CN14/248, February.
UNECA (1968), *Economic Bulletin for Africa*, vol. 7, no. 1-2.
Vallay, G. (1966), 'La Communauté Européenne et les Pays du Maghreb', *Revue de l'Occident Musulman et de la Méditerranée*, no. 2.
Wagner, R.H. (1988), 'Economic interdependence, bargaining power, and political influence', *International Organization*, vol. 42, no. 3, Summer.

Withol de Wenden, C. (1997), 'La politique de l'intégration', *Confluence-Méditerranée*, no. 22, Summer.
Wood, R. (1985), *From Marshall Plan to Debt Crisis: Foreign Debt and Development Choices in the World Economy*, University of California Press, Berkeley.
World Bank (1996), *Tunisia's Global Integration and Sustainable Development - Choices for the 21st Century*, World Bank, Washington, DC.
World Bank (1999), *Global Development Finance 1999*, World Bank, Washington, DC.
World Bank (2000), *World Development Indicators 2000*, World Bank, Washington, DC.
World Bank (various years), *World Development Report*, World Bank, Washington, DC.
World Bank (various years), *World Debt Tables*, World Bank, Washington, DC.
Yvoire (d'), J. (1965), 'Le Maghreb et la Communauté Economique Européenne', *Etudes Maghrébines*, no. 4, April.
Zaim, F. (1999), 'The Third Generation of Euro-Mediterranean association Agreements: A View from the South', *Mediterranean Politics*, vol. 4, no. 2, Summer.
Zartman, I.W. (1968), 'North Africa and the EEC negotiations', *The Middle East Journal*, vol. 22.
Zartman, I.W. (1971), *The Politics of Trade Negotiations between Africa and the European Economic Community*, Princeton University Press, New Jersey.
Zartman, I.W. (1976), 'Europe and Africa: Decolonisation or Dependency?', *Foreign Affairs*, vol. 54, no. 2.

Index

ACP-EU partnership agreement 29
Africa, Yaoundé Convention 52
agricultural exports 5, 36, 161
   association agreements 53, 57-8, 59-60, 64
   EC regulations 52
   EC trade agreements 29, 30-1
   Euro-Mediterranean association agreements 136, 137, 138-9, 140
   global Mediterranean policy 70, 73-5, 76, 83
   see also Common Agricultural Policy
aid *see* financial assistance
Alaoui, Bensalah 106
Algeria
   association agreement 186
   cooperation agreement 25
   debt *111*, 112
   demographic trends *105*, 106
   EC imports *80*
   EC relationship 26, 44-5, 47-51, 69
   economic development 20, 104
   employment 107-8, *108*, 109, 110
   export structure 81, *82*, 83
   financial assistance 85, *86*, 87, *88*
   gas 130
   instability 19, 36, 116
   intra-Maghreb trade *22*

   migrant workers *92*, *93*
   political liberalisation 117-18
   regional integration 17, 18
   state-society relations 114, 115
   trade balance 79, 156
Andresen, H. 52
Asian countries 81
association agreements 1, 25, 43, 63-4, 67
   CEEC 29, 32-4
   characteristics 55-6
   implications 58-60, 63
   negotiation process 51-5
   trade provisions 56-8
   see also Euro-Mediterranean association agreements
Azoulay, André 140

Baldwin, David A. 15
Barcelona Conference 6, 128
Barcelona Declaration 128, 132, 149, 158, 163-85
Belgium, migrant workers *92*
Ben Ali, Zine el-Abidine 27, 118-19
Ben Mustapha, Said, 145-6
Berrada, Abdallah 91
Boukhobza, M'hammed 114, 116
Boumediene, Houari 106
Bourguiba, Habib 53, 118
Bouteflika, Abdelaziz 118
Bouzidi, Abdelmajid 107
bread riots 116, 117

Brumberg, Daniel 115

Caporaso, James 12, 13
central and eastern European countries (CEEC) 6, 29, 32-4, 38, 127
cereals 52
China 81
citrus fruits 53, 54, 57-8, 74
Claes, Willy 129
clothing *see* textiles
Comité Permanent Consultatif du Maghreb (CPCM) 17, 24
Common Agricultural Policy (CAP) 4, 29, 156
  establishment 31, 46
  regulations 52, 53-4
  see also agricultural exports
Common Commercial Policy (CCP) 29
Common Foreign and Security Policy 127
Comptoir Maghrébin de l'Alfa 24
cooperation agreements 1-2, 25
cork 56, 70

Dahrendorf, Ralf 68, 132
Daoud, Zakia 121
debt 110, *111*, 112-13, 159
Declaration of Intent 44, 52, 55
demographic trends 104, *105*, 106
Denoeux, Guilain 119
dependence 11, 12-13, 14-15
dependency 13

EC *see* European Community
economic aid *see* financial assistance

economic development 2-3, 15, 16, 157-8
  association agreements 56, 58-60, 63, 136-7
  instability 103-4, 122-3
  liberalisation 116, 146-7, 159
  partnership initiative 132, 133-4
  regional integration 20, 25
EEC *see* European Economic Community
Egypt 186
energy policy 16, 130-1
  see also gas; oil
étatisation 114-16
EU *see* European Union
Euro-Mediterranean association agreements 2, 133, 134, 150-1, 155, 158, 186
  expected benefits 146-50
  features 135-7
  implications 159-61
  market access conditions 137-40
  potential costs 140-6
  see also partnership initiative
Euro-Mediterranean Stability Pact 133
Europe agreements 29, 33-4
European Agricultural Guidance and Guarantee Fund (EAGGF) 48
European Bank for Reconstruction and Development 33
European Coal and Steel Community Treaty 56
European Commission
  financial assistance 87
  The Future of Relations between the Community and the

Maghreb 26
  global Mediterranean policy 158
  migrant workers 91-2, 94-5, 131, 132
  olive oil 138
  partnership initiative 128
European Community
  CEEC 32-4, 38
  external trade policy 28-31, 38
  Maghreb regional cooperation 24-8
  Maghreb relationship 1-5, 14-17, 44-51
  member states' interests 34-7
  Single European Market 31-2
  see also association agreements; European Economic Community; European Union; global Mediterranean policy
European Council 127, 128, 131
European Development Fund (EDF) 48, 53
European Economic Area 29
European Economic Community 1, 24, 43, 44-5
  see also European Community
European Investment Bank (EIB) 85, 159
European Parliament 68, 120, 130
European Union 155-8
  see also European Community; partnership initiative
Evans, Graham 13
Evian Accords 49

Filali, Abdelatif 26
financial assistance 2, 3, 5, 155, 159

association agreements 63
Euro-Mediterranean association agreements 134, 137, 143-6, 151
global Mediterranean policy 67, 83, 85-90, 96-7
impact 4, 156-7, 158
fishing 85, 139
Fitouri, Mohamed 76-7
Five plus Five 35-6
Flory, M. 48-9
foreign direct investment 147, *148*, 149, 151, 160
France 34-6, 44-5
  Algeria 47-8, 49
  Common Agricultural Policy 46-7
  financial assistance 89, 157
  global Mediterranean policy 68
  migrant workers 90, 91, *92*, 95-6
  Morocco 45
  partnership initiative 127, 128, 133
  trade 36
  Tunisia 45-6
  Yaoundé Convention 52
free trade area
  association agreements 53
  CEEC 29
  Euro-Mediterranean association agreements 126, 129-30, 135, 150, 158
  expected benefits 146-50
  global Mediterranean policy 69
  market access conditions 137-40
  potential costs 140-6
  UMA 19
Front National (France) 95-6

gas 130
GDP 104
General Agreement on Tariffs and Trade (GATT) 30, 32, 56, 70-1
General System of Preferences (GSP) 29, 71, 81
Germany 36, 50, 51, 127
   migrant workers 92
Ghozali, Sid-Ahmed 73
global Mediterranean policy 64, 67-9, 96-7, 158
   financial assistance 83, 85-90
   migrant workers 90-6
   trade performance 77-83
   trade regime 69-77
Gonzales, Felipe 128
Les grandes lignes d'une stratégie maghrébine de développement 18-19
Greece 52, 55, 74, 138
Gulf War 113, 120, 127

Hassan, King, of Morocco 60
Hermassi, Elbaki 115, 116
Hollifield, James F. 91
hub-spoke effect 149
human rights 120, 122, 123

industry 4-5, 156
   association agreements 56, 58-9, 64
   Euro-Mediterranean association agreements 135-6, 138
   global Mediterranean policy 75-7, 81
   liberalisation costs 142-3, *145*
   regional cooperation 18
infrastructure 87, 89, 157

instability 16, 103, 122-3, 129
   economic factors 103-13
   social and political environment 114-22
interdependence 11, 12, 13-14
   Euro-Maghreb relationship 15-17
investment 147, *148*, 149, 151, 160
   association agreements 63
   and debt 110, 112
   dependency perspective 14, 15
   Single European Market 32
Israel 57-8, 186
Italy
   agricultural products 53, 138
   Algeria 50
   Five plus Five 35-6
   global Mediterranean policy 68
   migrant workers 92
   partnership initiative 127

Jordan 186
Juppé, Alain 127

Kahler, Miles 73
Keohane, Robert O. 12, 14
Koutla (Morocco) 120-1

Lall, Sanjaya 12-13, 15
Lebanon 186
Libya *22*, 26, 35
   regional integration 17, 18, 19
Les Lois Pasqua 96
Lomé Convention 2, 29

Maastricht Treaty 36
Maghreb Centre for Industrial

Studies 18
Maghreb Commission for Trade Relations 24
Malta 35-6
manufacturing industry *see* industry
market access conditions 137-40
Marocanisation 115
Mauritania 18, *22*, 26
Les mécanismes de concertation entre l'UMA et la CEE 26
Mediterranean agreements 29
migrant workers 2, 3-4, 16, 155, 157
   Algeria 48
   association agreements 53
   global Mediterranean policy 67, 90-6, 97
   partnership initiative 131-2
   remittances *93*, 159-60
La mise à niveau 143
Moada, Mohamed 120
Mohamed VI, king of Morocco 121
Morocco
   agricultural exports 31, 74, 76, 139
   association agreements 1, 2, 3, 25, 51-64
   clothing products 83, *84*
   cooperation agreements 25
   debt *111*, 112-13
   demographic trends *105*, 106
   EC relationship 26, 27, 28, 44
   EC trade 45, *46*, *61*, *80*
   economic development 20, 104
   employment 108, *108*, 109
   Euro-Mediterranean association agreements 135-7, 140, 186

   export structure *82*, 83
   financial assistance 85, *86*, 87, *88*
   industry 143
   intra-Maghreb trade 21, *22*
   investment 15, 147, *148*
   liberalisation costs 146
   migrant workers *92*, *93*
   political liberalisation 120-1
   regional integration 17, 18, 26
   social discontent 116
   state-society relations 115
   trade balance *62*, 79, 156
   trade taxes *141*
   value-added 72
most favoured nation status 30
Multi-Fibre Agreements (MFA) 31
multinational corporations 14, 15

NATO 129
Néo-Destour (Tunisia) 115
Netherlands, migrant workers *92*
Newham, Jeffrey 13
Niblock, Tim 130
Nye, Joseph S. 12, 14

oil 18, 56, 70, 81, 130
olive oil 54, 57, 138
Ordonez, M. 33
Oualalou, Fathallah 71, 75

Palestinian Authority 186
Parti Socialiste Destourien (PSD) (Tunisia) 115, 119
partnership initiative 29, 123, 126, 150, 155, 158, 159
   dimensions 132-4
   process leading to 126-32

see also Euro-Mediterranean association agreements
PHARE 33
politics 19, 114, 116, 117-22, 123
  partnership initiative 132-3, 155
  single-party system 115
Pompidou, Georges 68
Poos, Jacques 131
population 104, *105*, 106
Portugal 35-6, 74, 138
preferential trade agreements 67
Protocol 1/7 44, 45, 46, 47, 55

Rassemblement Constitutionnel Démocratique (RCD) (Tunisia) 119
regional integration 17-23, 72, 160-1
  external relations 23-8
  trade 149-50
Les relations de l'UMA et de la CEE: bases et axes 26
Rhein, Eberhardt 16
Rome Treaty 1, 44-5, 48-9, 55
Rosecrance, Richard 12, 13
Rossi, M. 68
rules of origin 71-2, 149

safeguard clause 71, 72-3, 76, 138
Santos, Theotonio Dos 13
Schumann, Maurice 69
security 129, 132-3
Seddon, David 114
services 161
Shaw, Timothy 12
Single European Market 31-2
single-party system 115
social dimension, partnership initiative 132, 134, 155
social discontent 114, 116, 117

Solana, Javier 133
South Commission, Single European Market 31-2
Spain
  agricultural exports 57-8, 74, 138
  Five plus Five 35-6
  migrant workers *92*
  partnership initiative 127, 128
state-society relations 114-16
steel industry 18
Stein, Arthur 12, 13
Stevens, Christopher 32
street politics 116
Syria 186

TACIS 33
technical cooperation 53
textiles 156
  Euro-Mediterranean association agreements 138, 140
  exports 36, 83, *84*
  global Mediterranean policy 76-7
  liberalisation costs 143
  trade agreements 29, 30-1
  voluntary restraint arrangements 73
Thorn, Gaston 54-5
tomatoes 74
trade 1-3, 4, 155, 156
  association agreements 55-8, 59-60
  EC imports *61*
  with EC member states 36, *37*
  EC policy 28-31
  EC trade balance *62*
  extra-EU 34, *34*
  global Mediterranean policy 67, 69-83, 96

intra-regional 20-1, *21*, *22*
liberalisation costs 140-6
partnership initiative 129-31, 133, 135-6, 150
regional integration 18-19, 24
Single European Market 31-2
trade agreements *see* association agreements
trade preferences 2-3, 158
Triptyque Révolutionnaire (Algeria) 115
Tunisia
  association agreements 1, 2, 3, 25, 51-64
  cooperation agreements 25
  debt *111*, 112, 113
  demographic trends *105*, 106
  EC imports *80*
  EC relationship 26, 27-8, 44
  EC trade 45-6, *46*, *61*
  economic development 20, 104
  employment 108-9, *108*, 110
  Euro-Mediterranean association agreements 135-7, 140, 186
  export structure *82*, 83
  financial assistance 85, *86*, 87, *88*
  industry 143
  intra-Maghreb trade 21, *22*
  investment 15, 147, *148*, 149
  migrant workers *92*, *93*
  olive oil 138-9
  political liberalisation 118-20, 122
  regional integration 17, 18, 26
  services 161
  social discontent 116
  state-society relations 115
  tax reform 142
  textile industry 77, 83, *84*

trade balance *62*, 79, 156
trade taxes *141*
value-added 72
Turkey 52, 55, 57-8

UNCTAD 31-2, 55-6
unemployment 95, 107-10, 146
Union du Maghreb Arabe (UMA) 18, 23, 25-8
United Kingdom 127
  migrant workers *92*
United Nations 19
United Nations Development Programme 18
United Nations Economic Commission for Africa (UNECA) 17

value-added rule 71-2
Vandewalle, Dirk 115, 116

Wagner, R. Harris 14
West Germany *see* Germany
Western Sahara 19-20
wine 49, 51
Wood, Robert 116
World Trade Organization (WTO)
  agricultural exports 139
  free trade areas 137
  Marrakech 32
  most favoured nation status 30
  Seattle 136
  textiles 138

Yaoundé Convention 52, 55, 64

Zeroual, Liamine 118